Self-Help Skills
for People with Autism

Self-Help Skills for People with Autism

A SYSTEMATIC TEACHING APPROACH

Stephen R. Anderson, Ph.D., BCBA
Amy L. Jablonski, Psy.D.
Marcus L. Thomeer, Ph.D.
Vicki Madaus Knapp, Ph.D., BCBA

Sandra L. Harris, Ph.D., series editor

Woodbine House ◊ 2007

Published in the United States of America by Woodbine House, Inc.,
6510 Bells Mill Rd., Bethesda, MD 20817. 800-843-7323. www.woodbinehouse.com.

Library of Congress Cataloging-in-Publication Data

Self-help skills for people with autism : a systematic teaching approach / Stephen R. Anderson ... [et al.].
    p. cm. -- (Topics in autism)
 Includes bibliographical references and index.
 ISBN 978-1-890627-41-6
 1. Autism in children. 2. Autistic children--Rehabilitation. 3. Self-help techniques. 4. Parents of autistic children. I. Anderson, Stephen R.
 RJ506.A9.S437 2007
 649'.154--dc22

2007018084

Manufactured in the United States of America

First edition

10 9 8 7 6 5 4 3 2

In dedication to our mothers and fathers

who taught us to believe we could accomplish anything

and to our husbands, wives, and children

for their continuous patience and encouragement.

Table of Contents

Preface

Raising children has unlimited rewards and some formidable challenges. Fortunately, many women and men willingly accept the responsibility and choose to become mothers and fathers. But no one chooses to have a child with an autism spectrum disorder (ASD) and the first news can be devastating. In the face of it all, so many parents of children with autism respond to the challenge with courage and commitment that is rarely observed in any other human endeavor. We have been blessed to work with so many such individuals and they have and will continue to motivate us.

As we watch children with autism grow, we are often struck by how many of them enter adulthood with little or no independence in the completion of daily self-help skills, like getting dressed in the morning or using the toilet. We wonder if the educational system failed them by focusing too much on academic learning and too little on practical skills that nearly all children learn by their early teens. We hope that this book encourages parents and professionals to continuously assess and balance learning in all areas of development and to not wait too long before addressing deficits in self-help.

We want to thank our colleagues at Summit Educational Resources who have been a source of support to us and who enhance the lives of children and families every day. We also want to thank the families of children we serve who have helped sharpen our insights and understanding of autism.

$\mathcal{I}$ntroduction

■ About This Book

This book is intended to provide practical advice that will enable parents and professionals to teach children with ASD skills in the areas of dressing, personal hygiene, eating, and toileting. As we prepared this book, we discovered with some surprise how much you need to know to successfully teach self-help skills. Although we encourage you to read this book and independently apply what you learn, from time to time you may need the advice of an experienced professional to help you get started with new objectives and to overcome some challenges along the way. If you are struggling to put your initial plan together or are not experiencing some progress after the first three or four weeks, you may want to seek some advice. Sometimes the first skill to be taught is the most difficult for you and your child. After the first, it often gets easier to add new skills.

Finding a qualified professional to help can be a challenge. It is our opinion that the most qualified individuals will have specific training and experience working with children with autism using research supported methods. One professional area that has shown great success in teaching a broad range of skills to individuals with autism is called applied behavior analysis, or ABA. People who work in this area are called behavior analysts. Formal credentialing as a behavior analyst through the Behavior Analyst Certification Board (BACB) can provide some confidence to consumers that a professional has the necessary competencies. The BACB maintains a list of certified individuals on their website (www.BACB.com). Unfortunately, the BACB is relatively new and it may be hard to find someone in your geographic area with this credential. A good resource for choosing a behavior analyst has been developed by the Autism Special Interest Group, a group linked to the

International Association for Behavior Analysis. Revised Guidelines for Consumers of Applied Behavior Analysis can be found at the Association's website (www.abainternational.org).

Some of the information in this book may be immediately useful to you and some may be more valuable as your child physically and intellectually develops. We suggest that you re-read relevant parts of the book as your child gets older and that you periodically assess how your child is doing against the benchmarks that we have provided. It has been our experience that most children with autism learn self-help skills and many become fully independent, but it requires persistence from each child's community of caregivers.

What this Book Plans to Accomplish

This book focuses on children with autism spectrum disorders aged twenty-four months to early teens, as well as older individuals with autism whose skill levels are within this age range. It is designed to be a practical handbook to guide parents to identify and teach basic self-help skills. Teachers and paraprofessionals who work in schools, daycare centers, and community residences also may benefit from the information and advice provided. The book will concentrate on four basic areas of development—eating, toileting, dressing, and personal hygiene. These are the areas most critical in the first ten years of life and form the foundation for other skills to follow. *Teaching skills to children with ASD involves five important parts: (1) specifying the goal, (2) breaking the skill to be taught into small steps for learning, (3) using a systematic approach to instruction, (4) evaluating progress, and (5) modifying the program as needed until goals are achieved.*

The approach that we will describe is a fluid and dynamic process that recognizes that every child is different. Although we provide some very specific recommendations, we must caution that significant individualization of the approach may be necessary to achieve the best results. We're confident that parents, paraprofessionals, and professionals will acquire new skills that enable them to assess and develop programs suited to their child or student.

As a parent or teacher of a child with autism, you are keenly aware that there are many opinions regarding the best way to instruct children with autism. Debate swirls around whether children who are fully included in general education classes (inclusion) progress more quickly than children who are taught in segregated special education classes; whether the symptoms of autism can be mollified through diet or dietary supplements; whether it is better to establish flexible environments that give the child greater control rather than highly adult-controlled situations; and so forth and so on. It is safe to say that these debates will not be solved within the pages of this book. Unfortunately, some professionals advocate personal philosophies (and resulting recommendations) before there is a complete understanding of the scientific merits or risks of the approach. In this book, we describe an approach that establishes first that instructional methods should be based upon generally accepted rules for scientific efficacy. The approach that we will describe is very optimistic in that it assumes that everyone is teachable, if we break skills into small enough steps and provide individualized and systematic instruction.

The recommendations are drawn from published scientific studies concerned with finding effective methods to assess and instruct children with developmental disabilities, including autism. The methods described are not passing fads, but have withstood the test of time and careful analysis, and are commonly found in effective home-based and school programs.

The basic principles of the approach will seem familiar to you since they're tools we use everyday. For example, we will discuss using a "task analysis" to teach new skills. A task analysis is a tool that breaks complex skills into manageable steps for learning. In day-to-day life, it is much like following a cooking recipe or instructions that accompany electronic equipment. From time to time, most of us have struggled with understanding these kinds of instructions and probably can identify with how a young child may feel tackling a new skill. Likewise, most of us have at some time used rewards to motivate others—also a tool we will discuss later. What will make our recommendations seem different is the level of detail, consistency, and analysis that will be required to be successful.

The Parents' Role

In today's busy lives, it seems like we need eight days each week to accomplish everything. At first blush it may seem like the recommendations in this book will serve only to increase the normal anxiety you already feel, rather than reduce it. It is important, however, that you make the time for this endeavor. We wish that it was simple, but the reality is that it will take much diligence to foster your child's independence. But "independence" is the key word. As your child acquires skills, it means independence for you as well—you no longer need to do everything for them! It may take weeks or months for your child to learn new skills, but most children with autism *do* acquire a greater level of independence after a period of systematic and consistent instruction. In most cases, you will be able to simply scaffold on top of the things you are doing already. For example, instead of taking the time to dress your son each day, you use that time to introduce a program to teach him to dress himself. It may take a little more of your time initially, but eventually you'll both gain greater freedom.

The School's Role

Many of you may want to ask a nagging question: "Why isn't my child's school helping to teach self-help skills? Shouldn't they be addressing skill deficits too?" Well, the quick answer is "Yes." Whether your child is in a general or special education setting in a public or private school, school personnel have a responsibility to provide a comprehensive program that addresses *all* areas of development, including self-help (Individuals with Disabilities Education Improvement Act—Revised, 2006).

But let us start by defending those school districts that may not have teaching self-help skills at the top of their list of things to accomplish. First, if your child is in a general education classroom, those rooms are not predisposed to teaching self-help skills. Most children come to school with the basic skills of dressing, toileting, and personal hygiene. Simply put, teaching self-help skills is not on most teachers' radar screens. Second, teaching self-help skills to children with autism often requires one-to-one attention. In contrast, most general education classrooms are set up to teach academic subjects within large and small groups. The emphasis here is on the phrase "academic subjects." Most classroom agendas are already pretty full each day, particularly now that most states have academic standards that must be achieved. Finally, some school environments are not very conducive to teaching self-help skills like dressing, while ensuring confidentiality and privacy.

Although historically many public schools have failed to understand their role in teaching basic self-help skills, some change appears to be occurring. (If you are a teacher reading this, we commend you on your efforts and we believe that you will find the results quite gratifying.) Regardless of your child's schools' current involvement, you needn't be discouraged from enlisting the district to help teach your child self-help skills. At a minimum, skills that are being addressed at home must transfer to school. For many children, this will not occur without specific efforts to program transfer of skills from home to school and vice versa. School district personnel must be closely involved with you to know your child's abilities and your expectations. As skills are acquired at home, the district staff must ensure that skills are practiced at school. In many cases, this is a small extension of what the school may be doing already. For example, once the child has achieved handwashing, the school personnel can add a handwashing routine to an already established bathroom schedule. Using a simple checklist of steps, the teacher or aide simply observes the child complete the routine (at the most natural moment), notes whether each step was completed independently, and, when needed, provides help. The good news is that once a skill is learned in one context, transfer and demonstration of the skill to a second context typically occurs with less effort.

If your child attends a special education classroom for some or all of his day, we are a little less sympathetic to the school district that is not actively planning and teaching self-help skills. These rooms should place the development of self-help skills on a level equal to other important areas of learning, including academics. In many situations, the special education classroom should be the origin of self-help instruction. We encourage you to work with your child's classroom team very closely. Include them in conducting the inventory of skills that we will discuss in Chapter 3. Seek their advice about the developmental readiness of your child and the age-appropriateness of identified skill targets.

Finally, make certain that your child's school "gets with the program" by incorporating agreed upon self-help goals into your child's IEP (Individualized Education Program). It's crucial that you set specific (not vague), measurable goals so that progress can be easily tracked. Be vigilant about maintaining daily or weekly home-school communication about your child's self-help skills program. Schedule team meetings beyond the regularly scheduled IEP meetings to ensure that everyone is on the same page and not inadvertently thwarting the efforts of others. Communication and collaboration are essential to ensure the success of programs between and across sites. This can be accomplished by recognizing that your child's school is your long-term partner and working to develop a healthy, mutually supportive relationship.

Overview

Hopefully by now you are rolling up your sleeves and excited to develop a program to teach your child or student skills for independence. Chapter 1 will provide an argument for why teaching self-help skills should be given greater emphasis. Chapter 2 will provide some basic background on autism spectrum disorders and explain how people with ASDs may learn differently. Chapter 3 will guide you through a process of determining what skills to teach and when. Chapter 4 will help you establish the best context for teaching. Chapters 5 and 6 will cover how to motivate your child to learn and provide detailed information on instructional methods. Chapter 7, "Evaluating Progress," is very important and should not be overlooked. Continuous evaluation of progress and using data to help guide you is key to making good decisions. Chapters 8–10 will provide specific recommendations for each of the major skill areas (dressing and personal hygiene, eating, and toileting). Chapter 11 discusses generalization and provides helpful hints to improve your child's ability to use newly acquired skills in a variety of situations. Finally, the appendices include many helpful materials including a self-help inventory, a general troubleshooting section, information on readiness skills, and instructions on planning for and writing lesson plans.

Please note that unless otherwise specified, we have used the terms autism, autism spectrum disorder, and ASD interchangeably throughout the text. Also, in the name of impartiality, we have alternated gender pronouns chapter by chapter. All bibliographical references are compiled in a master list at the back of the book.

Success is to be measured not so much by the position that one reached in life as by the obstacles which he has overcome.
—**Booker T. Washington**

Reducing Long-Term Dependence

The Keller Family

Janice and Mark Keller celebrated the birth of their son, Michael, like the parents of any first born. Both highly successful professionals, the Kellers had expectations that Michael would be healthy and bright and a success in school, sports, and relationships.

However, those expectations quickly turned to despair when Michael was diagnosed with autism at three years old. Reflecting back upon his early development, the Kellers realized that signs of autism seemed to always be there—the absence of words and his failure to play with toys. But most of all, there was always a sense that Michael was lost in another world, seemingly unaware of others, and unable to share pleasure or understand the feelings of others.

At four years old, the Kellers were most concerned with improving Michael's communication, social, and academic skills. Certainly, basic self-help skills such as feeding, dressing, and bathing himself were important, but they felt there was plenty of time to address those issues later.

The Kellers were fortunate enough to enroll Michael in an excellent preschool that

helped him to develop a functional communication system. Although using spoken words was still a challenge for Michael, he was quite proficient at indicating basic needs and could respond to simple questions using pictures organized in a small notebook. Michael would simply open his communication notebook and point to a picture (actually a line drawing) of the object that he wanted or to answer a question. He also acquired some academic skills including matching objects by color and shape, sequencing numbers and letters, and pointing to common objects upon request.

When Michael turned five years old, the Kellers decided together with the school district to place him in a regular kindergarten classroom with a one-to-one aide. Although supporting the plan, the school district expressed concern that Michael was still not toilet trained and lacked other basic skills, such as wiping his nose independently, and washing and drying his hands. He also still required significant help at lunch to use utensils consistently, pour from one container to another, and eat neatly. They agreed to try kindergarten but noted that these skills would become more important each successive year.

Although everyone acknowledged that Michael lacked many daily-life skills, very little attention was paid to improving his abilities. The school focused on academic skills and at home Michael's parents simply found it easier to do most things for him. After all, he was getting somewhat better; at least he now did not resist his parents' efforts to bathe and dress him daily.

Michael made some nice social gains in kindergarten and his communication and academic skills continued to improve, although he still lagged behind his peers. Each year thereafter, the school district emphasized Michael's differences from other students and noted that he lacked independence in the completion of basic self-help tasks. Eventually, it was decided that Michael would be better served in a special education classroom with some opportunities for integration. He was immediately excluded from several activities such as swimming because he was not fully toilet trained and he did not have independent undressing and dressing skills. The special education team attempted to address these issues but was unsystematic in its efforts and little progress was made.

Transition into adolescence and adulthood also became increasingly more challenging for the Kellers because of Michael's lack of independence. Mrs. Keller would not take Michael into the community without Mr. Keller because she could not comfortably take Michael into the women's bathroom and she did not trust that he could use the men's bathroom by himself. Frankly, the Kellers were tired—tired of having to assist Michael with of all the daily tasks of dressing, bathing, toileting, and food preparation.

As an adult, Michael moved into a small group home with three other young men. Although Michael was more competent in his communication and socialization than his housemates, he was rejected for placement in other homes because he was too dependent on others to complete basic self-help tasks. For the same reason, he was not hired for several jobs to which he applied.

Making a Case for Emphasizing Self-Help Skills

Do you see yourselves in a situation similar to the Kellers'? Although we are more successful than ever helping children overcome the severe deficits of autism, many children still require supports throughout their lifetime. Educators and families often correctly focus on communication, social, and academic delays in young children, but the failure to also address delays in the development of self-help skills can have short- and long-term consequences. Although Michael improved significantly and was able to participate in many typical school activities, full participation was not always possible. It is difficult to tease out what deficit areas most prevented full participation; however, it is likely that dependence in the completion of daily self-help skills contributed greatly. When a child is very young, no one seems to notice very much that a parent, grandparent, teacher, or aide helps her with most activities of daily living—dressing, bathing, eating, and toileting. After all, children are to be nurtured and protected. Furthermore, in our busy schedules, it is a lot easier to simply tie your child's shoes than it is to instruct, cue, prompt and, in short—wait—as she attempts to do it on her own. In addition, you probably feel very helpful and successful completing basic self-help tasks for your child. It is something that you can do successfully and easily, unlike helping your child to talk and socialize.

But as the Kellers help us to illustrate, your desire to assist can in fact prevent or thwart your child's development. Failure to address self-help skills may prevent your child from full participation in school functions, recreational activities, community integration, and eventually housing and job opportunities. Self-help skills signal the beginning of independence from parents and are critical for maintaining physical health and reducing dependence (Snell & Farlow, 1988). Moreover, appropriate dressing and hygiene skills are important for acceptance with peers. Concerned that we may have overstated the case and frightened you, let it be said that achieving greater independence in the completion of self-help skills *is* possible and may be one of the easiest areas (relatively speaking) to achieve success with your child with ASD.

> Failure to address self-help skills may prevent your child from full participation in school functions, recreational activities, community integration, and eventually housing and job opportunities.

A Different Way of Learning

As most of you know, autism is defined by deficits in three areas of development: (1) social interaction, (2) communication, and (3) range of interests. Deficits in one or more of these areas will likely interfere with the typical course of development of self-help skills. For young children, the development of self-help skills is closely related to their social and language development. Young, typically developing children often strive for the approval of their parents and teachers and love being recognized for their individual achievements. How many times have parents been heard to say, "You're such a big girl," when recognizing their child's attempt to complete a task independently. In fact, it is not uncommon for the child's desire for independence to be problematic, like when the child tries to pour her own milk and spills it. The typical child's extraordinary motivation to be independent makes the parent's task pretty simple—state and model expectations, provide ongoing support, and recognize (praise) the child's achievements.

When describing a child with classic autism, the story changes dramatically. We are unlikely to have a fully motivated child striving to please the adults around them. She is not likely to benefit vicariously from modeling provided by siblings, peers, and parents—hoping to match her behavior to others. In fact, she may appear unaware of others around her. Often the child appears disinterested and inattentive even after repeated requests to "watch" and "pay attention." It may even be unclear whether the child is processing the words spoken to them, particularly since many children do not follow the most basic instructions (e.g., "come here" and "sit down") consistently. A child with more significant impairments may also engage in a variety of repetitive mannerisms (e.g., hand-flapping or spinning the wheels of a toy car) that interfere with your attempts to help. For example, a child's fascination with fans may result in her flipping the switch on the bathroom fan repeatedly rather than assisting with brushing her teeth.

Because of the unique characteristics of children with ASD, the approach used to teach self-help skills will be different than teaching children without developmental disabilities. Based on an assumption that there is a relationship between the acquisition of skills and the language and intellectual strengths of each child, it makes intuitive sense that children with fewer developmental concerns are likely to learn self-help skills at an earlier age. For these children, teaching may rely on instructions, modeling, and frequent opportunities to practice skills.

In contrast, children with more significant developmental concerns are not likely to learn self-help skills by simply being exposed to tasks over and over again. However, an area of strength for many children with autism is their ability to successfully complete tasks that require little or no interpretation or discrimination of language, i.e., nonverbal tasks. Because self-help skills consist largely of fixed sequential actions (usually a strength for children with autism) and require little abstract thinking or social interactions (often weak areas), children with autism sometimes show relatively rapid learning and retention of self-help skills.

> Because self-help skills consist largely of fixed sequential actions (usually a strength for children with autism) and require little abstract thinking or social interactions (often weak areas), children with autism sometimes show relatively rapid learning and retention of self-help skills.

Although it would be helpful if you could explain and show the child your expectations for personal care, it is not necessary. Self-help skills rarely require language discriminations, so we can expect children to learn these tasks without having to completely understand language. Success for most children with autism will be achieved through a carefully crafted program that breaks the tasks into a series of small steps and uses direct and systematic means to instruct. Rest assured, this is precisely what this book will teach you to do.

■ Reducing Life's Stressors

Although a bit overused, we are reminded of the quote: "Give a child a fish and he will eat for a day. Teach a child to fish and he will eat for a lifetime." What is not stated is that if you give a child a fish without teaching her to fish, you may get stuck doing it forever. Clearly, many parents are stuck wanting their child to be more independent but lacking the resources, skills, and time to achieve their goal. As a result, they continue to do such tasks for their child and risk unwittingly making her more dependent. This dependency may ultimately foster resentment, particularly as the child grows older and reaches a chronological age when parents are generally relieved of some day-to-day responsibilities of care. Parents begin to realize that there may never come a day when they will be freed of these responsibilities. Also, there is a realization that there may not be adequate supports for their child once they are gone. As the years progress, these issues continue to irritate and create extraordinary stress.

If you've picked up this book, likely you've accepted that the "wait and see and hope" approach will not work. You've come to realize that some immediate efforts are needed to achieve greater solace later. With a well-crafted plan, you will find that some of the instruction you'll learn to provide can take place within the context of normal daily routines. Your child has to get dressed each morning anyway, so we'll show you how to overlay a program to teach her to dress. It may increase your time and effort initially, but as your child gains greater independence, your time commitment and stress level will thankfully be reduced. The siblings of a child with autism also may indirectly benefit from the increased independence of their brother or sister with autism by reducing the level of care they may have to provide as a potential long-term caregiver.

2

Success is where preparation and opportunity meet.
—**Bobby Unser**

Identifying Individual Differences

Susan

Susan is a ten-year-old child with autism who lives with her mother and younger sister. She attends a special education class in her local school district. She is nonverbal except for a few labels that she uses inconsistently. Fortunately, she is able to use a picture-symbol system to express her basic wants and needs and she is beginning to combine symbols to form short sentences ("I want a cookie," "Let's play"). She is able to recognize a few written words and she is working on identifying numbers. Susan is not yet toilet trained and she wears diapers, although her pediatrician indicates that she is physically capable of controlling her bladder and bowels. She requires significant assistance to dress and full assistance with buttons, zippers, and snaps. She uses a spoon to eat but has not yet mastered the use of a fork to spear food or a knife to cut and spread.

Mark

Mark is a four-and-a-half-year-old child with autism who attends a local community preschool program and receives home-based special education. Testing indi-

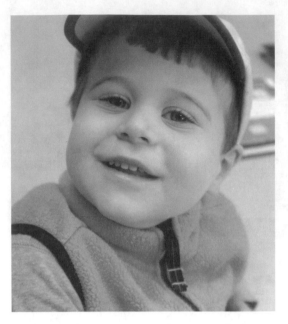

cates that his intellectual functioning is within the low average range. He has a large vocabulary of words and phrases but is rote and awkward when relating to other people. He has particular interest in anything associated with outer space and is unable to sustain a conversation about any other topic. He is able to follow basic instructions and routines, but frequently tantrums when asked to end a preferred activity or begin a less preferred task. He uses the toilet without direct help and rarely has accidents, as long as his parents frequently remind him to use the bathroom. He uses his fingers to eat most foods and still drinks from a covered cup to prevent spilling.

Although both Mark and Susan exhibit significant delays, Susan's mother probably feels the greater sense of urgency to ensure that her daughter acquires some basic self-help skills quickly. At ten years old, she should be dressing herself, independently toileting, and using eating utensils skillfully. Mark's parents may be a little more tolerant of their son's deficits because he is still very young and his abilities are within the normal age range for some skills (e.g., independent toileting). One thing is for sure, neither child is likely to improve very much without a carefully designed and systematic plan.

■ Typical Development—*When* Did They Learn That?

Although it is important to choose a self-help skill to teach that you are motivated to accomplish, it is also important to teach something that your child is developmentally ready to learn. If your child is not ready to learn, then your efforts may lead to initial failure. Determining what is developmentally "normal" is a little tricky when you are addressing the needs of children with general developmental delays. Looking at the benchmarks set by children who are developing normally will give you some general framework for what is considered age-appropriate. Most basic self-help skills are acquired by a child's sixth birthday; however, there is a broad developmental age span for any particular skill. For example, the typical age for learning to put on a T-shirt ranges from three years old to almost four years old. Many factors influence the age at which a specific skill is learned, including the child's physical development, attention span, and motivation, as well as the parent's tolerance. Nearly all children learn basic skills and do so within established age ranges (to be discussed in Chapter 3). Children with autism also can learn the identified skills when appropriate intervention is provided. However, for children with autism, there are significant individual differences as to *when* a skill is learned, beginning at the upper end of what is considered normal and extending into adulthood.

■ Typical Development—*How* Did They Learn That?

Very little research explains how typically developing children learn self-help skills. Children appear to learn largely from their parents' coaching, demonstration, and frequent gentle reminders. In most situations, parents simply show and tell children what they want them to do, then praise them for any reasonable attempts. Granted it's still not easy, but in most cases no extraordinary methods are required to ensure a positive result. Even the small number of children who develop problems (e.g., chronic bedwetting) typically improve as they physically mature and social consequences become more powerful. Only a small percentage of otherwise typically developing children require some form of systematic intervention.

Those of us who have spent time watching young children grow certainly observe a lot of activities that may be related to the development of daily living skills. An early skill observed in typically developing children is the ability to imitate the behavior modeled by a parent (Sebastian, 1998) or older sibling. Children spend a great deal of their time engaged in activities that mimic their parents and siblings and provide the context for learning social, communication, and, arguably, self-help skills. By imitating, children can learn a variety of basic and complex skills in a very short period of time without direct training being required. In fact, without imitation, how would language, play, and many academic skills be acquired? In short, it is a very important skill that can be used by an individual throughout his lifetime to acquire new skills.

Typically developing children not only have the ability to imitate but are naturally motivated to do so. Very early in life we see children engaged in pretend self activities such as brushing their own teeth or hair. Similarly, young children want to independently drink from a cup or pour from a pitcher. Whether it is the reward of matching or the praise they receive from their parents and teachers, the motivation to imitate seems to be present very early. Even when the parent discourages some independence (e.g., insisting that the child is too young to pour from the very full pitcher), the child's desire to do it independently persists—suggesting that the parents' attention may be important but not always necessary. How many times have we observed a child attempt to brush his hair, then reject a parent's attempt to help? It appears that the act of imitation is the goal, not one's physical appearance.

One of the first places that we observe imitation is in the context of play. It is possible that play may have a part in the early development of self-help skills. Very early in life, children begin to relate objects to themselves, imitating the behavior of others such as combing their hair, or later in a symbolic way, bringing an empty cup to their lips. These activities may map the way to greater independence in the completion of self-help skills.

■ Children With Autism—How Are They Different?

Anyone who has lived or worked with a child with autism is keenly aware that that child is unique—even when compared to other children with disabilities.

As a group, children within the autism spectrum exhibit a broad range of individual differences, from having no speech to mild speech and language disorders. When communication concerns are combined with impairments in social interactions and highly restricted interests, the triad of autism-defining characteristics is formed. Because autism may be characterized by a range of intellectual abilities from children with above average intelligence to children with severe intellectual delays, the disorder often presents differently each time. Clearly, different combinations of communication, social, and intellectual functioning may result in different developmental outcomes and may present very different challenges for teaching new skills.

In contrast to typically developing children, children with autism are not likely to learn by simply showing and telling them what is expected. Even those children with milder intellectual delays often struggle when skill requirements move beyond the very basic to advanced skills, such as coordinating clothing and choosing clothing consistent with age and community norms. These kids also may not recognize or respond to their peers' social "rules" for personal appearance and hygiene.

> In contrast to typically developing children, children with autism are not likely to learn by simply showing and telling them what is expected.

Many children with autism do not learn to imitate naturally and their play is described as less developed than that of other children, including those with developmental concerns other than autism (Lifter, Sulzer-Azaroff, Anderson & Edwards, 1993). These deficits are likely a result of neurological conditions that underlie autism and interfere with the child's ability to attend to, understand, and process information received. Most children with autism can be taught to imitate and play, but outcomes vary significantly. While most typically developing children learn rules (e.g., "Do as I do") that enable them to generalize regardless of the particular context (i.e., setting, task, example, and people), for some children with ASD, learning may be restricted to the specific examples taught (e.g., touching one's nose or rolling a ball) with little or no generalization to untaught examples (e.g., labeling body parts or playing catch).

After learning a skill (and in some cases simultaneous with learning), parents of children with autism must ensure that newly developed skills are frequently practiced and used in each of the settings in which their child will learn, play, and work. It is common for children with autism to learn a skill within a highly controlled set of conditions (e.g., washing their hands in their bathroom at home) and not be able to apply the same skill in another environment (e.g., in a busy community bathroom facility). This is commonly referred to as the failure to "generalize." The steps for teaching and recommendations for addressing generalization are something we will discuss in individual chapters and in detail in Chapter 11. For now, it is important to know that generalization is one of the challenges faced by parents of children with autism. In fact, learning is never complete until it can be shown that the child demonstrates the target skill in a variety of contexts (i.e., in different environments, and with different people and materials).

So what happens when imitation and play skills are absent or severely limited? The good news is that most children who do not learn generalized imitation still acquire basic and some advanced self-help skills. Although imitation is a highly useful way to learn (planned or natural), there is no evidence that its absence predicts failure for the development of daily-life skills. It just means that we must find another way to teach and for children to learn. Many children with autism require an approach that

> A newly learned skill is said to generalize if it can be performed in a wide variety of places, with many different people, and in the presence of a wide range of materials.

relies heavily on breaking the target skills into very small steps and directly teaching the skill one step at a time—often accompanied by direct physical prompts for desired responses that must later be faded. Of course, this approach may not seem as natural and fluid as simply showing and telling a child what you want, but it may be the only effective approach for children with significant developmental delays including autism. (We will discuss instructional methods in detail in Chapter 6.)

Not surprisingly, most things that Susan, from our earlier case sample, will learn will need to be taught directly. It's unlikely that she will borrow from one learning experience (e.g., buttoning her shirt) and apply it to another task (e.g., snapping her pants). It is also highly unlikely that learning to dress herself will immediately result in "independent dressing" or the ability to select her own clothing. The good news is that each skill can be learned if her parents' expectations are reasonable and their instructional methods are adequate. In contrast, Mark may show some generalization of learning from one basic activity to another without the benefit of direct instruction (e.g., use a variety of fasteners) or after only a few instructional opportunities and practice. But the limit of his ability to understand and spontaneously apply newly learned skills in novel situations is still unclear. Will he understand the importance of using deodorant daily or choosing clothing consistent with weather conditions? This will require his parents' frequent monitoring and intervention to ensure success.

Communication, particularly the ability to understand, process, and integrate information, is important for typical development. Once again, many children with autism experience significant delays in both the understanding and production of speech. As a result, methods that rely on verbal instructions and explanation may not work very well. Oddly, some children with autism may become unusually reliant on communication from adults and fail to gain a sufficient level of independence. For example, they are able to dress themselves, but only when the parent verbally prompts each step (e.g., "Now, put on your shirt").

Another characteristic of children with ASD is a restricted and stereotyped range of interests. This can present itself as an inflexible adherence to specific routines, stereotypic mannerisms (e.g., hand flapping), or preoccupation with facts (e.g., baseball statistics). Kids with significant nonfunctional verbal and body and hand mannerisms sometimes are the most challenging because these behaviors may interfere with getting and sustaining the child's attention. It also appears that some children use self-stimulatory behavior to help avoid tasks that may seem too challenging, at least initially. These problems are best overcome by attending closely to the information in Chapters 5 and 6 concerned with using reinforcers effectively and using good instructional methods that help elicit and keep the child's attention.

Finally, there are a variety of sensory and motor concerns that may interfere with learning self-help skills. These issues may be present at a very early age for some otherwise typically developing children but rarely persist beyond the first three or four years of life. In contrast, children with autism may have ongoing sensory and motor issues, such as an extreme sensitivity to the texture of toothpaste or difficulty with the fine motor skills needed for buttoning. Again, these problems will be discussed in later chapters.

Summary

It may seem that the issues discussed so far present a formidable and overwhelming challenge to parents and professionals. No doubt achieving greater independence will be a hurdle for some children with ASD but not an insurmountable one. The solution is to provide a planned and very systematic approach to instruction. It is difficult to predict which children with autism are likely to have the best outcomes and what variables are reliably associated with favorable results. However, we know that progress is likely to be achieved for most children only after a significant investment of time and effort. Certainly, there is existing and still emerging evidence that providing early intervention brings the greatest gains. At a young age, children are still developing intellectually and behaviorally, and expectations are being established. There is mounting information that the brain has the capacity to change in response to timely, intensive intervention (Shore, 1997). But rest assured, it is never too late to start. It may take a little more time for an older child or adult with autism to overcome behavioral patterns (his own and those of his parents) and behavioral concerns may be more challenging, but, there are hundreds of examples of adolescents and young adults that have learned to toilet, dress, and feed themselves.

> Rest assured, it is never too late to start teaching your child self-help skills.

As we have indicated, the range of outcomes for children with autism is broad and while some individuals will make very significant gains toward independence, some may remain dependent on their parents or caregivers for the rest of their lives. For some children, your primary goal may be to reduce their dependence rather than strive for complete independence. For example, if Susan, from our previous case study, eventually reaches a level when a single verbal prompt is required to ensure that she brushes her teeth each night before bed, that should be considered a success! Goals must be evaluated within the context of other individual accomplishments in social, communication, and vocational development. A minimum standard is that the development of self-help skills should never be an impediment to gaining productive employment and developing meaningful relationships. In this way, parents and professionals can make a significant difference in nearly every case.

3

Think you can, think you can't, either way you are right!
—**Henry Ford**

Determining What to Teach and When

The Miller Family

Daren and Cathy Miller have two children. Their oldest, a nine-year-old daughter, has some mild language delays and needs some extra help with academic subjects

at school. In spite of these problems, she has learned to dress, bathe, and feed herself like other children her age. The Miller's youngest child, Jeffrey, is a very different case. Jeffrey, diagnosed with autism, is five years old and will enter kindergarten this year. He is still almost completely dependent upon his parents for dressing, toothbrushing, and bathing. He has made progress in toileting but never independently initiates and still has many accidents. Jeffrey eats a reasonable range of foods but does not reliably use a spoon without significant spilling and never uses a fork to spear food.

Since a very early age, Jeffrey's parents have focused on his social and language development and have paid scant attention to the development of his self-help skills. Frankly, with so many issues and concerns, it is simply easier to do things for him. But with kindergarten looming, they have begun to think about basic day-to-day skills that most children are demonstrating by this time. The Millers don't know where to start. Unlike their daughter, Jeffrey shows very little interest in learning to be more independent and he sometimes resists their help to dress him and brush his teeth. The Millers wonder: Is it really worth struggling with these things now?

◼ Is Your Family Like the Millers?

The Millers reluctance to begin the process of teaching self-help skills is understandable, particularly given Jeffrey's lack of interest. Parents of children with autism will likely have to spend much more time and effort teaching self-help skills than parents of typically developing children. Even though the Millers' daughter has some mild language and academic concerns, she did not require extraordinary means to learn how to dress and bathe herself. Her parents simply needed to show and tell their daughter what to do, provide sufficient opportunity for practice, and—Presto! Well, maybe it wasn't *that* easy.

For parents and teachers, the challenges of teaching self-care skills to a child with autism are not fundamentally different from those faced teaching academic or communication skills. Research has demonstrated that children with autism learn best when the skill to be learned is broken into very small steps and each step is taught systematically (i.e., in a planned and methodical way). So, the quick answer to the Millers' question is, "yes," it is worth teaching Jeffrey some basic self-help skills now. Although it sounds a little trite to say, it's not going to get any easier. And although the Millers might be unenthusiastic, an early start will be especially useful since Jeffrey will shortly be expected to generalize these skills to his kindergarten classroom.

◼ Overview of this Chapter

This chapter will guide you to identify and prioritize the self-care skills that are most important for your child to learn at this time. We have divided the broad domain of self-help into four areas—undressing and dressing, personal hygiene, eating and drinking, and toileting. Chapters 8-10 will address each of these areas specifically. Our goal here is to help you determine what skills you should teach and when is the right time, developmentally, to teach them. We also plan to give you helpful recommendations on how to set realistic goals for learning and establish reasonable expectations for your child's independence. We will argue that learning will be a very individualized developmental process for each child, in which achievements build on each other over months and years.

◼ Deciding What to Teach
Determining What is Normal or Age-Appropriate

It is common for parents to frequently compare their young child with autism to nieces, nephews, and friends' children. Even parents whose children appear to be progressing typically, may quietly observe and compare their child to other children and discreetly probe for differences. Knowing how other children are developing seems to help validate that our children are growing normally or, maybe, more quickly than other children. This behavior may have some value when a parent has some legitimate reason to think their child is not developing normally but otherwise it is not a very healthy practice, and the information can be easily misinterpreted. Why would we say that? Well for one thing, same-aged children develop skills at different points in time but within acceptable age ranges that may be months apart. This occurs because genetic, biological, and/or environmental variability exists within and across families. As much as some parents try to accelerate their child's learning by providing enriched learning experiences, each child brings to a situation his or her own disposition and interests, as well as behavioral and developmental history, and these differences may significantly influence how development unfolds.

> The term "age-appropriate" refers to concepts, skills, and activities that most children are able to demonstrate within an observed age range (e.g., most children, age eighteen months old to two years old, are able to put two words together, such as "more cookie").

Experts also have reported that learning has a natural ebb and flow—it is not always fluid and uninterrupted (Bloom & Tinker, 2001). Typically developing children may show tremendous progress in one developmental area, then, suddenly, stop when another area begins to emerge or expand. For example, a child may begin approximating simple words, but suddenly show very little additional language growth for several months. At the same moment, the child may demonstrate rapid growth in his or her motor development, for example, learning to crawl up stairs or walk independently. The point to be made here is that, at any given time, two children of the same age may have distinctively different developmental profiles, but both are considered within the normal range of acceptable growth.

It must be recognized that children with autism may have even more irregular or scattered developmental profiles, showing progress in one developmental domain and little or no progress in another. For example, they may have normal or slightly delayed motor development (e.g., jumping, climbing, and running) and show little or no growth in another area (e.g., remain completely nonverbal). These differences are not just a matter of the natural ebb and flow of development, as we described above. As an analogy, instead of high and low rolling hills that define typical development, children with autism have tall peaks and deep valleys defining their development. Even when compared to children with developmental disabilities other than autism, children with autism often show very uneven development within and across domains (e.g., excellent gross motor skills but very immature fine motor skills).

Probing to see how your child with autism stacks up to other chil-

> Instead of high and low rolling hills that define typical development, children with autism have tall peaks and deep valleys defining their development.

dren may be extremely discouraging if you discover that your child is significantly off the normal path. On the other hand, knowing the age and order that children typically learn specific skills may help you decide where you should start with your child's instruction and may provide important insight into which order to teach specific skills. We recommend that typical developmental milestones be used as a guide for determining readiness, but should not be used to measure your child's progress. We suggest that the best approach to evaluating progress is to continuously evaluate your child against himself or herself, much like a runner who is trying to improve his time running a 10k race. The goal is continuous personal improvement, not taking first place in the race. Too much focus on normal development may discourage you from taking action. We will provide some objective ways to measure progress in Chapter 7.

> We recommend that typical developmental milestones be used as a guide for determining readiness, but should not be used to measure your child's progress.

Table 3-1 on page 17 provides a list of developmental milestones, that is, the age by which most children (not specifically children with autism) have acquired the skill indicated. For example, by age two, most children can drink from a cup unassisted and use a spoon with some reasonable independence (although spilling may still occur). What it does *not* show, but is important to note again, is that the specific age that these skills may be acquired varies considerably across children. While one child may be able to independently drink from a cup at fourteen months of age, another child may not acquire this skill until twenty-two months of age. Still, both are considered "normal." Thus, there is considerable range in normal development. Nevertheless, this table provides a frame of reference for the identification and prioritization of self-help skills to teach your child with autism. One easy guideline is to teach only age-appropriate skills, or those skills that most children your child's age use already. Thus, if your child is not drinking from a cup by age twenty-two months, then this is an area that needs attention soon.

Age-appropriateness is only one way to determine what to teach and when. Other considerations include your child's developmental readiness (developmentally-appropriate), the presence of pivotal learning-to-learn skills, her interests and abilities, as well as what is important (functional) for your child to know at the time. And, of course, *you* have to be sufficiently motivated and be willing to invest the time and energy needed to teach the skill. Let's take a moment to talk about each of these.

> Developmental milestones are a set of skills or tasks that most children can do within a certain age range.

Determining What Is Developmentally-Appropriate

Developmental appropriateness or readiness considers where the individual child is functioning within known developmental sequences. For example, chil-

■ Table 3-1   Developmental Milestones

The following table identifies the age at which most typically developing children have acquired the skill identified (best estimates).

BY AGE:	MOST CHILDREN:
1 year	■ Hold and drink from a bottle ■ Eat solid foods ■ Feed self most of a meal (finger foods)
2 years	■ Drink from a cup ■ Use a spoon or fork (with spilling) ■ Suck liquid from a straw ■ Remove shoes, socks, pants
3 years	■ Feed self with spoon (without spilling) ■ Pour well from pitcher ■ Ask to use toilet ■ Urinate in toilet ■ Wash and dry hands ■ Bathe with assistance ■ Take off coat ■ Put on coat (not including fasteners) ■ Pull up pants with elastic waistbands ■ Put on shoes (not necessarily correct feet)
4 years	■ Prepare simple snacks (i.e., fix a bowl of cereal) ■ Brush teeth ■ Wash and dry hands and face ■ Are toilet trained during day with some accidents ■ Remove most clothing independently ■ Put on socks independently ■ Put shoes on correct feet ■ Dress themselves, except laces and buttons ■ Unbutton clothing ■ Put on clothing in correct front/back position
5 years	■ Prepare simple foods (sandwich) ■ Apply soap to washcloth ■ Use toilet without help ■ Care for nose without assistance (blow and wipe) ■ Use towel to dry body ■ Get dressed without help ■ Button front-opening clothing ■ Use all fasteners
6 years	■ Spread with a knife ■ Cut with a knife ■ Cover mouth with tissue or hand when sneezing or coughing ■ Remember to wash hands after using the toilet ■ Brush hair acceptably ■ Dress without reminders including opening and closing fasteners ■ Tie shoe laces
7 years	■ Cut with knife and fork simultaneously ■ Use proper utensil for eating food ■ Wash self acceptably without help (shower or bath)
8 years	■ Choose proper clothing for occasion ■ Coordinate clothing

dren do not run until they know first how to walk. Once you know what is considered a normal sequence of skills development, you can assess your child against this sequence and follow the typical order of development. In a sense, age is irrelevant. Readiness is defined by the presence of requisite skills within a developmental domain (like our example of walking before running) or across developmental domains (learning to play leads to greater socialization with peers).

A small number of studies have shown that children with autism are more likely to learn and generalize a skill when it is within the child's current ability, as defined by a normal developmental sequence. For example, researchers who have studied language and play development (Dyer, Santarcangelo, & Luce, 1987; Lifter, Sulzer-Azaroff, Anderson, and Cowdery, 1993) have reported that children with autism are more likely to acquire skills based on each child's level of functioning within known developmental sequences rather than on the basis of their age. If a boy plays with objects indiscriminately (e.g., all objects are mouthed), he may not be ready to learn pretend self activities (e.g., child brings a cup to his own lips to pretend to drink) (Lifter et al., 1998). On the other hand, he may be ready for learning specific actions like hugging a stuffed animal or rolling a car. We do not know of any similar studies that have examined developmental readiness in the acquisition of self-help skills. However, relying on research from other areas, most professionals recommend that you follow a developmental sequence.

> Each child is unique with individual patterns and rates of growth. Learning opportunities should challenge but match the child's developing abilities (Brendekamp & Copple, 1997).

Referring again to Table 3-1, self-help skills are presented in a developmental sequence that starts with the most basic skills and gradually moves to more complex skills. For example, most children learn to remove their pants before they become completely toilet trained. This list used in combination with the skills inventory that we will present later in this chapter (and in Appendix A) will help guide your decision-making as to what to teach and when.

Assessing Whether Your Child Has the Building Blocks for Learning

Table 3-2 provides a list of questions you can use to help determine if your child has important learning readiness skills. We must admit that we're a bit hesitant to include this section here. We're concerned that if you determine your child doesn't have the "learning-to-learn" skills, you may decide this is not the time to begin teaching self-help skills. Although we cannot absolutely say that the absence of these skills leads to failure, logic tells us that certain skills are very likely to make teaching (that is, learning) more successful. That said, we are not recommending that you wait until everything is perfectly in place before beginning. Some of these learning-to-learn skills may improve as you begin to teach self-help skills (e.g., your child may gradually become more accepting of physical prompts).

How many of these questions can you safely answer "yes" to? If your answer is "very few" or "none," then you may want to begin by teaching a few basic learn-

---

■ **Table 3-2   Learning-to-Learn Skills—Determining Your Child's Readiness to Learn**

Does your child:

1. Consistently look when you call her name?

2. Pay attention when you give a direction by stopping what she is doing and orienting her body or head toward you (brief eye contact preferred)?

3. Follow simple one-step directions such as "come here," "sit down," "wait," "stand up," "give me _____"?

4. Consistently make and sustain eye-contact with you for at least three seconds?

5. Look at objects or materials when asked to do so?

6. Sit or remain for at least ten minutes in a defined area while engaged in an activity (with or without close parent supervision)?

7. Communicate simple wants and needs (e.g., pointing to a desired object) using words, gestures, sign language, drawings, or pictures?

8. Point to common body parts when asked (e.g., eyes, ears, nose, head)?

9. Respond to physical guidance without resisting?

10. Imitate your simple motor actions such as pointing to your nose or touching your head?

---

ing-to-learn behaviors before tackling the problem of self-help skills. If pushed to identify the most significant learning-to-learn skills, we would identify five skills that your child should acquire: (1) pay attention to an activity (five to ten minutes); (2) respond to name and the instruction "look"; (3) follow simple instructions; (4) imitate the actions of others; and (5) make choices.

You may wonder why "making choices" is a readiness skill. This ability allows your child to identify what rewards he values most. We often begin a lesson by asking the child "What do you want to earn?" She then selects by pointing to one object from a choice of two to four items. Throughout the session, we remind her what she is earning. This is often important when you are looking for the most natural and effective ways to motivate a child to complete self-help tasks. For example, if you ask your child to select what she wants for breakfast, she might be encouraged to dress herself so she can go eat.

A detailed discussion of how to teach these important requisite skills is beyond the scope of this book. We have tried to be helpful by including a brief description of how to teach them in Appendix C. We suggest that you look at this after you have read Chapters 4, 5, and 6, which describe instructional tools that are helpful for teaching learning-to-learn skills. Most often these skills are taught within highly structured situations in the home or school where distractions are minimized, materials and cues are systematically used to help the child learn, and behavioral concerns are more easily addressed. This context is most conducive to helping the child acquire learning-to-learn skills. As the child becomes more compliant and understands that good things result from following directions and being successful at task completion, then learning in less structured contexts is likely to be more successful. Helpful resources for learning to teach basic skills include Harris & Weiss (1998), Lovaas (2003), and two books edited by Catherine Maurice & colleagues (1996, 2001). The complete references are included at the end of this book.

Considering Your Child's Interests and Abilities

Consider the significant challenges faced by the Millers in our earlier case study. Their son, Jeffrey, shows very little interest in being independent or pleasing his parents and teachers. In addition, Jeffrey often resists their attempts to help him complete even simple tasks, such as brushing his teeth. As such, there is a tendency for everyone to say, let's just wait a little longer to teach these skills and maybe he will be more interested in a few months. Well, it is certainly true that children must be physically and emotionally ready for some skill targets. On the other hand, many children with autism do not automatically become more interested as they get older. The goal is to find a balance point between what your child is interested in doing and what he or she needs to do, based on their age and developmental profile.

You may find it easier to start with a skill that is emerging or that your child shows some interest in performing. For example, if Jeffrey sometimes helps put on his shirt by raising his arms without prompting, that should signal to his parents that he may be ready to learn to put on a pullover shirt independently. Similarly, if he seems highly interested when his parents make him a sandwich for lunch, they might begin to teach him to spread jelly with a knife, even before he learns other skills that typically emerge earlier.

> In deciding which skills to teach first, the goal is to find a balance point between what your child is interested in doing and what he or she needs to do, based on their age and developmental profile.

Assessing *Your* Readiness to Teach

Your readiness as a parent is also essential to choosing the skill to be taught and the timing of that instruction. As we indicated before, it must be a skill that is developmentally-appropriate, meaning it is a skill likely to be acquired by a typically developing child during that period of life. Your two-year-old child should not be expected to tie her own shoes. Parents often target skills that will reduce their aggravation and make life easier for them. For example, you may accept that your child eats with her fingers, even if other children her age are eating with a spoon. At least this is one way that your child is relatively independent. At the same time, you may be highly motivated to address toilet accidents because of their immediate consequences to you and your home (e.g., urine soaked clothing and furniture). But if you begin too early, before your child has some basic readiness skills, you may unwittingly set the stage for failure. You must search for the balance between your child's readiness to learn a specific skill and your interest in teaching it. Having said that, we also recommend that you *begin* with something developmentally-appropriate and that involves only a few steps or component skills. Teaching a child to pour from a pitcher has far fewer steps and fewer component skills than toileting (e.g., recognizing the need, locating the bathroom, pulling pants down, and so on).

> You must search for the balance between your child's readiness to learn a specific skill and your interest in teaching it.

Selecting Functional Skills to Teach

It is additionally important to consider what is most functional for your child to learn at a given time. In our example, Jeffrey Miller is preparing for entry into kindergarten. His family and school professionals should consider which of the deficit areas are most important for kindergarten integration. Although bathing may be age-appropriate, learning to independently pull up pants or put on shoes may be more important for fitting in at school. Thus we have defined functional skills as those skills your child needs in order to fully integrate and participate at home, school, or work. In the case of self-help skills, almost everything is a functional skill, but you cannot teach everything at once. So how do you determine what is really functional at this point in time? Consider the questions in Table 3-3 on the next page. These questions are not ranked in order of importance. If none of these questions can be answered positively, then the skill is probably not important to teach at this time. If some of the questions can be answered with a "yes," then whether to teach the skill or not must be considered

> Functional skills: Those skills your child needs in order to fully integrate and participate at home, school, or work.

within the context of the child's age, readiness, and other skills to be addressed.

In Jeffrey's case, his parents are considering teaching him to dress, brush his teeth, initiate toileting, and use a spoon with minimal spilling. The Millers applied each of the questions in Table 3-3 to each target skill and produced the profile shown in Table 3-4 on the next page. These answers apply to Jeffrey's situation and might look very different for another child even at the same age.

Toileting and spoon skills received the most "yes" answers. Based upon these results, the Millers decide to address these two skill sets and wait on the other areas until later. They've also consulted with school district staff who agreed that these were functional areas of importance. We do not recommend that you work on more than one or two skills at a time. If you decide to teach more than one skill, choose skills that have very little in common. For example toothbrushing and cutting with scissors share very little in terms of the component skills required and the materials used. On the other hand, toothbrushing and face washing often have common materials (e.g., towel, sink, and mirror) and a common setting (bathroom) and may create confusion for some children.

■ Table 3-3   Determining What is Functional for Your Child to Learn Now

1. Does the absence of the skill prevent the child from full participation in activities with peers or siblings (e.g., inability to swim in public pool because she is not toilet trained)?

2. Does doing the skill for your child underscore the child's weaknesses and lead to her being less accepted by her peers (e.g., requires an aide in the bathroom)?

3. Is the skill necessary or important for teaching another skill (e.g., pulling pants up and down is important for toilet training)?

4. Is this a skill that must be performed independently in public (e.g., when a male child becomes too old to accompany his mother into a public bathroom)?

5. Is this a skill that, when absent, may create embarrassment for the child or her family (e.g., inability to use a spoon successfully limits restaurant outings with her family)?

6. Is this a skill that, when absent, may result in unsanitary conditions or create health concerns (e.g., not knowing how to blow her nose)?

■ Table 3-4   Jeffrey's Profile

	Dressing	Brush Teeth	Toileting	Use of Spoon
Question 1:	No	No	Yes	No
Question 2:	No	No	Yes	Yes
Question 3:	Yes	No	No	Yes
Question 4:	N/A*	N/A*	N/A*	N/A*
Question 5:	No	Yes	Yes	Yes
Question 6:	No	Yes	Yes	No

*Assumes that Jeffrey is still young enough that independence in public is not expected.

■ Conducting a Skills Inventory

Take a moment to flip to Appendix A in the back of this book, which provides a Self-Help Skills Inventory that you can use to assess your child's development. The column labeled *Functional Area* identifies the four areas of self-help that we are addressing in this book: eating and drinking, undressing and dressing, toileting, and personal hygiene. Each *Functional Area* is further divided into *Tasks* and these are subdivided into *Skill Targets*. This instrument is designed to help you determine your child's strengths and weaknesses and help prioritize skills to be taught. We suggest that you make several photocopies of this inventory, one you can use now and more for later reassessing your child periodically to note any significant changes. Consider sharing copies with your child's classroom teacher, aides, specialists, and resource teachers. Although they won't be able to speak to all functional areas addressed, they may be able to shed some light on what skills or deficits your child is exhibiting in the school environment. This will also encourage better dialogue between home and school in the area of teaching self-help skills.

There are detailed instructions on the first page of the self-help inventory. In general, your goal is to look at each of the skill targets and determine whether your child is able to perform that skill and to indicate the level of help that she requires. If your child is unable to complete a skill target without significant help, then you next need to consider whether her current ability is age-appropriate. For example, most very young children require help with cutting and spreading with a knife. These would not be good skill targets until the child is six or seven years old. As you look through the list of skill targets, you can quickly eliminate those that are not age-appropriate. Once the inventory is complete, we recommend you narrow the list to five or six skill targets. These should then be considered within the larger picture of other goals being addressed at the same time (i.e., academic, behavioral, play, social) and the questions discussed previously and presented again in Table 3-5. After considering these questions, reduce the number of skill targets further to only one or two. At this point, you are ready to develop specific goals for learning and a plan to achieve each. We will talk about these steps in greater detail later in this chapter and in Chapters 4 and 5.

■ Table 3-5 Questions to Ask When Finalizing Goals for Instruction

1. Is the skill expected of a child this age (age-appropriate)?

2. Has your child learned skills that are typically learned before the skill you are thinking about teaching (developmentally-appropriate)?

3. Is the skill important for the child to learn at this time (most functional), when considered against everything else she needs to learn?

4. Does your child have the necessary readiness skills (e.g., following instructions or accepting physical guidance, or fine motor abilities)? (Refer to Appendix C.) If no, can she learn them while you are teaching the target skill?

5. Has your child shown some interest in learning this activity?

6. Is there a natural reward associated with completing or learning the skill (e.g., your child puts on coat and can go outside; learning to toilet reduces annoyance of feeling wet after a toilet accident)?

7. Is this one of the first skills being taught? If yes, is it relatively simple to teach (i.e., involves only a few steps and component skills)?

8. Does your child present any physical limitations to achieving this skill? If yes, are there accommodations that you can make?

Setting Reasonable Expectations

The goal for most parents is to help our children achieve productive, independent lives. As our children achieve greater independence, we are freed from the daily tasks of cooking, cleaning, and physically caring for them. But what, exactly, does improved independence mean for parents of children with autism? We know that a large number of children with autism will require supports long into their adulthood, and many will never achieve full independence.

Although individuals with autism share broad similarities (impairments in communication, socialization, and limited range of interests), significant individual differences exist within these areas. As we mentioned earlier, one child with autism may understand and engage in basic conversation, and make her needs known, while another may understand very little of what is spoken to her and may not talk at all. While one child may have reasonably well-developed motor skills that enable her to complete complex skill targets such as buttoning, another child may not achieve success without significant accommodations to compensate for fine motor challenges.

As you are developing realistic expectations for your child, you need to consider many factors. First, it is the rare child who learns a new skill and never experiences another error. Learning is a slow, incremental process and typical children may take weeks, months, and maybe years to reach complete independence. It is common for a typically developing three-year-old child, who has successfully learned to indicate her need to go to the bathroom, to occasionally forget and wet her pants. This may happen for some children until they are five or six years old. Thus, if we expect perfection from children at a very young age, we may be very disappointed.

We often establish goals for learning that allow some room for errors at first, and then gradually we modify our expectations as the child continues to show intellectual and physical growth. Thus, our goals often leave a little wiggle room: *"When given a toothbrush and toothpaste, Jeffrey will complete **most** of the steps (80 percent or better) without help."* Note that this goal does not require Jeffrey to remember to brush his teeth—his mother or father reminds him to do it. It does not require that he find the toothpaste and toothbrush; Mom or Dad also does that for him. And, it accepts that he will need occasional verbal or physical reminders (prompts) to complete the functional skill, at least for now. But as he gets older, this expectation will change—more independence will be expected. For example, at some point, his parents will add the requirement that he remove the toothbrush and toothpaste from the cabinet and apply toothpaste to the toothbrush. Again, that may not be age-appropriate for a four-year-old, but it would be a reasonable expectation for an eight-year-old.

Another variable to consider is your child's physical and intellectual abilities. You may have to set the *initial* goal a little lower if your child has significant delays. We don't necessarily recommend that you establish a long-term goal that achieves less than other children, but you may have to work on several short-term goals first. You must also acknowledge that it may take a long time to achieve your long-term goals. In fact, many children with autism may take months and sometimes years to achieve independence in the development of even the most basic skills. So don't get discouraged after a few weeks if things seem to be moving slowly.

Even with adequate instruction, some children with autism do not reach young adulthood having achieved complete independence in the demonstration of self-help skills. For this group of individuals, we recommend that goals be adjusted to incorporate more realistic expectations. We certainly would not set the bar low for a four-year-old, but by late adolescence, we have a pretty good estimate of the child's physical and intellectual potential. For some children, we may be reasonably satisfied knowing that monitoring or verbal reminders are sufficient to ensure that the task is completed. It is not that we have given up on the goal of complete independence, but most of our energy and focus becomes dedicated to reducing the individual's dependence on *physical help* from another adult. If you have very young children now, you do not need to worry about this yet and you may never need to worry about it.

> Many children with autism may take months and sometimes years to achieve independence in the development of even the most basic skills. So don't be easily discouraged.

Another variable to consider is your child's physical ability to complete some of the tasks. Children with fine motor challenges may struggle to remove toothpaste caps, remove the lid from a jar of peanut butter, and button or snap. Sometimes materials can be modified, such as using oversized buttons or using shoes that fasten with hook and loop tape (Velcro) instead of shoestrings. In some instances, the use of modified materials may be temporary, such as the child who gradually moves from oversized buttons to normal buttons as she acquires greater motor dexterity. We will discuss the use of physical accommodations in Chapter 4.

In short, and we find ourselves saying this often, you need to find a reasonable balance between your child's age, general abilities, and what is considered normal. You can always increase expectations later. If you set your expectations too high initially, your child and you may conclude that you have failed. There are no quick and easy outcomes. Successfully helping children with autism is a long journey, but in the end, the rewards are plentiful if you are patient and systematic.

Summary

By carefully planning what to teach, you can help your child acquire greater independence. It is the gift that keeps on giving. With greater independence comes greater opportunity to function as a full and participating member of a family and community. As we have argued, teaching self-care skills is not fundamentally different than teaching anything else. But before beginning, identify a skill target that has a high probability of being learned by your child. This can be determined by completing some of the checklists that we have included that assess your child's interests and readiness. If your child has already learned some basic attending skills (e.g., following simple commands, imitation, and sustained engagement), then she is in great shape to move forward with self-help training. If these skills are still absent, then it may make sense to take a step back and teach a few readiness skills first. We have provided some strategies for teaching readiness skills in Appendix C. The good news is that children with autism can learn if we break tasks into small enough steps and we teach systematically.

*The child provides the power but the parents have
to provide the steering.*
—Benjamin Spock

4

Establishing a Context for Learning

The Murphy Family

*Mark Murphy is determined to teach his eight-year-old
son, Trevor, to independently dress himself. Each morning he
lays clothes on the bed for Trevor and asks him to get dressed. He
peppers Trevor with instructions (e.g., "Put your arms through
the sleeves; now put your head through this hole"), physically
prods, and continually encourages. If Trevor is not focusing, his
dad commands him to pay attention. Mr. Murphy has taught
his daughter to dress herself by simply showing her what to do
and occasionally reminding her how to do it. He is confident
that with enough practice he can teach Trevor the same way.
But, after several weeks of instruction, he realizes that he has
wound up simply dressing Trevor himself each day.*

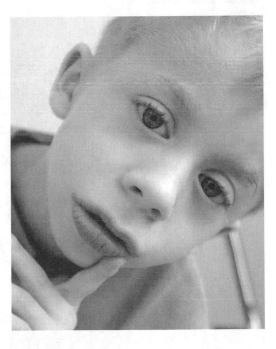

■ Why Won't This Work?

Telling and showing alone will not successfully teach most children with autism to dress themselves. So, what is the magical solution to accomplishing change?
Well, the first thing to know is that there is no magical solution. For most children,
it will take a consistent approach applied over many weeks and months to realize
success. Fortunately, there are general strategies and many scientifically validated

tools for change that have been shown to work for most children with disabilities, including autism. But before we talk about specific teaching methods, we want to first talk about setting up the learning environment.

■ Finding the Best Context for Learning

The context that you select for learning may be as important as how you plan to teach. Choosing "context" is more than just a matter of deciding where and when to teach; it also involves considerations of the most natural situation for learning and specific child variables such as attention, fine motor skills, motivation, and compliance. Your goal is to create an environment that maximizes attention and provides sufficient support and motivation, but does not result in the child's reliance on you forever. Failure to set the stage for learning may inhibit learning and prevent your child from using the desired skill in a variety of situations or conditions. This is referred to as a failure to generalize.

Many children with autism have difficulty generalizing newly learned skills. Generalization means that the child learns a new skill under one set of conditions (at a certain time, in a certain place, or with certain people) and then he uses the skill under a different set of conditions. For example, if the Murphys teach Mark to independently dress himself in his bedroom, they may discover that he is unable to independently dress himself after gym class at school—thus a failure to generalize has occurred. Their effort was not wasted, but they must spend additional time to complete the teaching process. So, how do you determine the place and time that you can maximize learning, minimize distractions, and foster generalization? Begin by considering the questions presented in Table 4-1.

> Your goal is to create an environment that maximizes attention and provides sufficient support and motivation, but does not result in the child's reliance on you forever.

Everything being equal, the most natural place and time for a skill to be displayed is also the best location and time for teaching that skill. For example, Mark needs to get dressed each morning in his bedroom before going downstairs to eat breakfast, so it stands to reason that this is when and where he should be taught this skill. However, none of us live or work in perfectly stable environments without time constraints, and there are many variables that eventually influence the context you chose. Teaching a young boy to use the urinal at school between classes may be the most natural time, but it creates extraordinary challenges including privacy issues. On the other hand, teaching him to stand at the toilet at home may not transfer to using the urinal at school. If this skill is going to be taught at school, then it makes sense to choose a time and place that is private and distractions

> The most natural place and time for a skill to be displayed is also the best location and time for teaching that skill.

■ Table 4-1	Questions to Ask When Establishing the Context for Learning

1. Where is the most natural place to perform this particular skill?

2. What is the most natural consequence that results from performing this skill (e.g., putting on a coat results in going outside)?

3. Where is your child most likely to demonstrate this behavior in the future?

4. What are other settings where this skill needs to be performed? Will a different skill-set be required in those settings (e.g., a paper towel dispenser vs. a cloth towel for drying)?

5. Considering the child's age and abilities, what is the most natural signal for your child to know to perform this skill (e.g., using the toilet signals that his hands should be washed after)?

6. Does your child have the physical ability needed to perform this skill or will accommodations be required (e.g., oversized buttons or modified spoon)?

7. What skill components are required at this time and which ones may be added later (e.g., providing a toothbrush with toothpaste already on it)?

8. Have you selected and organized all the materials that you will need to teach the skill?

are minimal. If the skill is going to be taught at home, then his parents need to develop a plan to ensure that the skill will generalize to school, even during busy and confusing times.

Physical Environment

While self-help skills are most often performed at home (e.g., dressing and bathing), there are many times that a skill target must be used in another context (e.g., homes of relatives or friends, school, and work). Often, these other environments have subtle, and sometimes not so subtle, variations in the physical environment and social expectations. Although these differences may seem small and insignificant to you, they may form significant barriers for your child with autism. For example, if at school, children are expected to remove their lunch from a bag and unwrap individual items, at some point these additional requirements need to be factored into your thinking about a suitable instructional goal for eating independently. Although you may start by simply getting your child to independently eat an unwrapped sandwich placed on a plate, at some point, you may add a requirement to unwrap the sandwich first.

You probably won't think of everything, but you need to identify as many conditions as possible and actively help the child respond appropriately to each. We recall observing an adult with a disability become very anxious and upset in a public bathroom because he could not find the faucet handles to turn on the water. There were no handles because the flow of water was controlled by a sensor triggered when his hands were placed under the faucet.

Social Environment

Similarly, the social environment may affect your instructional goal. It may be okay for a boy to let his pants drop completely to the floor and stand at the toilet at home, but that would be considered odd by peers while standing at the urinal at school. Again, while it may be impossible to think of everything, you should take a few minutes before you begin to clearly describe what the target skill will look like when you are done and whether it meets a community standard. The point is that what may seem completely innocent in one context may seem inappropriate in another environment. A little planning up front might prevent the need to reverse an undesirable or embarrassing habit later.

As hard as it may seem to accomplish, you also need to look ahead and think about where your child may live, go to school, or work in the future. For example, an adolescent may need one set of mealtime skills if he will be entering a group home (e.g., setting the table, selecting the appropriate amount of food, eating neatly and quietly) and yet a set of additional skills if he will be living independently (e.g., preparing a grocery list, shopping, and preparing meals). As we mentioned in Chapter 1, the absence of age-appropriate self-help skills often prevents a person from achieving the highest level of independent living possible. As challenging as it may be, making an educated and realistic prediction of your child's living and work conditions when he becomes an adult is the first and maybe the best thing you can do to help him or her achieve self-sufficiency. Completing this step gives you the capacity to contrast current abilities with future expectations and to set goals for learning. Obviously, it will be easier to do this at age fifteen than at age eight, but use your best judgment now, then reassess periodically to see if things have changed.

Once you have identified other significant environments where your child is likely to live or work or recreate, the best thing you can do is to visit those places and talk with the people who set the conditions and expectations in those settings. Try to discern the level of independence that is expected and how often staff support and reward individuals for reasonable attempts to demonstrate the desired skills and behaviors. If you observe that there are high expectations for independence but little help and praise, you will need to establish a goal for learning that is matched to that environment.

> Making an educated and realistic prediction of your child's living and work conditions when he becomes an adult gives you the capacity to contrast current abilities with future expectations and to set goals for learning.

■ Selecting a Natural Signal or Cue

It is important to consider what event should signal your child to engage in the target skill. For example, a ringing alarm clock is a natural and age-appropriate signal for a young adult to get out of bed and get dressed. In contrast, it would not be good preparation for adult life if the parent chose to wake their young adult child and remind him to get dressed each day. We're reminded of an adolescent with autism who would begin eating only when an adult told him to eat. Although only a minor inconvenience for his family, instructing him to eat was not the most natural cue and the family expressed concerns about his long-term survival. Because he had not been taught to respond to more natural cues (e.g., food served and others beginning to eat), he was at risk of always being dependent on others.

We encourage you to think about the most natural signal before starting to teach a specific skill. Selecting a natural or age-appropriate signal may influence how you write an objective for learning and how you teach. Obviously, there will be different expectations based on the child's age and developmental readiness. Referring to the example of getting out of bed and dressed each day, the objective for an eight-year-old child might begin with the phase, "*When instructed to get dressed*, Mark will dress himself." In contrast, an objective for an eighteen-year-old might read, "*After the alarm sounds*, Jessica will turn off the alarm and dress herself."

We also encourage you to think about what natural consequence will motivate your child to demonstrate the desired skill target. We will discuss in more detail ways to motivate your child in the next chapter. At this point and to the degree possible, we want you to consider ways to set up the environment so that the most natural consequence follows the completion of the skill target. Just learning to put on a coat is not very exciting, but if doing so results in going outside to play, this natural reward could increase your child's motivation to cooperate. Similarly, washing one's hands before snack may be more motivating than a contrived hand-washing routine that has no immediate natural consequence. In each case, the consequence must be fairly obvious to your child and occur as quickly as possible following the completion of the activity.

Making Physical Accommodations

For children that are easily distracted and children who have physical challenges, you will need to modify the context and materials. As we mentioned before, some settings may be too distracting or provide very little privacy, even if they are the most natural context for learning. When the teaching environment is not the natural context for performing the target skill, try to set up the contrived context to match as closely as possible. This is not typically a problem at home, but it can be a little complicated at school when space and human resources are limited. When looking for similarities, consider the materials you will use and the instructions you provide, as well as the physical environment.

If your child has significant fine motor limitations or significant attention deficits, modify the instructional materials, at least in the beginning, to meet his individual situation. For example, learning to tie shoes is a complex task with a lot of fine motor requirements. It also requires that the child engage in the sequence of steps while leaning down over his shoes. For some children, this is simply too challenging. As a result, they lose interest very quickly and try to avoid or escape the task (e.g., passively resisting prompts or constantly sitting or standing up). As an alternative, you may want to start with an oversized shoe that sits on a table in front of the child. Additionally, the shoestrings can be color coded to help the child discriminate. Clearly, this is not the end point, but think about it as learning to drive in a parking lot before you try the highway. It is a starting point to gain better motor skills, learn the expectations, and, importantly, be successful. Frankly, it is also easier for you to physically prompt the child through the steps when you are not also leaning toward the floor. As you will learn later, you can gradually increase expectations as your child's skills improve.

When and How Often to Conduct Training

As we discussed in Chapter 3, we recommend that you teach no more than one or two skills at a time and that you try to pick skills that are very different from each other (e.g., toothbrushing and cutting with a knife instead of toothbrushing and face washing). This will reduce any confusion that may be created by having some common materials (e.g., towel, sink, and mirror) and a common setting (bathroom).

Once you have decided what and where to teach, identify the best time to conduct the program and do it consistently. There is sufficient evidence that children with autism require a great deal of repetition to learn new things. Implementing the program once a week will probably not be enough to produce the desired result. At first it may seem like a lot, but try to run each Instructional Program <u>at least</u> once a day and preferably two or three times a day. Most programs for teaching basic self-help skills should take only about ten to fifteen minutes per opportunity. Whenever possible, you can incorporate your instruction into existing routines. For example, learning to pull up his pants can be incorporated into your son's morning dressing routine, toileting activities, and putting on his pajamas at night. Like all of us, the more we practice a newly developing skill, the better we get at it.

Preparing for Each Instructional Lesson

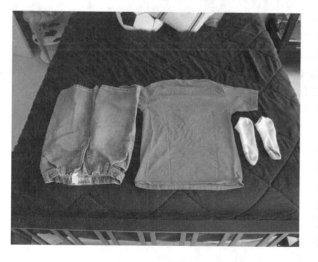

Before each session, be prepared with any materials you will need, including a copy of the steps of the instructional program. (We will discuss writing programs in Chapter 6.) If physical accommodations (e.g., modified spoon or bowl for eating) are necessary, get those materials ready. If the context is going to be set up so that some steps are completed for the child (e.g., clothes laid on the bed in the order and position that the child will dress), prepare before bringing the child to the room. If you intend to reward the child with food, toys, or other tangible materials, have those on hand as well. See Table 4-2 for a list of considerations in preparing for each instructional session.

Summary

As we have noted in the previous paragraphs, there are a lot of things to think about before you even begin instruction. Establishing the best context for learning

■ Table 4-2   Considerations when Preparing for Each Instructional Session

1. Review the instructional program prior to beginning each session.

2. Organize materials for the lesson (e.g., put toothpaste on toothbrush and lay it near the sink).

3. Identify and have available any rewards for the child.

4. Make sure that your record keeping system is ready (will be discussed in Chapter 7).

5. Clear the area of any distractions, e.g., unnecessary materials, toys, or other small objects that your child may find desirable.

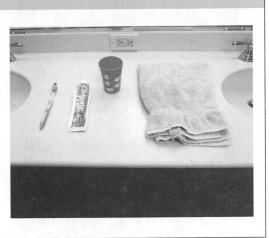

self-help skills is as important as the methods you choose to use to teach them. Thoughtful planning sets the stage for your child's learning and helps to ensure that newly learned skills are acquired and consistently used in a variety of contexts and situations. Like so many things we have and will discuss in this book, your planning will require a great deal of individualization. That is, given **your** child's specific strengths and weaknesses, what is the most functional thing for him to learn at this time? What physical context will maximize your child's learning?

> Establishing the best context for learning self-help skills is as important as the methods you choose to use to teach them.

What is a reasonable and appropriate expectation for his current level of independence? Taking the time to consider these questions will be time well spent.

5

Motivating Your Child to Learn

The Jones

Kevin and Mary Jones are determined to find a way to improve their son's ability to sit at the kitchen table and eat using utensils. Tom, their seven-year-old son with

autism, rarely sits for more than a minute or two, preferring instead to grab food from his plate and eat it while running or pacing back and forth. His parents have tried a lot of things including pleading, nagging, using loud commands, and scolding to make him sit at the table and use utensils. But nothing seems to work.

Mrs. Jones has heard that it is important to reward her child in order to help him learn to do what she wants. Although Mr. Jones thinks this sounds like bribing and refuses to participate, Mrs. Jones has decided to try it anyway. So, when she asked Tom to sit at the table and he did it, she immediately gave him a bite of his favorite candy bar. At first, this approach seemed to work really well. Each time she asked Tom to come to the table he seemed more alert and motivated and quickly responded to her request. But after a few days, Mrs. Jones was less consistent in her resolve to require Tom to sit at the table. Tom either sat only for a few seconds (long enough to receive the candy) or ignored his mother entirely. In the meantime, he continued his practice of running into the kitchen and standing at the table long just enough to grab a few bites of food in his hand. Then, he'd be off again. When Mrs. Jones threatened Tom by saying he would not get candy unless he followed her directions, half the time he just didn't seem to care. In fact, sometimes the more his mother repeated her demands, the more defiant Tom became.

Tom's failure to follow directions is not limited just to sitting at the table. In fact, he fails to follow most directions, whether they are given by his mother, father, or teachers. After three weeks of using rewards, this kind of behavior still persists and everyone is feeling stretched to their limits.

Why didn't Mrs. Jones' attempts work? Maybe you've tried similar techniques with your child or student and been frustrated by the same outcome. In this chapter we'll discuss how to set the stage for success by determining what motivates your child and reinforces desirable behavior.

Rewarding Your Child for Learning

Brushing teeth, bathing, and combing hair are not at the top of the list of things children most like to do. Many typically developing young children resist their parents' attempts to help them complete these tasks. Even into early adolescence, parents often have to remind their child to brush her teeth and take a shower, sometimes against the child's strenuous verbal objections. So, why do children eventually get more independent? First, it is important to understand that independence occurs gradually over many years. Children first acquire the component skills of a task under their parent's watchful eye and supervision. As they get older, there are negative social and health consequences, such as bad breath, body odor, or possible tooth decay, that often motivate older adolescents. Most children also are rewarded simply by the completion of the task and doing a good job (as recognized by parents and teachers). But the feeling of accomplishment and the fear of undesired social consequences may not be sufficient motivation for a child with autism.

> A reinforcer (also called reward) is something provided after a desired behavior that makes the behavior more likely to occur again.

So how do you get your child sufficiently motivated to learn? One important tool is the use of reinforcement or rewards. (We will use these words interchangeably). When a behavior results in reinforcement, we are more likely to do it again. This is the principle and purpose of reinforcement. We are all more likely to repeat behavior when it results in attention from people we respect, and material items like toys or money, and provides necessary things like food. There are many ways to reward children for learning, but the strength of the reward (i.e., its ability to increase behavior) must be determined individually. It is not just a matter of giving pleasurable things (e.g., praise and toys) to your child. There are a variety of factors that influence the effectiveness of rewards. In our example, Mrs. Jones has the right idea about the principle of reinforcement but fails to consider the many variables that strengthen or diminish the power of reinforcement. We will discuss these now. The principle of reinforcement may seem simple, but as Mrs. Jones showed us, it is not that easy, and proper use takes a lot of planning and good timing.

> The feeling of accomplishment and the fear of undesired social consequences may not be sufficient motivation for a child with autism.

Using Praise

Parent and teacher praise is a powerful reward that can be used to motivate many children to learn. Praise is usually given very enthusiastically—"Wow! You did that all by *yourself*"—so that it can be easily discriminated from other words spoken to the child and is likely to capture the child's attention. It is important that your praise and attention be given *immediately* following demonstration of the desired behavior, so that the child understands that there is a contingent relationship, i.e., their behavior—and not something else—resulted in your praise and attention. Initially, we encourage you to verbally reward your child (e.g., "Nice try") for any reasonable attempts at task completion. This accomplishes two things. First, the child begins to understand the expectations of the task and, second, they immediately experience success and are more likely to repeat the behavior.

In addition to following the desired behavior immediately, your attention must be given only for preferred behavior—not behaviors that interfere or compete with learning. For example, be careful not to reward the child's attempts to leave the area or unintentionally reward her inattention. When behavior problems occur, calmly redirect the child using the least amount of physical and verbal guidance necessary to get him back on task. It may be necessary to start with very small expectations, then gradually increase them.

Again returning to our example of the Jones family, Mrs. Jones might have had more success if she had gradually increased the expectations for Tom to sit at the table (this is a technique called *shaping* and it will be discussed in Chapter 6). Initially, asking Tom to simply come to the table and sit for one or two seconds was a reasonable short-term goal. But gradually, the expectation should have been increased to sit for progressively longer and longer periods of time (maybe in increments as short as thirty seconds to a minute) before the reinforcer, in this case, a candy bar, was made available. Gradually increasing the behavioral expectation to receive a reinforcer is one of the tools the Jones could have used to prevent Tom from simply sitting long enough to get the candy, then quickly standing and leaving.

All being equal, social reinforcers (e.g., praise and physical touch such as hugs, kisses, and high fives) are the most practical potential reinforcers. (We refer to them as "potential" because we don't know if they will actually be perceived by the child as pleasant and result in an increase in the target skill.) Unlike toys and food, social reinforcers are always immediately available and can be delivered and received very quickly. And, most importantly, they are a natural part of everyone's daily lives. Therefore, we recommend that social reinforcers always be used even if they must be paired initially with food, toys, or other events. Over time, this constant pairing may result in social reinforcers (particularly praise) acquiring reinforcing value for the child with autism.

> Social reinforcers are actions or words (e.g., tickles, praise, high fives) used to reward a child's desired behavior.

Using Food Reinforcers

Because food is necessary to our survival, it also is naturally reinforcing to most people. Unlike praise and attention, food is not a very convenient reward. First, it is not always with you. You have to plan ahead. Second, it may break the continuity of your lesson, while the child consumes the reward. Third, the value of food to the child is very dependent upon other factors such as how hungry or full the child is. Fourth, some parents are not anxious to fill their child up with sugary treats or "extra" food beyond normal meals. We recommend the use of food in some limited situations, particularly when other methods have not worked very well in the past. Food can also be beneficial because your child does not have to relinquish it (like she would a toy). She simply consumes it and then it is gone. When food is used as a reinforcer, you should not depend upon it exclusively; pair it with praise and physical contact. Over time, these activities may acquire greater reinforcement value because they have been paired with food.

In our earlier example of the Jones family, Mrs. Jones had the right idea about using food, but did not execute her plan very systematically. For example, Mrs. Jones selected a candy bar as a reinforcer. But, candy bars are highly filling and, depending upon the timing (e.g., following lunch) and how much candy is delivered each time, it may or may not be a good motivator. She also failed to pair it with praise and attention, thus she ran the risk of long-term dependence on food as a motivator.

> When food is used as a reinforcer, you should not depend upon it exclusively; pair it with praise and physical contact.

If you choose to use food, also consider such variables as nutritional value of the foods (e.g., fruits and juices over candy and soda), foods that can be consumed pretty quickly (e.g., raisins vs. a candy bar), and possible food allergies. Because self-help targets usually consist of a series of small steps linked together to make a more complex skill, it would be counterproductive to interrupt each step to deliver an edible reward. Thus food is typically delivered at the end of all steps and praise is given between steps. From this point forward, we will refer to the reinforcer provided at the end of all steps as the "super reward." Super rewards typically involve attention, activities, and/or food delivered after the entire task is complete and contingent upon good performance.

For some children, food may be a distraction. The child may continuously reach for the food or talk about the food. In the worst case, you may not be able to use food as a reward for some children. In less severe cases, simply keep the food concealed or out of the child's reach until it is time to give it to him.

> "Super Rewards" are food, toys, activities, or free time that a child receives after she successfully completes all the steps of a task.

Again, one of the most important things is that you always pair the delivery of food with praise, smiles, and/or physical contact. We have found that food reinforcers can be faded pretty quickly as attention and other reinforcers are introduced.

Using Activity Reinforcers and Preferred Objects

You may recall we briefly discussed activity reinforcers when we talked about finding natural consequences for the completion of the target skill (e.g., putting on a coat results in going outside to play). There are hundreds of things that can be identified as activity reinforcers, but it will take a little creativity on your part. For some children, the most effective activities are those that stimulate the senses of sight, touch, and smell. The important things to consider are that the activity must be delivered as immediately as possible and that it be contingent upon the child's cooperation and success. Review the suggestions for activity reinforcers given in Table 5-1, and then make a list for your child of activities you think may be reinforcing to her. Remember that what may be reinforcing for one child may not be rewarding to another. Also, the value of the reinforcer can change, so it may be necessary to periodically update this list of reinforcers for your child.

When using preferred activities as reinforcers, you need to make sure that the activity (or parts of the activity) can be completed within a reasonable amount of time so as not to delay further task completion. Some children are motivated by completing small parts of an activity at a time (e.g., receiving one piece of a puzzle after each completed step of a task, leading to a completed puzzle at the end), but others are upset if the activity is not fully completed (e.g., they are only interested in building puzzles if they can dump the pieces out and put the puzzle together right away). Often activity reinforcers are best used as a super reward (given after the completion of a target skill).

When using preferred objects as reinforcers, keep in mind that you will need to allow your child to access the object for a brief period of time and then she will need to relinquish it. Many children quickly catch on to a routine of brief play with an object after each completed task. Others become very upset and refuse to give the object back. If the latter is the case, the object is not likely going to be a useful reinforcer.

■ Table 5-1 Examples of Activity Reinforcers

■ Jumping on a trampoline	■ Playing with a favorite toy
■ Going outside	■ Helping to make a snack or meal
■ Turning lights on and off	■ Singing a song
■ Sitting in an adult's lap	■ Reading a story
■ Going on a special outing with an adult	■ Playing a musical instrument
■ Eating out at a favorite restaurant	■ Drawing a picture
■ Being twirled in a circle	■ Jumping up and down with an adult
■ Dancing	■ Looking in the mirror
■ Playing in water	■ Patting or rubbing head
■ Using a flashlight	■ Inhaling favorite smells (e.g., perfume, soap)
■ Blowing bubbles	■ Blowing up or playing with balloons
■ Listening to music	■ Getting massaged
■ Being spun around	■ Taking a walk
■ Free time	■ Watching television
■ Watching a videotape or DVD	■ Playing a computer game
■ Painting or coloring	■ Holding a stuffed animal
■ Hugs and kisses	■ Getting tickled
■ High fives	■ Wrestling; rough play

Using Stickers & Token Economies

Stickers are commonly used with young children to improve preschool performance. Although there may be some children with autism who respond to stickers, it is unlikely that stickers alone will be reinforcing. The exception to this statement is the use of stickers within a "token economy." A token economy works much like money. Stickers or other currency (e.g., stars, points, plastic chips) are earned immediately after performing the target skill and can be exchanged later for a reinforcer (e.g., a desired toy). This technique can be applied with older children, but is unlikely to work for very young children with autism. For more information on token economies, see the book *Incentives for Change* by Delmolino & Harris (2004), part of Woodbine House's Topics in Autism series.

■ Reinforcement vs. Bribery

It is very important to distinguish reinforcers from bribes. Some parents, like Mr. Jones, worry that they may be bribing their children if they reward them for desired behaviors. Reinforcement and bribes differ in many important ways. The first is that bribes are given as a means to incite a corrupt or illegal activity or behavior. Reinforcement is used to increase desirable behavior and facilitate learning. Additionally, bribes are given **before** a behavior occurs (again, as a way to incite behavior). Reinforcement, on the other hand, is only given **after** the desired behavior has already occurred to communicate to the child that more of the same behavior is desired and expected. Returning to our previous example, if Mrs. Jones asked Tom to come to the table, Tom refused, and then Mrs. Jones asked him again while dangling the promise of candy, then the process certainly has the appearance of a bribe. On the other hand, if the expectations are clear that following Mrs. Jones' direction the first time results in a reward, and the reward is given only if Tom immediately follows her request, then there is greater hope that a small piece of candy can be used to motivate and increase desired behavior.

◾ Identifying Reinforcers

The simplest way to identify reinforcers is to watch your child and make a list of things she eats, activities she seeks or responds to positively, and toys she plays with. Frequently update the list, based on additional observations and discussions with other people who know your child well. Although this may be the easiest way, it may not be the most accurate way to identify effective reinforcers. First, parents' perceptions of what is reinforcing to their children may be clouded by their own biases. Second, unless you update the list weekly, it may not include your child's most recent preferences.

In addition to creating a master list of reinforcers, we suggest that you periodically conduct a reinforcer assessment (Dyer, 1987; Fisher, Piazza, Bowman & Amari, 1996). A reinforcer assessment begins by selecting toys and materials that you think are reinforcing (or potentially reinforcing) to your child. Items that are new and exciting and those that stimulate the senses tend to be most preferred by children (Bandura, 1969). We provided some examples of objects and activities in Table 5-1. Next, sit at a table or on the floor in a location free from distractions. Place a few items one at time in front of your child and wait for her reaction. Make a note of items that she picks up and examines or plays with for more than just a few seconds. After a little while, try to remove an item from her, and observe her reaction. If your child provides some resistance, it is a good sign that she finds the object desirable. Place one or more objects just beyond her reach and note how motivated she is to get them. Systematically present and remove items until you have a list of five to ten things that appear to be most reinforcing for your child.

> A reinforcer assessment is a means to systematically identify items that are desired by your child and can be used to motivate her to attend and work to learn new things.

A somewhat modified reinforcer assessment can be used to identify preferred foods as well. Present two food items to your child and ask her to choose one. Give your child a very small piece of the chosen item and wait until she has completely consumed it. Repeat the procedure several times, mixing new foods and previously selected items and continue in this manner until you have developed a list of preferred items.

Because it is not practical to conduct a reinforcer survey every day, we recommend that you try to find a large number of objectives, activities, and food items and

rotate the things you use each day. Once you have identified some potentially powerful reinforcers, it is important to place them away and out of reach when you are not instructing. If your child has free access to the materials at other times, she is not likely to work very hard to earn them. Although withholding highly rewarding items may seem difficult, if you rotate them regularly, individual items only need to be restricted for a few days.

When you begin teaching new skills to your child, present two or three choices from the list of reinforcers that you have identified (can be any combination of food, activities, toys, etc.) and ask your child to choose which one she wants to "earn." (For activities, use visual representations so your child can actually "see" them.) If she doesn't understand this concept in the beginning, gradually over days and weeks most children come to understand it. Once she has chosen an item, set it aside but within view and remove the other choices entirely from sight. Present the chosen item by pointing to it, tell the child that she is working to earn it, and then begin your instructional lesson. Periodically, you may want to remind your child what she is working to earn.

As we discussed previously, initially you should reward your child with praise and/or another identified reinforcer (e.g., food or activity) for all reasonable attempts. But as the child begins to respond correctly, provide the reinforcer *only if the attempt progressively builds on the previous level of responding.* Again, we will talk about this more in the section on "shaping" in Chapter 6. Use praise very liberally, more liberally than food, materials, or activities. One tip is to praise your child for all reasonable attempts but to deliver food and activity reinforcers (the super reward) only when your child does something particularly noteworthy. *Again, remember that a lot of food and long engagement with activities are not necessarily better motivators.* If your child eats too much food, she may be less responsive to any additional instruction you may want to do later. Similarly, a short period of time with a preferred toy or activity (one to five minutes) helps to keep the child's interest

piqued and ready to earn it again. As previously mentioned, if your child will not relinquish the reinforcer after a reasonable amount of time, you may need to use hand-over-hand guidance to remove it or choose to use a different reinforcer. The key is to use the smallest, yet most effective amount of reinforcer. We wish there was a formula we could give you, but there isn't one. You may have to use a little trial-and-error to strike the right balance.

Using Then Fading Rewards

It is very important to understand that the frequent use of rewards is a tool for teaching and not meant to be part of the end result. In the beginning, we use lots of rewards (praise, toys, food) to build the desired behavior. As your child becomes more competent at the target skill, you should begin rewarding less frequently each time the skill is exhibited—this is called *reinforcer fading*. One practical approach is to fade food and activity reinforcers first, since they are the least natural. So, instead of delivering food after each successful completion of a dressing routine, provide food after every other successful session. Gradually, increase the number of sessions without food, while maintaining praise as a reward each time, until food is no longer being used at all. This is not as easy as it sounds since your child may regress if reinforcers are withdrawn too quickly. In this case, you will need to back up the process a bit. The process is a balancing act and can take several weeks or many months, depending on the needs of your child. Ideally, you need to fade the type and amount of reinforcement to a level observed or expected to occur in the setting where you child will be using the skill in the future. This match will help to ensure that the behavior is maintained over time.

> As your child becomes more competent at the target skill, you should begin rewarding less frequently each time the skill is exhibited—this is called *reinforcer fading*.

The Jones Family's Revised Plan

After some initial spotty success and then disappointment, Mr. and Mrs. Jones are still determined to find an effective way to increase Tom's compliance to simple instructions, ability to sit at the table to eat, and to consistently use a spoon. At seven years old, learning these skills is long overdue. Mr. Jones, who initially thought Tom's behavior would get better with age, has finally agreed that change is going to happen only if he and his wife take dramatic action.

First, they introduced a plan to improve Tom's compliance to general instructions—not just mealtime behaviors. They began each and every interaction with Tom by first getting his attention, delivering a clear and concise instruction (given as a statement, not a question), and providing a brief opportunity for him to respond (three to five seconds). Initially, they helped him by physically guiding him to respond as the instruction was delivered. His response was immediately rewarded with praise and a small amount of food, even though they were helping him to comply. This was the first step in building his understanding of the relationship between following instructions and getting something he wanted (e.g., attention, praise, food).

While they were addressing Tom's compliance to general instructions, the Jones family began a program to teach Tom to sit at the table and eat his meals. They did not focus initially on using utensils. This would come later. After thinking about it for awhile, they realized that Tom liked most of the foods they served to him. Rather than using candy to reward sitting at the table as they had tried before, maybe the meal itself could be used to reward sitting. They also conducted a reinforcer assessment and put together a small box of preferred toys that Tom could get only if he ate his meal.

They began by instructing Tom to sit at the table, which he now did because he had been rewarded for following general instructions. When he was seated, he was praised and provided with only the smallest amount of food on his plate, which he could eat with his fingers in one bite. After eating the one bite, he was praised and allowed to leave the table and given one toy from his toy box to play with. After about five minutes of play, Tom was asked to put the toy back in the box. Some hand-over-hand assistance was initially required to return the toy, but he did it without getting too upset. Then he was instructed to sit at the table again, and once more provided with a small item of food that he quickly consumed. As before, he was praised and allowed to leave the table with a toy he had selected. Since Mr. and Mrs. Jones generally spent about forty-five minutes at the dinner table, they were able to repeat this sequence with Tom approximately five or six times at dinner. Mr. and Mrs. Jones decided not to practice these skills at breakfast since their time was too limited and they felt it would cause undue stress on the family. They decided to practice at both lunch- and dinnertime over the weekends.

At mealtime the next day, Mrs. Jones placed a bit more food on Tom's plate, necessitating that he remain at the table for a slightly longer period of time. She carefully increased the amount of food and extended the time he needed to sit each day, as he made steady progress. She kept a careful record of his progress to make sure she wasn't moving along too fast. (We will discuss data collection in Chapter 7.) Because Tom generally enjoyed his food and quickly understood the expectations that were placed on him, he was sitting for ten minutes at a time within two weeks. Mr. and Mrs. Jones were very happy with their success and decided that it was now time to teach Tom to eat using a spoon with the principles of task analysis and chaining that will be discussed in Chapter 6.

▮ Summary

We have tried directly and indirectly to make the point that good intentions and common parenting practices alone likely will be insufficient to teach self-help skills to children with autism. It will take a coordinated and highly systematic approach that includes ways to motivate your child to want to learn. We all can identify with what it is like to motivate ourselves to complete a difficult or challenging task. We seem to find creative ways to avoid and procrastinate getting the job done when the going gets tough. It is our sense that children with autism experience challenging situations everyday and motivation to overcome those situations is not easily found. It is your (our) job to find ways to sufficiently help motivate your child to gain the needed skills and acquire greater confidence.

In this chapter we have identified a variety of tried and true ways to motivate children with autism. It is important to remember first that any approach must be individualized to your son or daughter. What may work for one child at a given time and place may not work for another child or even the same child at another time and place, so your reinforcer options must be reassessed frequently. Second, rewards must be applied highly systematically with clearly identified expectations for learning and a plan for achieving your goals. Third, parents and professionals must demonstrate incredible patience. In most cases, desired skills will be acquired in very small, incremental stages over a long period of time. The good news is that you will achieve your goals if you remain persistent and demonstrate patience.

6

Using Effective Tools for Change

The Cruz Family

Ms. Cruz finally mustered up the courage and energy to toilet train her eight-year-old son, Ricky. She decided to follow his teacher's advice and instruct him to use the toilet every thirty minutes, hoping that she would catch him at the right time and he would experience some success with urinating in the toilet. But things didn't quite go the way she had planned. Almost from the beginning, he didn't follow her instruction to stop what he was doing and go to the bathroom. When she attempted to physically guide him, Ricky cried and tried to hit and kick her. After several back-wrenching attempts, Ms. Cruz was finally successful in getting Ricky into  *the bathroom. However, he did not seem to understand that he had to pull down his pants and he resisted by making his body limp when she tried to do it for him. Even when she eventually was successful in getting him to sit on the toilet, he immediately wanted to get up and run away. Maybe, she thought, he just isn't ready for this and she should wait until he is a little older. He didn't even seem to know when he was about to urinate or have a bowel movement, so why even bother?*

■ Selecting a Systematic Approach to Teaching

Ms. Cruz's experience is not atypical. When common parenting practices do not work, what do you do next? The good news is that there are a number of instructional tools that have been shown experimentally to work for most children with autism. But, before we talk about specific instructional tools, let's begin with a general approach. In our opinion, a successful approach involves the five steps that were listed in the introduction:

1. Clearly specifying the goal for learning;
2. Breaking complex skills to be taught into small steps for learning;
3. Using a systematic approach to instruction;
4. Evaluating progress (collecting and using data); and
5. Modifying your approach as needed to achieve the target goal.

This system of goal setting, teaching, evaluation, and modification provides a highly systematic approach to instruction that has repeatedly worked for most children with autism. This approach presumes that we may not hit a home run the first time we come to bat, but over time, if we follow the steps indicated, we are likely to produce desired change.

Step 1: Specifying the Goal

The first teaching step is to determine the exact goal (or target) that you hope to achieve. The goal helps to define what you are going to teach and it pinpoints expectations for learning. What are reasonable expectations for your child's learning? Obviously, our job as parents is to help our children acquire skills that lead to greater self sufficiency. But, as we have discussed, a realistic goal must also consider the child's age and physical and intellectual abilities when establishing expectations. Your first goals for your child should be reasonably achievable, even if he initially falls short of complete independence. You can always add additional goals that target greater independence after your child accomplishes some basic things. If your goals are beyond the child's abilities, you and your child are likely to become frustrated and discouraged. A teaching goal contains four basic components:

1. The goal should specify an ***instructional context*** in which the skill target will occur.
2. The goal should pinpoint behaviors or activities that are ***observable and measurable.***
3. The goal should specify behaviors that are ***realistically attainable*** by your child within a few months or less.
4. The goal should specify how and when you will know that your child has acquired the skill (***mastery criteria***).

Instructional Context

As we have discussed, your expectations should vary depending upon the age and ability of your child. We would not expect a four-year-old child to complete all the steps of a toothbrushing routine without some prodding and help from his parents. On the other hand, we might expect a twelve-year-old child to complete a toothbrushing routine with little or no help. The *instructional context* is the part of the goal that helps to define expectations and it establishes the conditions and limitations under which the target skill will occur. The concept of instructional context was expanded on in Chapter 4 as part of *Establishing the Context for Learning*. As we mentioned then, establishing an instructional context is more than just *where* to teach; it also involves considerations of the most natural situation for learning, and child variables such age, ability, need for accommodation, and attention. The following are some examples of how the context could change for the target skill of dressing:

1. *With his pants already pulled over his feet,* Sam will pull his pants to his waist.
2. *Given a pull-over shirt and elastic pants,* Sam will dress himself.
3. *With clothes laid on the bed in sequence (e.g., underwear, pants, shirt, socks, shoes),* Sam will dress himself.
4. *With clothing neatly stacked on his dresser,* Sam will dress himself.
5. *Hearing an instruction from one of his parents to get dressed,* Sam will dress himself.
6. *After gym class,* Sam will remove his clothes from the locker and dress himself.
7. *After hearing and responding to an alarm clock,* Sam will dress himself.

As you can see, these conditions each describe a different context for the child's response and are sensitive to the child's prerequisite abilities and the specific setting where the behavior is expected to occur. They also can be combined to provide even greater specification of the instructional context such as the phrase: *"With clothing laid on the bed in sequence, and after hearing his parent instruct him to get dressed,* Sam will dress himself." We need to know a lot about Sam before we know which instructional context is right for him. Remember, it is better to start with a simple context or condition that is likely to result in progress. You can always increase your expectations as your child achieves some initial success.

Observable and Measurable Behavior

The skill that you choose to teach should be clearly stated, immediately observable, and reliably measurable. This is a relatively direct task as it is applied to self-help skills. Most of the goals for learning are highly specific and directly related to the target skill. An example of a vague behavioral target would be "improving eating skills." A set of motivated parents could waste a lot of valuable time trying to improve their child's eating skills only to discover that each of them had interpreted the target and measured progress differently. Rather than start with a hazy goal of improving eating skills, it would be better to identify a couple of specific skills that will eventually lead to improved eating skills, such as using a fork to spear food, and learning to cut with a knife. The same rules apply for your child's self-help skill IEP goals.

Realistically Attainable Goals

As we have discussed many times so far, begin with a skill that your child has a good chance of obtaining within a few months. This involves setting the instructional context so that the conditions are favorable for success, recognizing your child's physical and intellectual limitations, and factoring in your child's age. Remember that complex skills are achieved by mastering many smaller goals first.

Mastery Criteria

Setting mastery criteria is a way of objectively determining whether a goal has been achieved. We recommend that the mastery criteria consist of two parts, an *acquisition criterion* and a *maintenance criterion*. The acquisition criterion pinpoints a specific dimension of behavior, such as how often it should occur, the number of steps the child completes, the number of times that someone has to help, how long it takes, or how accurately the child responds. Table 6-1 provides some examples of these behavioral measures and mastery criteria. We also will discuss measurement more in Chapter 7.

The mastery criterion should also indicate over what period of time your child should demonstrate the skill before you consider it mastered (this is sometimes referred to as maintenance criterion). Is doing it once enough? How about twice? Should he always be correct or is there room for some error? We need to remind ourselves often that almost no one does something 100 percent of the time and we all make mistakes sometimes. Therefore, we have to give ourselves, and our children, room for less than perfect results.

> Mastery criteria let you know when a goal has been achieved.

Based on our collective experiences, we have concluded that you need to keep moving forward all the time. Once the child achieves a reasonable mastery of the first skill (or skill step), move on to the next one. Otherwise you run a risk of getting locked in place for long periods of time and the child eventually quits engaging completely. If a child demonstrates the target skill with a reasonable degree of accuracy over three or four sessions or days, he has mastered it (maintenance has been achieved). Referring to Table 6-1 and adding a maintenance criterion to the first example, the objective would now read: "Miles will have *no more than one toilet accident in a week for three consecutive weeks*."

Once you have considered each of the parts separately, you can now put the parts together to form a coherent and presumably achievable goal for learning. The following are some illustrations of complete goals for learning.

Goal examples:

MILES—TOILETING

Target Skill Goal: *While prompted every thirty minutes to use the toilet, Miles will have no more than one toilet accident per week for three consecutive weeks.*

1. *Instructional context:* prompted every thirty minutes to use the toilet
2. *Observable and measurable behavior:* toilet accidents
3. *Realistically attainable goal:* reduced number of accidents while on a toileting schedule
4. *Mastery criteria:* no more than one toilet accident per week for three consecutive weeks

AARON—SHAVING

Target Goal: *Given an electric razor prominently displayed next to the bathroom sink, Aaron will shave his face, completing 80 percent of the steps without help for three consecutive days.*

1. *Instructional context:* an electric razor prominently displayed next to the bathroom sink
2. *Observable and measurable behavior:* shaving his face
3. *Realistically attainable goal:* improved but not complete independence (yet)
4. *Mastery criteria:* complete 80 percent of the steps without help for three consecutive days

If a child demonstrates the target skill with reasonable degree of accuracy over three or four sessions or days, he has mastered it.

Table 6-1 Examples of Objective Measures of Progress

BEHAVIORAL MEASURE	EXPLANATION	EXAMPLE OF MASTERY CRITERION
Frequency, or *how often* the behavior occurs	How many toilet accidents occur within an identified time period (e.g., block of hours, day, week)	Miles will have no more than one toilet accident a week
Number of steps successfully completed This is often converted to a percentage (e.g., number successfully completed steps divided by the total number of steps × 100).	Most self-help programs include a series of sequenced steps (e.g., pick up t-shirt, put head through hole, put arms into shirt sleeves, and so on). Each step is scored as correct or incorrect	Aaron will shave, completing 80 percent of the steps with no help
Number of times you must help (prompt)	The number of times an adult has to help (prompt) the child toward completion of the target skill	James will tie his shoes with two or fewer prompts
Duration, or *how long* it takes	The length of time it takes the child to complete the task. This is useful when the child has most of the component skills but is slow to complete them	Keri will eat her lunch and clear her plate and utensils within thirty minutes
How accurately the child responds	For example, a record of whether the child can put a spoonful of food into his mouth without spilling	John will eat one cup of yogurt with a spoon without spilling any
Combined criteria	Combining two or more dimensions into a single criterion	Terri will brush her hair and teeth within fifteen minutes with two or fewer prompts

Ms. Cruz Writes a Behavioral Goal for Ricky

Ms. Cruz decides that she needs to set goals for learning that will prepare Ricky for toilet training. She sets her first teaching goal as follows: "When I call his name, Ricky will walk into the bathroom without hitting or kicking for three days in a row." Ms. Cruz specified an *observable behavior*: Ricky will "walk without hitting or kicking." She can easily observe this and write down whether or not it occurs. Notice that she did not begin to address his physical sensation to use the bathroom, since that is not something she can directly observe. Ms. Cruz knows that Ricky has been successful walking to the bathroom several times in the past and feels confident that the goal is small enough to attain within a week or two. Finally, she decides that she will be confident that Ricky has acquired the skill when he does it for three days in a row. Now that Ms. Cruz knows how to write a goal, it is time to begin breaking the skill that she wants to teach into small teaching steps.

Step 2: Breaking Complex Skills Into Smaller Steps for Learning

A complex skill target may consist of many component skills, steps, or sub-skills (we will use these words interchangeably). For example, learning to wash your hands can be broken down into very few steps or many steps depending on your child's needs. (See Table 6-2 for examples of a short and long task analysis for handwashing.) If your child cannot complete much of the task then more steps are better because it helps break the complex skill into smaller, learnable actions. This will increase your child's chances of success. Breaking skills into many steps is even more important if the goal is broad, such as, "Sam will learn to dress himself, including underwear, pants, shirt, socks, and shoes," versus a more specific goal such as, "Sam will learn to put on his socks and shoes."

Breaking complex target skills into small, learnable steps or actions is called a task analysis. Typically the steps are arranged in sequence or order in which they are to be performed (again, see Table 6-2). Although a task analysis is a common and very effective tool for teaching children with autism, it also is the way that we all learn many complex things. A set of directions to assemble a new swing set is an example of a task analysis. Manufacturers often break the task into a series of steps with illustrations. Each step builds on the previous step and sets the conditions for the step to follow.

A task analysis breaks a complex skill into multiple steps.

An even more complex behavior that is broken into steps is learning to drive a car. Think about how you learned to do it. You probably did not immediately turn on the car and start driving down the highway—or at least we hope you didn't! After you break the skill into its many component parts, you have to marvel at how anyone ever learns to drive! It involves gross motor actions including opening the door, sitting in the seat, and moving the gear shift; precise fine motor tasks, including steering and breaking; visual perceptual skills, including judging distance, making turns, and maintaining speed; and cognitive tasks involving split-second decision-making that link the entire process together.

■ Table 6-2   Task Analyses of Handwashing

BASIC TASK ANALYSIS		EXPANDED TASK ANALYSIS	
Step	Component Task	Step	Component Task
1	Turns on cold water	1	Places right hand on cold water handle
2	Turns on hot water	2	Turns on cold water
3	Places hands under water	3	Places left hand on hot water handle
4	Places one hand under and other hand on soap dispenser	4	Turns on hot water
5	Pushes pump down	5	Places right hand on soap pump
6	Rubs soap between hands	6	Places left hand under soap pump
7	Rubs back of right hand	7	Pushes pump down twice
8	Rubs back of left hand	8	Rubs soap between hands for three seconds
9	Rinses hands under water	9	Rubs back of right hand for three seconds
10	Turns off hot water	10	Rubs back of left hand for three seconds
11	Turns off cold water	11	Places both hands together under water
12	Finds hanging cloth towel	12	Rubs right and left palm together under water for three seconds
13	Dries palms of both hands	13	Places one hand on top of other hand under water and rubs for three seconds
14	Dries backs of both hands	14	Places opposite hand on top of other hand under water and rubs for three seconds
		15	Places left hand on hot water handle
		16	Turns off hot water
		17	Places right hand on cold water handle
		18	Turns off cold water
		19	Finds hanging cloth towel
		20	Rubs palms of both hands with towel between them
		21	Rubs back of one hand with towel
		22	Rubs back of opposite hand with towel

So, you probably began by simply sitting in the driver's seat, studying the instruments on the dashboard, experimenting with the lights and turn signals, and pushing the break and gas pedal a few times. Next, you turned the key and started the engine and once you mustered up the nerve, you took it in and out of gear a few times. And so on. But amazingly, most adults learn to drive, and after a few years most are hardly conscious of all the component steps. Well, this is the same thing that we are trying to accomplish by writing and using a task analysis. It breaks complex skills into smaller steps for learning.

Now, you may not intend to teach your child to drive, but teaching self-help skills involves a similar approach, i.e., breaking the complex tasks into smaller steps for learning. Unlike you, however, children with autism may spend a lot more time on each step before mastering the entire sequence of sub-skills. An added benefit of breaking complex skills into smaller steps for learning is that it increases the number of opportunities to reward your child's accomplishments. Very few children are able to sustain attention and motivation to complete a difficult and lengthy task, and children with autism find it even more challenging. It is not quite an errorless process (i.e., occurs with few or no errors), but it comes close, as you will see later. A task analysis also helps you organize your teaching approach and establishes many check points to either praise your child for good work or help if he is struggling to be successful. As your child masters one step and links it to the previously learned step, he is more motivated to continue learning and soon will form strings of individual skills or actions into complex behaviors.

Task Analysis

Mr. Turner & Charlie

Mr. Turner was determined to teach his son, Charlie, to remove his pajama bottoms and put on his underwear independently each morning. He began with a reasonable goal, "When he is told to get dressed and his underwear is placed on the bed next to him, Charlie will remove his pajama bottoms and put his underwear on with one or no prompts for three consecutive days." It seemed like a simple, achievable goal. But no matter how much Mr. Turner coached and prodded, after two months, Charlie was still completely dependent upon his dad. What Mr. Turner began to realize was that it was not enough just to set a goal and start teaching. He also needed to break the target skill into a series of smaller, learnable steps. Although learning to remove pajamas and put on underwear seemed simple enough, Charlie really didn't understand what was expected of him and he lacked some of the component skills. Mr. Turner decided that the task had to be broken into smaller steps for learning, so he developed the task analysis shown in Table 6-3.

Mr. Turner clearly numbered the steps so they were easily taught in sequence each time. Numbers also made it easy for him to monitor progress on each of the steps (something we will discuss further in Chapter 7). Once he began teaching these small steps systematically, he discovered that Charlie was significantly more interested and responsive. And, of course, greater responsiveness resulted in more frequent praise and attention—a formula for ultimate success.

Table 6-3	Task Analysis for Changing from Pajamas to Underwear

SKILL TARGET: CHANGING FROM PAJAMAS TO UNDERWEAR	
Step	**Component Skill**
1	Grasp pajama bottoms with both hands at opposite sides of the waistband.
2	Pull pajama bottoms down while bending forward at the waist.
3	While sitting, remove one leg from the pajama bottoms.
4	While sitting, remove the other leg from the pajama bottoms.
5	Grasp clean underpants with both hands at opposite sides of the waistband. Make sure tag is at the back.
6	While sitting, bend forward.
7	While sitting, place leg into one opening of the underwear and slide through.
8	While sitting, place other left leg into remaining opening of the underwear and slide through.
9	Pull underwear to waist while slowly standing up.

Developing a Task Analysis

The best way to develop a task analysis is to perform the task yourself while writing down each component step. The number of steps can vary widely depending upon the level of support your child or student needs. In the task analysis provided in Table 6-3, the task of changing from pajamas to underwear was broken down into nine steps. For another child, more or fewer steps may be needed. Again, please review Table 6-2 for an example of a short and expanded lesson plan for handwashing. When developing the steps, try to make sure that each step requires a similar amount of your child's time and effort. The overall number of steps should be manageable (generally less than twenty-five).

When developing the steps of a task analysis, try to make sure that each step requires a similar amount of your child's time and effort. The overall number of steps should be manageable (generally less than twenty-five).

Another way to create a task analysis is to observe another person performing the task or to talk to those that are familiar with the steps that are involved in the task. Teachers, therapists, and special educators may be able to assist you in this process. Several books and other reference materials also contain task analyses for many skills, including Baker & Brightman (2004), and Wheeler, Miller, Springer, Pittard, Phillips, & Myers (1997). When considering a task analysis that has been written by someone else, make sure that the target skill has been broken into enough steps for your child. Even if you can find an "off-the-shelf" task analysis, you may have to individualize it a little for your child or student.

Reinforcing Steps in the Task Analysis

In order for your child to achieve success early on, he will need to receive a reinforcer after each step in the task analysis. The concept of reinforcement as well as an outline of ways to select reinforcers was discussed in Chapter 5. Although it might be tempting to provide a highly rewarding item (such as a favorite toy) after each step, this is generally not practical and may slow down progress. Referring to Table 6-4, you will begin to see why it would be nearly impossible to provide a favorite toy or activity after each successfully completed step of the program (and, for obvious reasons, food would not be a very good selection). On the other hand, a simple social reinforcer, such as a smile, high five, pat on the back, or brief praise, can be used after each step if your child is responsive to this type of reinforcement and if it will not distract him from the task at hand. Use whichever makes the most sense for your child, with the goal of always trying to fade this reward when it is no longer needed.

Mrs. Bartolo & Giovanni

Mrs. Bartolo has been working on teaching her son Giovanni to brush his teeth independently for almost three weeks now. (Table 6-4 illustrates how praise and toys in combination can be used to teach toothbrushing for a child who has been working on this skill for some time.) *Mrs. Bartolo provides praise after each independently completed step, but withholds it for any step that requires a prompt. The toy (super reward) is delivered at the end if, subjectively, she feels that Giovanni was attending, trying to respond correctly, and was successful most of the time. Notice that no reinforcer is delivered after some of the steps because it is no longer needed. Eventually, as Giovani progresses, he will only receive the super reward when the entire task is completed independently.*

Step 3: Using a Systematic Approach to Instruction

A variety of teaching tools will be presented here, along with descriptions of the potential benefits of each. While there may be some flexibility to try different tools, make sure that you give any one method a long enough period of evaluation before you change it. Children with autism often respond only after a lot of repetition. You should be prepared to commit to a particular approach to teaching until you can clearly determine whether or not it is working. This can take from a few sessions to a few weeks depending on how quickly your child learns. If you abandon an approach too quickly, you may waste valuable time starting and stopping. Expect that learning will be a long process and give you and your child sufficient time to respond. Practice and patience are the keys to success. Some basic criteria

■ Table 6-4   Task Analysis of Toothbrushing and Example of Using Rewards

Step	Expected Response	Child's Response	Praise or Super Reward
1	Find and pick up toothpaste	Correctly performed	"Great, you found the toothpaste."
2	Remove cap from toothpaste and hold tube in one hand	Correctly performed	"I like the way you are working."
3	Find and pick up toothbrush and hold in other hand	Must be prompted to find toothbrush	Nothing
4	Place a small amount of toothpaste on toothbrush	Must be prompted	Nothing
5	Turn on cold water	Correctly performed	"Good job. You turned on the water by yourself."
6	Wet toothbrush	Correctly performed	"Wonderful, keep up the good work."
7	Place toothbrush on teeth	Doesn't respond, so he is prompted	Very moderated, "Good."
8	Move toothbrush up and down five times in various positions	Must be prompted some of the time	Use praise when he is moving toothbrush, prompt when he is not.
9	Spit toothpaste into sink	Correctly performed	"Wonderful."
10	Rise mouth with water	Correctly performed	"Nice job. You are doing great."
11	Place toothbrush in holder	Correctly performed	"Good job brushing your teeth. You earned time to play with your dinosaurs" (super reward).

for choosing the most suitable teaching method (or at least the first to try) will be provided later in this chapter.

Developing New Skills Using Prompts and Shaping

Prompting

For most children with autism, progress is unlikely without the effective use of prompts. Sometimes we expect a child to perform a skill independently and become frustrated when they are unable to even get started. At other times, we do things for our children before giving them a chance to do it on their own. Either way, you run the risk of perpetuating dependence on you. Fortunately, the effective use of prompts encourages independence and reduces frustration for you and your child. Prompts must be utilized frequently in the early stages of teaching and then systematically reduced (faded) over time. "*Use them then lose them*" as quickly as possible.

Prompting is essential when you are attempting to teach a skill to your child that is not presently in his repertoire. Try to imagine teaching someone to play golf without prompts. We certainly would use a lot of modeling and verbal directions, and we might use gestures to get our point across. Physical prompts would likely be used very sparingly. Praise and correctional feedback (e.g., "Don't bring your club back so far next time") would be used often. Now let's imagine another scenario in which the person learning to play golf does not understand the language you are speaking and does not know how to imitate your actions. Now, physical prompts and gestures become much more important, and verbal prompts and modeling may provide little help. And without some physical prompting, there may be little or no behavior to reward—how does the individual know what you want? In our opinion, children with autism are much like the second golfer, i.e., not understanding all of the language and not very skilled at imitating the behaviors of another person. There are a variety of prompts that can be used with your child.

Prompts can come in many forms including verbal (such as instructions, hints, or cues), gestural (such as pointing), modeling (showing the child what you want him to do), visual cues (such as photos or picture representations that show the steps of the task to be completed), and physical (hand-over-hand guiding the child or lightly or intermittently touching the child). Which type you choose to use is largely dependent upon which method works best for your particular child. You may need to

> A prompt is assistance given to help your child complete a task. A prompt can range from complete physical guidance to simple gestures or cues.

■ Table 6-5   Examples of Various Prompts to Teach Spoon Use

TYPE OF PROMPT	EXAMPLE
Physical guidance	*Hand-over-hand:* Place your hand on top of your child's hand, pick up the spoon and bring it to your child's mouth. *Partial Guidance:* Tap the child's arm to assist him in bringing the spoon to his mouth.
Visual cue	Show photographs of another child completing each step.
Modeling	Get the child's attention; pick up a spoon while simultaneously asking the child to imitate your actions.
Gestural	Point to your child's spoon or get his attention and glance at the spoon.
Verbal	Say "pick up your spoon" before your child begins to eat with his fingers.

experiment some to determine this. Table 6-5 provides examples of these various prompting strategies and how each might be applied to teach the actions of "eating with a spoon."

Prompting Steps in the Task Analysis

While progressing through the steps in a task analysis, you may find that your child is making errors on steps or simply not doing anything at all. It is during these instances where prompts must be introduced. We generally recommend that you apply a "most-to-least" prompting strategy. This means that you provide the greatest assistance initially, in order to achieve success and then slowly move to reduce your assistance as your child makes progress. In most-to-least prompting you guide your child through the entire chain of steps, thus minimizing errors. Therefore you provide "hand-over-hand" assistance and then gradually, the amount of physical guidance is faded by moving from hand-over-hand to partial physical guidance (such as touching your child's hand) to gestures (pointing to materials) to brief verbal direction ("keep going"). (Figure 6-1 provides several examples of various levels of prompts.)

When the desired response is occurring reliably (as specified by the mastery criteria on your goal) with prompts, the prompts must be gradually removed, or faded. Unfortunately, removing prompts without significantly affecting performance is more of an art than a scripted approach. A little trial and error is in order. On one hand, if you fade too quickly, your child may backslide. On the other hand, if you delay too long, you may increase your child's dependence on you. Remember, you ultimately want a natural cue or signal to control your child's response such as an alarm clock signaling that it is time to get dressed in the morning and eating triggered by hunger and the presence of food.

Another prompting method available to you is called least-to-most prompting. In least-to-most prompting you provide the minimum (least) amount of assistance needed initially

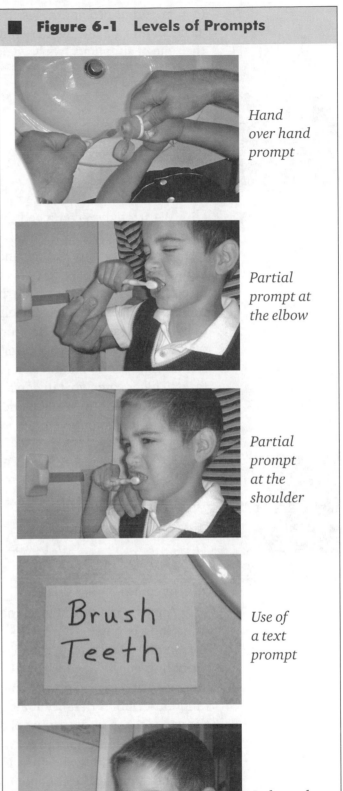

■ Figure 6-1   Levels of Prompts

Hand over hand prompt

Partial prompt at the elbow

Partial prompt at the shoulder

Use of a text prompt

Independence

(e.g., a verbal prompt or gesture) and then increase the level of prompting only as needed (e.g., adding more physical guidance if the child does not respond). For the sake of simplicity, we have decided not to elaborate on this method very much here. Our decision is supported in part by emerging evidence suggesting that most-to-least prompting methods may result in less long-term prompt dependence, at least for many of the kind of tasks that we will discuss. Therefore, in this book we recommend that you use a most-to-least prompting strategy, except in the case of intensive toilet training, which we will be discussing in Chapter 10.

> Prompt fading is a method of systematically reducing the amount of help you give your child.

We strongly recommend that regardless of prompt level used, you use verbal prompts sparingly. Often verbal prompts are the most challenging to fade and result in the greatest degree of dependence. A good rule to follow is to minimize adding any prompts that are unnecessary and eventually must be faded. Begin with prompts and then begin fading the prompts for those individual actions (steps) that are the strongest (i.e., most likely to be consistently performed). Remember, if you didn't really need the prompt or praise to ensure success, don't add it in the first place. There is no obligation for you to talk throughout the session. We have observed that parents and teachers have a tendency to talk while teaching self-help tasks. That is somewhat understandable because there are so many opportunities to socialize, label things, and model appropriate language. But self-help activities are not typically the context for socializing. The goal is to get your child to do the target skill without you. If you insert yourself where you are not needed, you run the risk of unintentionally creating dependency. It also is important to refrain from using multiple instructions and verbal prompts for your child. It is better to only use physical or gestural prompts with these tasks as they are easier to remove over time.

> If you insert yourself where you are not needed, you run the risk of unintentionally creating dependency.

Shaping

Another important teaching technique is called shaping. Shaping involves reinforcing a behavior that occurs very rarely or, when it occurs, it is not very refined. For example, learning to color is a skill that is often gradually shaped from random scribbling on the page to smooth stokes within lines. Parents often begin by modeling coloring in a coloring book. When the child initially imitates, his strokes are random scribbles that occur across the page without reference to printed lines on the page (e.g., a line drawing of a horse). Over time, some of the scribbles actually fall within the lines of the drawing. Parents often selectively praise the child for coloring more within the lines. Over time (usually weeks and months), the parents continue to praise the child for coloring that begins to fill within lines and respond less to random scribbles. This behavior of reinforcing closer and closer approximations to the desired coloring actions is an example of shaping. When teaching self-help skills we rarely use shaping in isolation. It would be long and arduous to ask a child to wash and dry his face, then selectively reinforce only those responses that approximate the desired sequence of actions. In most cases, the prerequisite skill set simply does not exist. Instead, we combine prompts with shaping. This combination ensures that the behavior is exhibited (even if it has to be prompted) so that it can be reinforced.

When teaching a new skill, our expectation is that the child will demonstrate all of the steps of a target skill fluidly and with little or no help. Although that is our expectation, we don't begin with that. Instead, we require only that the child demonstrate one step and we gradually add one additional step at a time as the child demonstrates mastery of the previous one.

> Shaping involves reinforcing close approximations of a desired behavior using selective praise.

Within each step of our task analysis, prompting and shaping is important. We begin by accepting almost any response, even if it is physically prompted. The immediate goal is to help the child be successful, demonstrate to him our expectations, and set up the conditions for earning rewards. If we expect the child to demonstrate all of the steps in a fluid manner from the beginning, we almost always will be disappointed by the outcome. It is somewhat like learning to walk. The child begins by pulling themselves to standing position. Then they learn to hold onto furniture and slowly take steps. Next they learn to take a few clumsy steps and immediately fall to the floor. And the process continues until the child is walking fluidly and eventually is able to run. Along the way, parents praise, support, and model the desired behavior. Children with autism learn most things in the same way. But, unlike typically developing children, it will take a more systematic approach and a great deal of practice.

Within a step of our task analysis, we initially accept and praise a response that is completed even if it takes a great deal of our help. But gradually, we expect and reward selectively based on the child's improving performance. Consider the following shaping sequence to teach a child to dry his face with a cloth towel in which prompts and praise are used then faded over a series of trials:

1. Parent places his hands over child's hands, brings towel to child's face and wipes forehead, cheek, and chin.
2. Parent places his hands over child's hands, brings towel to child's face, and applies less pressure to wipe face (selectively verbally reinforce greater effort on the child's part).
3. Parent places his hands over child's hands, brings towel to child's face, and continues to gradually diminish the pressure so that child is moving towel on face (selectively verbally reinforce greater effort).
4. When the child is responding without resisting prompts, parent helps by touching or nudging the child's hand (selectively verbally reinforce when the child is wiping his face and withholding praise when he is not).
5. Parent provides some verbal prompts and encouragement, uses gestures if needed, but withholds physical prompts unless child fails to move towel on face.
6. Parent gradually fades the use of verbal prompts and gestures.
7. Parent fades praise.
8. Combine this step with previous and next steps to be learned.

Chaining: Linking Steps to Form More Complex Behavior

Chaining is a method of linking relatively simple behaviors to form a more complex task. Chaining starts with a task analysis (the foundation), then we use a number of other building blocks, or tools that we have already discussed (e.g., reinforcement, prompting, shaping) to link the steps together in a coherent and meaningful way. In a chain, each action (or step) in the chain signals the next action to be completed and reinforces the action that has just occurred. Referring back to our example of toothbrushing in Table 6-4, if Mrs. Bartolo consistently praises Giovanni for turning on the cold water (Step 5), that step will become reinforcing itself *and* signal Giovanni to wet the toothbrush (Step 6) because additional rewards are imminent.

In our own lives, we learn many things in a chain. Try to quickly recite the last couple lines of the U.S. Pledge of Allegiance. What most people may discover is that they began at the beginning of the pledge and worked their way to the end. That is because we learned the pledge as a chain of individual phrases that built on each other. In the case of Giovanni, once he learns all of the steps, it becomes almost automatic—much like the pledge of allegiance or our learning to drive example presented earlier.

Chaining allows you to take the task analysis that you have previously developed and directly present it to your child. Chaining is a way of linking the component steps that you developed in your task analysis into one fluid skill. Instead of just presenting all of the steps at once to your child, we recommend you systematically introduce them one at a time until all of the steps are linked into one skill. Sometimes we do this by starting at the end and working backwards and sometimes by starting at the beginning and working forward. We are going to talk about two chaining methods: backward chaining, and forward chaining.

> Chaining is a method of linking simple behaviors together to form a more complex task.

Backward Chaining

In the toothbrushing example (Table 6-4) Giovanni earns time playing with a favorite toy for completing the chain of toothbrushing steps. Mrs. Bartolo makes sure Giovanni moves successfully through the eleven steps as quickly as possible so that he experiences the super reward. If the toy or activity is truly reinforcing, Giovanni is more likely in the future to cooperate with toothbrushing. Initially, the goal is to make sure Giovanni understands the relationship between his cooperation and getting the super reward. In this case, completing the last step—placing the toothbrush in the holder—immediately signals that the super reward is available (praise and the toy). To ensure that this connection develops, Mrs. Bartolo places her hands on top of Giovanni's hand(s) and physically prompts him through Steps 1–11 so that he makes no errors and the super reward is given as quickly as possible following completion of the last step (Step 11). This teaching approach provides almost immediate access to the reinforcer (a motivating toy, activity, or food) and enables Giovanni to experience success—nearly error free.

The next time that Mrs. Bartolo works on toothbrushing (either at the end of the first day when Giovanni is getting ready for bed or the following morning when he wakes up) she will give him an opportunity to accomplish Step 11 without her help. As before, she will physically prompt him through the first steps, this time stopping after Step 10. After Step 10, Mrs. Bartolo will remove her hands and pause to see if Giovanni will put his toothbrush back in the holder independently (Step 11). If he does not respond within three seconds, she will again place her hands on the back of Giovanni's hand(s) and guide him to place the toothbrush in the holder. If he completes Step 11 without help, she will praise him and deliver the super reward. If he requires help to complete Step 11, she will praise him if it requires less effort to prompt him (meaning he assists), but will not deliver the super reward.

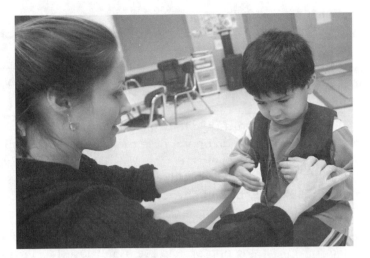

Hand-over-hand prompting involves placing your hands on top of your child's hands and physically guiding him through the task.

Each time she will conduct the session in the same way, using less and less physical help, until he is reliably placing the toothbrush into the holder (Step 11) without help for three consecutive times. It is likely that it will take five to ten days before he is independent on this one step of the chain of steps. Once Giovanni is able to independently complete Step 11 and has demonstrated that he can do so over the course of three separate toothbrushing opportunities, Mrs. Bartolo will begin teaching Step 10 *with* Step 11. That is, she hand-over-hand prompts Giovanni through Steps 1–9, pausing before Step 10 and waiting for Giovanni to complete Steps 10 and 11 independently. As before, if he fails to respond within three seconds or responds incorrectly, she quickly places her hand on his and helps him complete the step. Once he achieves independent responding for Steps 10 and 11, she adds Step 9 and repeats the just described process. Mrs. Bartolo continues in the manner until all eleven steps are learned.

Table 6-6 (on page 64) provides an example of how training would progress through the steps using backward chaining. For economy of space, we will describe only a five step program. We also have included a step for programming generalization. We will discuss this later in this chapter and again in Chapter 11.

The parent (or teacher) physically guides using only the amount of pressure needed to help the child succeed.

Forward Chaining

Simply put, forward chaining is the opposite of backward chaining. In forward chaining, you focus instruction on the first step until it is learned. The remaining steps are prompted hand-over-hand until you reach the end. Like backward chaining, once the target step is being reliably demonstrated, you move to the next step, in this case, Step 2. You continue adding a step as each step is achieved, going forward, until all steps are independently demonstrated. We have included a template for teaching using a forward chain approach in Table 6-7 (on page 65).

■ Table 6-6 Template for the Backward Chain Approach

Phase	What You Do	What Your Child Should Do	Criteria for Moving to the Next Phase
1	■ Instruct child to begin skill target using an appropriate cue (words, picture, etc.). ■ Place your hands on the child's hands and physically guide him through all steps.	Your child should cooperate with your assistance.	Move to Phase 2 after one or two practice runs (Phase 1).
2	■ Instruct child to begin skill target using appropriate cue as in Phase 1. ■ Place your hands on the child's hands and physically guide him through steps. ■ Just before the last step, remove your hands, pause, and allow your child to attempt last step. ■ If your child responds correctly, praise enthusiastically and provide super reward. If he does not respond or responds incorrectly, physically guide using only pressure needed. ■ Gradually diminish the pressure with each trial so that your child is moving toward independence.	Your child should independently demonstrate the <u>last</u> step without help.	Move to Phase 3 when your child can complete the last step without prompts for three consecutive opportunities.
3	Follow instructions above and remove support for last two steps.	Your child should independently demonstrate the <u>last two</u> steps without help.	Move to Phase 4 when your child can complete the last two steps without prompts for three consecutive opportunities.
4	Follow instructions above and remove support for last three steps.	Your child should independently demonstrate the <u>last three</u> steps without help.	Move to Phase 5 when your child can complete the last three steps without prompts for three consecutive opportunities.
5	Follow instructions above for each remaining step in order until all are complete.	The child should independently demonstrate <u>all steps</u> without help.	Move to the generalization phase after your child completes all steps with two or fewer prompts for three consecutive opportunities.
6	Generalization phase (see Chapter 11).	Your child should demonstrate target skill in various settings, using a variety of materials, and with various people.	Program is complete when your child demonstrates the ability to use skill target in most settings and with all familiar adults with little or no help.

■ Table 6-7 Template for the Forward Chain Approach

Phase	What You Do	What Your Child Should Do	Criteria for Moving to the Next Phase
1	■ Instruct child to begin skill target using an appropriate cue (words, picture, etc.). ■ Place your hands on the child's hands and physically guide him through all steps.	Your child should cooperate with your assistance.	Move to Phase 2 after one or two practice runs (Phase 1).
2	■ Instruct child to begin skill target using an appropriate cue as in Phase 1. ■ Pause and give your child a chance to complete the first step. If your child responds correctly, praise enthusiastically and provide super reward. If he does not respond, or responds incorrectly, physically guide him using only the amount of pressure needed. ■ Gradually diminish the pressure so that the child is moving toward independence. ■ Once the first step is complete, place your hands on your child's hands and physically guide through all remaining steps.	Your child should independently demonstrate the <u>first</u> step without help.	Move to Phase 3 when your child can complete the first step without prompts for three consecutive opportunities.
3	■ Follow instructions above and remove support for the first two steps. ■ Praise child after completion of Step 1 and deliver the super reward after completion of Step 2.	Your child should independently demonstrate the <u>first two</u> steps without help.	Move to Phase 4 when your child can complete the first two steps without prompts for three consecutive opportunities.
4	■ Follow instructions above and remove support for the first three steps. ■ Continue to praise for completion of previous steps and provide the super reward for completion of Step 3.	Your child should independently demonstrate the <u>first three</u> steps without help.	Move to Phase 5 when your child can complete the first three steps without prompts for three consecutive opportunities.
5	Follow instructions above for each remaining step in order until all are complete.	Your child should independently demonstrate <u>all steps</u> without help.	Move to the generalization phase after your child completes all steps with two or fewer prompts for three consecutive opportunities.
6	Generalization phase (see Chapter 11).	Your child should demonstrate target skill in various settings, using variety of materials, and with various people.	Program is complete when your child demonstrates the ability to use skill target in most settings and with all familiar adults with little or no help.

This approach has a simplicity and logic that is appealing to many parents and teachers—moving forward from the beginning to the end. On the other hand, problems can arise due to delivery of the super reward being significantly delayed after the child's demonstration of the target step—at least in the beginning. Consider a ten-step program. You give the child an opportunity to demonstrate Step 1 and he does it independently. You immediately praise him, then following the tenants of a forward chain, you prompt him hand-over-hand through the remaining nine steps. At the end, you deliver the super reward (food or an activity) for cooperation and attention. For some children with autism, this delay in reinforcement may be too long to wait. It may also create some confusion regarding what is most valued by the parent, since the super reward comes after a series of *prompted* actions. One solution is to deliver the super reward after the target trial (as described in Table 6-7). Although this approach interrupts the flow of steps from start to end, it does communicate to the child that greater independence is what is valued by you.

If you use this approach, you must select reinforcers that can be consumed pretty quickly (e.g., food) or are unobtrusive (e.g., high five) so that you get back to the task and continue through the rest of the steps. It should be emphasized that some children may have no problem delaying reinforcement and understanding the desired contingency between independence and recognition. For this group of children, forward chaining is an excellent choice.

Determining Which Chaining Method is Best for You

There is no perfect way to determine the best teaching approach for you and your child. The first thing you need to do before you start is to determine what your child can do already, prior to beginning instruction. This is called getting a baseline and will be discussed again in Chapter 7. First, model the steps of the program, drawing your child's attention to what you are doing. Next, ask him to complete the task (e.g., "Wash your hands.") and give him a few seconds to start. If he fails to begin or responds only a little, gently guide him (hand-over-hand) through the steps. We recommend using physical prompts rather than more verbal prompts at this stage. (Note: You will need the task analysis at this point.) Experiment with the types of prompts you use and back away some of the time to see what he can do on his own. You may have to repeat this sequence over two or three days to get a good picture of what he can do. As you are doing this, consider a few questions: Can he do any of the steps on his own? Is he cooperative when I physically prompt? Does he pay attention to the modeling I provide? Does he seem to respond to my verbal instructions (e.g., "Rub the back of your hand")? Does he respond to gestures with and without verbal prompts (e.g., pointing to facet handle to signal that water should be turned on)? Based on the answers to these types of questions consider the following guidelines:

- If your child cannot complete most of the steps, but understands the relationship between his actions and rewards, even when the rewards are delayed several minutes, then use a **forward chaining** approach.
- If your child cannot complete most or all of the steps and does not understand the relationship between his actions and delayed reinforcement, then use **backward chaining**.

Within either the forward or backward chaining approach, if you discover in obtaining a baseline that your child can reliably complete some steps independently, then allow him to do so during teaching. If he begins to make errors, though, continue with full prompting for all steps that have not yet been taught.

Developing New Skills Using Video-Modeling

As we have indicated, one type of prompt that may help some children is modeling. In its simplest form, the adult simply shows the child what he wants the child to do, then expects the observing child to imitate. As we have mentioned before, this alone is not likely to be an effective strategy for most children with autism. When combined with physical prompts and the systematic use of rewards, greater success is possible, but still only a small number of children may respond. One particular creative modified approach to using modeling is to videotape the model and show it to the child with autism. Many children with autism are highly interested in the content of videotapes and are more likely to imitate the words and actions that they observe in this medium. In addition to the increased motivation that some children show, another benefit of video modeling is that the model in the video will perform the exact same actions each time they are viewed. This consistency may help some children to recognize the critical actions. In general, this approach will work only for those children who (1) have a high interest in videotapes and (2) demonstrate the ability to imitate the actions of another person.

Videos can be developed by parents using a peer or sibling as the model on the video. If your child performs a skill inconsistently, you may also want to catch them performing the desired skill on video and then allow them to watch themselves and practice the skill. This technique, called video self-modeling (VSM), is gaining popularity as recent research reveals the effectiveness of this method for teaching children and adolescents with ASD social and daily living skills. Some skills that video-modeling can be useful for include: asking an adult for assistance, sharing with a peer, asking to join into a group activity, and most of the self-help skills that are discussed in this book.

Increasing Independence

We have discussed teaching new skills, thus far, as a highly parent-directed approach. We recommend that you develop a task analysis by writing down all component steps involved in a complex task. We suggest that you link the list of steps when teaching by utilizing a backward or forward chaining approach. We also recommend ways to signal your child that a self-help skill needs to be completed (e.g., mom tells Giovanni that it is time to brush his teeth). This highly adult-directed model is often useful during the initial phases to teach the skill; however, you do not want to be an active participant in your child's completion of self-care routines for life. There may be some children who will never be capable of achieving full independence but most individuals with autism can achieve a significant level of independence and free parents and caregivers from daily involvement. The suggestions below will allow you to help increase your child's level of independence.

    1. Generalize (also see Chapter 11)— Once your child is beginning to show some success, attempt to practice skills frequently every day in different locations throughout the home (to the extent practical) and with different adults (e.g., Mom, Dad, Grandma). This process will assist in facilitating generalization of new skills. It is also important to find and use every reasonable natural opportunity to practice emerging skills. If your child's teacher is working on the same skill, make sure that the same or similar tools are being applied in each context. If disagreements occur regarding the best approach, seek common ground so that your child is not receiving mixed messages. Schedule specific times to conduct the program; keep in mind that more is typically better. Given the considerable demands on all families, take advantage of existing natural opportunities to work on the target skills, even if it is simply to informally practice what is being more formally taught at another time. Below are examples of how handwashing might be embedded into many existing opportunities:

- Before breakfast, lunch, and dinner
- After using the bathroom
- After playing outside
- After an art project
- Before and after helping with cooking
- After wiping or blowing nose

2. **Utilize visual supports**—As previously mentioned, verbal prompts (verbally instructing a child) are difficult to fade and can inhibit independence. Instead of verbal prompts, consider using visual cues to provide support to your child that may not require that you be present.

Step	Picture
Use toilet	
Wipe	
Wash hands	
Dry hands	

One type of visual cue involves presenting your task analysis in picture form to your child. Let's suppose that you developed a simple task analysis for your son on independent toileting and decided to use a picture to represent each step as shown at left.

The pictures could simply be pasted into a horizontal or vertical strip, laminated, and hung in the bathroom for continued reference by your son. He no longer needs to rely on you to remember the steps.

Visual cues can also be used to instruct your child to begin a task. Instead of telling Giovanni that it is time to brush his teeth, his mother could simply show him a picture of a toothbrush, further reducing the number of verbal instructions that she has to provide. Some students who are nonverbal may require visual supports throughout much of the teaching process. Remember, that the amount of visual support given should be specified as part of the context in your initial goal (e.g., *When shown a picture of a toothbrush, Giovanni will brush his teeth without assistance 90 percent of the time*). For more information on creating and using visual supports, see the book *Visual Supports for People with Autism* by Cohen & Sloan (2007), part of Woodbine House's Topics in Autism series.

3. **Fade reinforcement**—As has been discussed many times before, it is essential to fade the reinforcers that your child receives for skill completion, ultimately to the most natural level. Praise or other social reinforcers given during steps of a task analysis should ideally be removed as the child progresses. The super reward should be faded once the skill is mastered and reliably used in many situations. Ideally, the completion of the task should be rewarding in and of itself, although we know that is not a reasonable outcome for many children who will continue to need some assistance throughout their lives.

Step 4: Evaluating Progress

Let's quickly review where we are now. The first three steps for teaching self skills were (1) specify the skill that you want to teach (the goal), (2) break complex skills into smaller steps for learning (the task analysis), and (3) use a systematic approach to instruction (e.g., chaining, prompting, and prompt fading). The next step (4) is to collect and use data. We will offer specific methods for monitoring and evaluating progress in greater detail in Chapter 7. Until then, it is important to state that progress must be consistently monitored. It is the interplay between intervention and evaluation that enables you to know when to continue with your current approach and when modifications to your plan are needed. If you have selected and specified teaching goals as outlined in this chapter, it will be easy for you to compare the progress data that you have been tracking with the goals that you have set. Progress occurs very rapidly in some children and slowly in others. Progress for an individual child may also vary depending on the complexity or type of skill being taught. Do not become alarmed if it takes a while for your child to meet his goals. However, if little or no progress is evident within two to three weeks, it is time to make some teaching modifications.

> If little or no progress toward you specified goal is evident within two to three weeks, it is time to make some teaching modifications.

Step 5: Analyzing Data and Modifying Your Approach as Needed

After collecting some data on your child's progress (e.g., number of steps he completes independently) you can graph the data so that you have a visual representation of progress. Again, we will talk about this more in Chapter 7. It is highly unusual that your first plan will be completely successful. The typical pattern involves implementing one or more strategies that you believe are best for your child, giving them sufficient time to work (two to three weeks), then assessing your child's progress. In many cases, simple modifications are all that are needed. Appendix B provides a summary of common problems that you may confront when teaching any type of skill and possible solutions to attempt. We also have included the section entitled "Troubleshooting Common Problems" in Chapter 7 and additional troubleshooting strategies specific to individual skill areas in other chapters of this book.

Writing an Instructional Plan

In this and prior chapters, we have laid out all the component parts of an instructional plan for teaching your child self-help skills. Now, let's take a moment to pull all of these pieces together into a comprehensive written plan. We have provided instructions for writing a plan and a blank template in Appendices D and E respectively. As you can see, the instructions direct you to detail the various parts of the plan (e.g., objective for learning, the place and time for instruction, the instructional cue, and rewards). Before you begin teaching, take a few minutes to complete each section of the instructional plan template. Please note that we also have attached the specific phases of intervention for each type of chaining approach (i.e., backward chain and forward chain) that we just discussed. Almost any self-help skill that you choose to teach can be plugged into one of these plan templates. Thus, all you have to do is choose *one* of them, insert the skill that you plan to teach into the model, and get started.

Summary

We realize that we have provided a lot of information in the last few chapters. Table 6-8 attempts to put all of the pieces together for you by providing practical pointers for teaching self-help skills. As we mentioned in the beginning of this chapter, follow the five steps that we outlined and your chances of success are good. Begin by establishing a clear and achievable goal for learning. Next, examine the skill that you are teaching and break it into small steps for learning. This may be the most important thing that you do to ensure your child's success. Breaking the skill into smaller actions allows you to work on one step at a time, carefully linking them together to form the more complex skill. Third, select and consistently use the variety of proven methods that are available for teaching children with autism. Pay particular attention to motivating your child to learn by using praise and super rewards. If your child is easily distracted and responding inconsistently from one day to the next, it is probably time to reassess rewards and find some new things to motivate him. Fourth, it is very important to continually collect and use data. The best way to do that is to collect objective information, such as how many times you have to prompt each step of the program. And finally, whatever plan you develop will likely require a little bit (and sometimes a lot) of alterations along the way. Hardly anyone hits a home run his first time up to bat.

Table 6-8   Some Practical Pointers for Teaching Self-Help Skills

1. Make sure that the skill you've chosen to teach is developmentally appropriate for your child. Don't frustrate your child or yourself by teaching something before your child is ready.

2. Analyze the skill you want to teach by doing it yourself slowly and writing down the steps.

3. Remember to set up a consistent time and place every day to conduct the program. Typically the most natural time and place are best.

4. Get your child's attention before you provide an instruction. After the initial run-through, minimize verbal comments and instructions. Remember that anything you add (e.g., physical guidance, verbal cues, and pointing) will eventually have to be removed (faded) if you want your child to achieve independence. The rule to remember is you shouldn't add anything that your child doesn't need to be successful.

5. Remember to set up the environment (e.g., materials and their arrangement) before you begin the instructional lesson.

6. Be patient and consistent. Most children with autism learn from a lot of repetition. It may take weeks and even months to teach one skill.

7. Continually evaluate how your child is doing and be willing to make changes as needed.

8. Early in teaching, make sure that your child gets praise for any reasonable attempt to complete the task.

A life spent making mistakes is not only more honorable but more useful than a life spent doing nothing.
—George Bernard Shaw

7

Evaluating Progress

The Richards Family

Tyshawn Richards is a very active young boy with autism who touches everything and often puts things into his mouth, whether it is dirt from a potted plant or the dust bunnies from under the couch. Tyshawn's parents, Martha and Tyrone Richards, are constantly asking Tyshawn to spit things out and washing his hands, since he is unable to do this independently. Frustrated and impatient for results, they decide to create a simple task analysis for handwashing and dive in to the training process without much preparation. They identify four instructional steps: (1) turning on the water, (2) rubbing his hands with soap, (3) rinsing his hands with water, and (4) drying his hands.

They start by going through the four-step program with Tyshawn at least three to four times a day, when he is getting ready to eat or when he comes in from outside. After a week, Tyshawn's parents are feeling even more frustrated. It occurs to them that they are each going about the training differently, have a different set of expectations for Tyshawn, and are defining success differently. They can't determine whether

Tyshawn is making any progress internalizing the handwashing process or simply following their many verbal and physical prompts. They stick it out for four weeks of on-and-off training in handwashing, but begin to think that maybe Tyshawn just isn't ready to wash his hands independently. With little information as to what is working and not working for Tyshawn, his parents lose heart in the effort and resort to simply washing Tyshawn's hands for him.

■ Is Your Child Really Learning?

Let's start with the assumption that you are about to begin teaching a skill to your son or daughter and that you plan to use the strategies and tools laid out in previous chapters. I am glad you are here because this is a must-read chapter. If you have committed yourself to teaching self-help skills to your child with autism, it's important that your time, efforts, and energy are not wasted. We understand that while you are willing to do anything for your children, there are things other than teaching handwashing and shoe-tying that also need your attention during the course of a typical day. One of the best ways to ensure that your time is well spent is to collect information on how your child is doing along the way. We call this information "data." Data will enable you to know whether or not your child is learning the skill you are trying to teach and help guide you to make appropriate modifications to your efforts if progress is not evident.

> Data will enable you to know whether or not your child is learning the skill you are trying to teach and help guide you to make appropriate modifications to your efforts if progress is not evident.

■ Why Should You Collect Data?

The Richards had the best intentions to teach Tyshawn to wash his hands. By targeting three or four opportunities a day to instruct and practice, it appeared that they had made a significant commitment to teaching the skill. But after a few weeks, Mrs. Richards was convinced that Tyshawn was progressing but Mr. Richards was not. Neither parent was clear as to what prompts the other was using or what step was the focus of their attention. The Richards should be commended for attempting to teach Tyshawn to wash his hands, yet they lacked a systematic way to collect information that would objectively tell them whether or not their son was learning and what modifications might be needed to ensure progress.

Does collecting data mean that you must walk around with a clipboard all day recording everything your child does? No. Collecting data means that you will periodically record information regarding your child's performance on a particular task or step that you are teaching. Does it have to be written down? Preferably yes, because if you are like most of us, your memory for details is not always accurate or objective, especially when you have thousands of other things on your mind.

Teaching skills systematically is critical but equally important is objectively evaluating your child's progress and the effectiveness of your teaching methods. The purpose of this chapter is to provide the specifics on how to collect data reliably and quickly, and how to use the data to help guide your instruction.

What are data?

Data are snapshots of information that provide details about the occurrence or nonoccurrence of a precisely identified event or action. When some people think of data collection they think of a person holding a clipboard and making a tally mark each time a child engages in a previously defined skill or behavior. Yet this is clearly an exaggeration of data collection as it is used in most teaching instances. Whether we realize it or not, we use data all the time. Our banking accounts, electric and gas meters, and cell phones collect and use data on a daily basis. Take a bank statement. Every time you use your credit or debit card, the amount is recorded. This is critical information, or data, that lets you know plain and simply if you have enough money to pay your next bill or make the next purchase. In the same way, when teaching children, particularly children with autism, we need information on how much the child is learning and to assess whether our teaching methods are working. Do we keep teaching a skill to a child in a specific way if no progress is being made? Just as we change our spending habits when our bank statements indicate that we have no money, we change our instructional plan when the data tell us the child is not acquiring the target skill. In the example above, Tyshawn's parents did not have data to tell them whether their son was getting more independent in his handwashing. Without data, we often allow our biases and wishes to interfere with our objective evaluation of how things are going.

Making Data Collection Simple

Typically, when we collect data on a child's progress, we record whether or not a particular behavior occurs within a particular context (e.g., the child hangs up her coat upon arrival home) or the number of times a particular behavior occurs (e.g., how many times the child hangs up her coat in all settings) or how long it takes to complete a task (e.g., how long it takes to eat lunch). We might also record the number of prompts needed for a child to exhibit a desired behavior (e.g., how many times a parent has to prompt her to hang up her coat). Or we might record the number of correct and incorrect responses (e.g., whether the child hangs up her coat vs. drops it on the floor). Typically, this kind of information is collected over several opportunities, days, or instructional sessions and allows us to quickly evaluate whether or not a child is making progress. Frequency data (i.e., the number of times that something is observed) can also be summarized as a percentage of opportunity to respond (e.g., the number of steps completed independently can be converted into the percentage of steps completed by dividing the number correct by the total number of steps).

Most parents of typically developing children do not take data because learning occurs quickly over a short period of time using the same instructional methods used by their parents. Take, for example, a child without disabilities who is learning to ride a bike. We take off the training wheels and we hold the child's bike firmly as the child pedals. After a yard or two we gradually release our grip on the bike, the child continues to pedal for one to three yards, and then we quickly renew our grip on the bike as the child begins to lose balance and fall. We make sure she is okay and praise her for going the one to three yards and then get her back on the bike. We hold the bike as she pedals and then once again gradually release our grip. Again, the child may go one to three yards or may even make it five yards before she begins to lose balance. We repeat this cycle a few times until the child indicates that she wants to do something else. Each time we practice during the next week or so, the child goes a little further until one day she is off and riding away on her own. This is a learning ritual that goes on every spring and summer on countless driveways and sidewalks. Parents teach but they don't collect data and yet the child still learns to ride her bike without training wheels in a relatively short amount of time.

Unfortunately, most children with autism do not learn by the same methods used for generations to teach basic skills. As we have indicated previously, only when skills are broken into small component steps (a task analysis) and are taught very systematically across weeks and months of practice is learning realized. Data allow you to objectively assess subtle changes in your child's behavior that enable you to conclude that she is progressing or whether your approach to instruction needs to change. For example, if you are teaching your daughter to wash her hands and she is making little or no progress with the step that requires her to pump the soap dispenser, you may decide to break that step into a number of smaller steps for learning. Or you decide to provide more practice on the one step where she is most often failing (pumping the soap) so that the entire sequence of steps is not held up every time she attempts to wash her hands. Another option is to provide more physical guidance to your child for the step that involves pumping the soap. In short, if the data indicate that over a period of two to three weeks you are still using prompts on a particular target step, then the step or your approach needs to be modified.

■ Using the Task Analysis Data Sheet

The key to collecting data is to develop a method that is easy and gives the most amount of information with the least amount of effort. The Task Analysis Data Sheet (TADS) should meet these criteria. (See Table 7-1, page 78.) The Task Analysis Data Sheet lists the verbal instruction to be given in each teaching session (e.g., "Tyshawn, wash your hands"), the teaching method (e.g., backward chaining or forward chaining), and the steps needed to complete the task (the task analysis). You simply record how the child performs each step of the overall task. Specifically, you record whether or not your child requires a prompt or completes the step independently without a prompt. If your child performs the step without any help, then a "+" is written in the column corresponding to the task and the date observed. If your child requires a prompt (verbal, visual, gestural, or physical) then a "-" is recorded. (See Table 7-3, page 81.) The only exception to the rule of recording a minus when a prompt is needed is when the program is written to include a specific cue for each step, such as your child following a series of photographs or drawings depicting each step. Although it is certainly desired that visual cues will eventually be unnecessary, that may not be the initial goal. As we described in Chapter 6, you may set up the context initially to make it easier for your child to achieve the objective: "*Given a set of photographs that depict handwashing and drying,* Tyshawn will complete all of the steps with two or fewer prompts."

Tyshawn's parents have decided to take a more systematic approach to teaching handwashing and data collection. Using the TADS, Mr. and Mrs. Richards start by filling in the top of the data sheet including the goal and verbal instruction they plan to use: "Tyshawn, wash your hands." They then record the type of teaching method they are going to use: backward chaining. All the steps for washing hands are then recorded under the column heading "Component Skill." (See Table 7-2.) In this new task analysis, handwashing has been broken down into fourteen steps, instead of the parent's original four-step plan. Each step is numbered on the sheet. As noted before, the number of steps is dependent upon your child's ability level and her experience with the particular skill being taught. Whether using backward or forward chaining, you number the very first step as number one. In this example, the first step is "Turns on cold water." In the beginning, nothing is recorded in the column labeled "Mastery." We will get to this later.

■ Determining What Your Child May Already Know—Collecting Baseline Data

Ideally, when you create a list of self-help skills that you want your child to learn, you have a pretty good sense of your child's ability in each area. That is to say, you choose to teach your child how to put on a t-shirt, brush her teeth, or use eating utensils believing that your child cannot do these things independently. You base this assumption on your recollection of always having to do these tasks for your child or having to remind and prod your child continuously to dress, brush her teeth, and eat with a spoon. It is possible, however, that while your child may not be able to do the whole skill independently, she may be able to do some or many of the component skills (e.g., can push arms through the sleeves of a t-shirt). The reason your child may not have willingly displayed these abilities is that she has learned that if she does not perform the tasks independently, you will do them for her.

For this reason and others to be discussed, it is recommended that prior to teaching a self-help skill, you collect information (data) about your son's or daughter's ability to accomplish the skill that you have targeted for instruction. This initial collection of data is called a "baseline" assessment. (See Table 7-3.) Collecting baseline data is one of the best ways to maximize your teaching time. A baseline assessment provides a wealth of information that will guide your planning and instruction. First, as we have discussed, it will tell you whether your child is able to complete all, or most, of the component steps of the skill without your help. Simply put, if your child can perform *all* of a particular skill, then you obviously don't need to teach it. Or, if your child can do *part* of the task that you intend to teach, it may alter your task analysis (e.g., number of steps) and/or the teaching tools that you select to use (e.g., level of prompts and type of reinforcers). Second, a baseline provides a

■ Table 7-1 Task Analysis Data Sheet

SKILL TARGET _____

      GOAL _____

YOUR INSTRUCTION TO CHILD

(e.g., "Brush your teeth."): _____

TEACHING METHOD (Circle)   BACKWARD   FORWARD

Mastery	Step	Component Skill (e.g., Turn on water)	Date													

■ **Table 7-2**   **Task Analysis Data Sheet: Setting Up the Data**

SKILL TARGET   Handwashing

GOAL   When given the instruction, wash your hands, Tyshawn will completely wash his hands independently for three consecutive sessions.

YOUR INSTRUCTION TO CHILD
(e.g., "Brush your teeth."):   "Tyshawn, wash your hands."

TEACHING METHOD (Circle)   BACKWARD   FORWARD

Mastery	Step	Component Skill (e.g., Turn on water)	9/17	9/18	9/19	Date							
			BSL	BSL	BSL								
	1	Turns on cold water											
	2	Turns on hot water											
	3	Places hands under water											
	4	Places right hand under and left hand on soap dispenser											
	5	Pushes pump down twice											
	6	Rubs soap between hands for 3 sec											
	7	Rubs back of right for 3 seconds											
	8	Rubs back of left hand for 3 sec											
	9	Rinses hands under water											
	10	Turns off hot water											
	11	Turns off cold water											
	12	Finds hanging cloth towel											
	13	Dries palms of both hands											
	14	Dries backs of both hands											

Record instruction to be used and circle teaching method.

Record date that baseline is collected and the letters BSL to indicate baseline.

Record the numbers of the steps and the corresponding task to be taught.

reference for comparing future progress. If you know where your child is starting from and you know where you hope to go (the goals or mastery criteria), you are able to continuously assess your child's progress against this initial reference point.

> A baseline assessment provides a wealth of information that will guide your planning and instruction.

The procedure for collecting and running baseline is as follows. Complete the Task Analysis Data sheet as described above including delineating the steps (even if these steps have to be modified after the initial baseline assessment). Then, in the first column below the word "Date," you write the date of your first baseline session, and below that box, you write the abbreviation for baseline, "BSL" (see Table 7-2). This will indicate that the marks (i.e., "+" or "-") recorded in that column are baseline data. It is generally recommended that you gather at least three sessions of baseline data collected over two to three consecutive days.

Please note that we use a variety of different ways to describe a time interval for teaching (e.g., days, opportunities, and sessions). The definition of days refers to calendar days (e.g., Monday, Tuesday, and Wednesday). Sessions and opportunities are often used interchangeably to refer to a period of time in which you focus on teaching a specific skill. Mr. and Mrs. Richards chose to have Tyshawn wash his hands whenever he came indoors. Each of these was an "opportunity" to run through the fourteen steps of the handwashing program they had developed. (This may also be referred to as a handwashing "session.")

Again, we recommend that you conduct at least three baseline sessions over the course of at least two days, before you begin instruction. This will provide a reasonably accurate measure of your son's or daughter's ability. If your child can perform any of the steps of the skill consistently without prompts for three sessions consecutively, you can be fairly certain that she knows how to do it. In fact, we consider the step mastered if the child can perform the skill for at least three consecutive sessions without any prompts.

Determining What Tyshawn Can Do

As noted previously, Tyshawn's parents are tired of having to wash their son's hands. They write a new task analysis with fourteen steps and decide to conduct a baseline assessment to determine what Tyshawn is actually capable of doing. The baseline assessment unfolded as follows and the data were captured in Table 7-3:

1. They began by recording the first day of baseline assessment (9/17) and wrote BSL for baseline on the data sheet.
2. Next, Mrs. Richards directed Tyshawn to the sink and said, "Tyshawn, wash your hands," then paused.
3. She waited about three seconds and when Tyshawn didn't respond she used a hand-over-hand prompt to complete the first step (turn on the cold water). She was likewise prepared to use hand-over-hand prompting if Tyshawn tried to leave the area, attempted a later step such as beginning to dry his hands before washing them, or engaged in a competing behavior such as playing with the mirror.

■ Table 7-3 Task Analysis Data Sheet: Collecting and Recording Baseline

SKILL TARGET Handwashing

GOAL When given the instruction, wash your hands, Tyshawn will completely wash his hands independently for three consecutive sessions.

YOUR INSTRUCTION TO CHILD "Tyshawn, wash your hands."
(e.g., "Brush your teeth."):

TEACHING METHOD (Circle) (BACKWARD)   FORWARD

Mastery	Step	Component Skill (e.g., Turn on water)	9/17 BSL	9/18 BSL	9/19 BSL												
	1	Turns on cold water	−	−	−												
	2	Turns on hot water	−	−	−												
	3	Places hands under water	−	−	−												
	4	Places right hand under and left hand on soap dispenser	−	−	−												
	5	Pushes pump down twice	−	−	−												
	6	Rubs soap between hands for 3 sec	−	−	−												
	7	Rubs back of right for 3 seconds	−	−	−												
	8	Rubs back of left hand for 3 sec	−	−	−												
	9	Rinses hands under water	−	−	−												
	10	Turns off hot water	+	+	+												
	11	Turns off cold water	+	+	+												
	12	Finds hanging cloth towel	−	−	−												
	13	Dries palms of both hands	−	−	−												
	14	Dries backs of both hands	−	−	−												

Record a minus ("-") for each step in which a prompt is given to the child.

Record a plus ("+") if child completes step independently.

4. Since Mrs. Richards had to physically place Tyshawn's right hand on the cold water handle and turn the handle with him, she recorded a minus sign ("-") in the cell below the 9/17 date next to the corresponding step.

5. After helping Tyshawn to complete the step to turn on the cold water, Mrs. Richards removed her own hand and gave Tyshawn an opportunity to complete the next step independently (i.e., turn on the hot water).

6. After three seconds, Tyshawn had not turned on the hot water, so she once again applied a hand-over-hand prompt.

7. As with Step 1, Mrs. Richards recorded a minus sign ("-") for Step 2 indicating that Tyshawn accomplished the step with her help.

8. The process continued like this for each step of the task until they reached the end. If Tyshawn required no prompts, physical or verbal, for a particular step, then a plus sign ("+") was recorded to indicate Tyshawn did the step independently.

9. Periodically throughout the session, Mrs. Richards praised Tyshawn for trying his best, following instructions or whatever behavior she could identify as praiseworthy.

As shown in Table 7-4, data were collected during three baseline sessions on 9/17, 9/18, and 9/19. Tyshawn's parents examined the three baseline sessions to determine how much of the task Tyshawn could do independently. Looking at the chart in Table 7-4, it appears Tyshawn needed prompts for most of the steps, except for turning the cold and hot water off. We can be somewhat assured, based on this data, that Tyshawn does not know how to wash his hands completely independently. However, he did appear to know how to do Steps 10 and 11, so his parents indicated that these steps were mastered by putting an "M" in the "Mastery" column. Because Tyshawn appears to know these steps already, his parents will not have to teach them. He will still need to complete these two steps each time but his parents should not have to prompt or provide immediate rewards for completing them independently. As we mentioned in Chapter 6, if for some reason Tyshawn begins to make errors on Steps 10 and 11 (including failing to respond in a timely manner), we recommend adding a full physical prompt to avoid errors and then treat these steps in the same manner as others in the forward or backward chaining method. With baseline completed, teaching can now begin.

Collecting Instructional Data

The methods of collecting teaching data are the same as for collecting baseline. Each session begins with the parent or teacher recording the date and then delivering the initial instruction (e.g., "Wash your hands"). Unlike baseline, however, when using backward or forward chaining teaching procedures, you only have to record your child's performance for the specific step(s) of the task that you are teaching as well as any steps that are mastered. The reason is that in a backward or forward chaining approach, your focus is on the steps that you are teaching (or have taught) while the steps yet to be learned are being prompted so that no errors occur. For example, if teaching your child using forward chaining, you would record whether your child independently completed the first step of the task

■ **Table 7-4** **Task Analysis Data Sheet: Analyzing Baseline Data**

SKILL TARGET: Handwashing

OBJECTIVE: When given the instruction, wash your hands, Tyshawn will completely wash his hands independently for three consecutive sessions.

YOUR INSTRUCTION TO CHILD: "Tyshawn, wash your hands."
(e.g., "Brush your teeth."):

TEACHING METHOD (Circle) (BACKWARD)   FORWARD

Mastery	Step	Component Skill (e.g., Turn on water)	9/17	9/18	9/19												
			BSL	BSL	BSL												
	1	Turns on cold water	−	−	−												
	2	Turns on hot water	−	−	−												
	3	Places hands under water	−	−	−												
	4	Places right hand under and left hand on soap dispenser	−	−	−												
	5	Pushes pump down twice	−	−	−												
	6	Rubs soap between hands for 3 sec	−	−	−												
	7	Rubs back of right for 3 seconds	−	−	−												
	8	Rubs back of left hand for 3 sec	−	−	−												
	9	Rinses hands under water	−	−	−												
M	10̶	Turns off hot water	+	+	+												
M	11̶	Turns off cold water	+	+	+												
	12	Finds hanging cloth towel	−	−	−												
	13	Dries palms of both hands	−	−	−												
	(14)	Dries backs of both hands	−	−	−												

Baseline data reveals that Tyshawn needed some type of prompting to complete these tasks for levels 1-9 and levels 12-14.

Baseline data reveals that Tyshawn can do levels 10 and 11 independently.

Based on baseline data, level 14 will be taught first. The step is circled to denote that this is the first step to be taught with backward chaining.

Write an "M" next to the level numbers 10 and 11 to indicate child completed these steps independently without any prompts throughout baseline.

■ Table 7-5 Task Analysis Data Sheet: Scoring the First Teaching Session

SKILL TARGET Handwashing

GOAL When given the instruction, wash your hands, Tyshawn will completely wash his hands independently for three consecutive sessions.

YOUR INSTRUCTION TO CHILD (e.g., "Brush your teeth."): "Tyshawn, wash your hands."

TEACHING METHOD (Circle) (BACKWARD) FORWARD

Mastery	Step	Component Skill (e.g., Turn on water)	9/17 BSL	9/18 BSL	9/19 BSL	9/20								
	1	Turns on cold water	−	−	−									
	2	Turns on hot water	−	−	−									
	3	Places hands under water	−	−	−									
	4	Places right hand under and left hand on soap dispenser	−	−	−									
	5	Pushes pump down twice	−	−	−									
	6	Rubs soap between hands for 3 sec	−	−	−									
	7	Rubs back of right for 3 seconds	−	−	−									
	8	Rubs back of left hand for 3 sec	−	−	−									
	9	Rinses hands under water	−	−	−									
M	10	Turns off hot water	+	+	+	+								
M	11	Turns off cold water	+	+	+	+								
	12	Finds hanging cloth towel	−	−	−									
	13	Dries palms of both hands	−	−	−									
	(14)	Dries backs of both hands	−	−	−	−								

Date — First date a teaching session is conducted is recorded here.

In this example, Tyshawn needed prompts to dry both his hands. A minus is recorded.

Level 14 is the primary focus of teaching when starting backward chaining. The instructor will provide some prompts if necessary but as quickly as possible will fade the prompts so child completes level on his own.

and then prompt your child through the remaining steps (except Step 10 and 11, which he already knows). As with baseline data, you record a minus sign whenever a prompt is necessary for the step(s) you are teaching and a plus sign whenever the child completes the step(s) being taught independently (See Table 7-5). You do not need to record anything for the steps that you are not teaching yet, but if you prefer, you can put a "P" for prompt in each corresponding cell.

Measuring Tyshawn's Progress with Teaching Sessions

After completing baseline and determining that teaching handwashing is necessary, the Richards settle on using the backward chaining approach. As we discussed in Chapter 6, backward chaining allows the Richards to go through the nonmastered steps rapidly so that Tyshawn can quickly access the super reward at the end. Referring to Table 7-5, you can see that the Richards record the date they begin teaching on 9/20, in the column right after the last baseline session. The first step they will teach him is Step 14. To denote this, they circle Step 14 on the TADS. (If the Richards were teaching this task via forward chaining, they would have circled Step 1 on the chart.) The Richards gave the verbal cue, "Tyshawn, wash your hands" and then proceeded to guide him through all fourteen steps (except 10 and 11), and then immediately provide the super reward. The Richards do this so that Tyshawn learns that going to the sink and washing his hands will result in receiving the super reward. They go through this process three or four times to establish this relationship in Tyshawn's mind.

After a few sessions, the Richards prompt Tyshawn through the first nine steps, pause so that he can complete Steps 10 and 11, prompt Steps 12 and 13, and pause again just before Step 14 to see if he will complete it himself. If he completes it independently or is more cooperative (meaning he requires less prompting or resists the prompt less), then he receives the super reward. (Refer back to Chapters 5 and 6 for a complete explanation of reinforcement and chaining methods.) Beginning on 9/21 (see Table 7-6, page 86), the Richards paused after Step 13 and Tyshawn completed Step 14 on his own. (Tyshawn's learning of this step is probably a little faster than you will experience and is used only to provide an example.)

Continuing the training over five sessions, as illustrated in Table 7-6, reveals that Tyshawn completed Step 14 independently for three days and thus mastered this step. The parents cross out the circled Step 14 and write "M" in its mastery column. The parents then circle Step 13 to note that Step 13 will now be the primary focus of instruction. On 9/24, the Richards work to teach Tyshawn to complete Step 13 *and* 14 while assisting him as necessary for Steps 1-9 and 12. On 9/24, Tyshawn is taught to dry the palms of both hands as well as the backs of both hands. He does both steps without a prompt and thus both cells are marked with a plus. The next six sessions of training with Tyshawn are shown in Table 7-7. In this example, Tyshawn mastered Step 13 and so training is now focused on Step 12. Since this sheet had been filled out completely, the Richards start a new data sheet. Tyshawn's parents will transfer the mastered steps, the step numbers, and the tasks onto the new data sheet. They then record the next training session, 9/29, on the new TADS.

Note that in this example, the Richards were completing a session at least once a day. Whenever possible you should try to conduct training sessions more

■ Table 7-6 Task Analysis Data Sheet: Scoring the First Five Teaching Sessions

SKILL TARGET Handwashing

GOAL When given the instruction, wash your hands, Tyshawn will completely wash his hands independently for three consecutive sessions.

YOUR INSTRUCTION TO CHILD (e.g., "Brush your teeth."): "Tyshawn, wash your hands."

TEACHING METHOD (Circle) ~~BACKWARD~~ (circled) FORWARD

First 5 sessions of teaching.

Mastery	Step	Component Skill (e.g., Turn on water)	9/17	9/18	9/19	9/20	9/21	9/22	9/23	9/24		
			BSL	BSL	BSL							
	1	Turns on cold water	−	−	−							
	2	Turns on hot water	−	−	−							
	3	Places hands under water	−	−	−							
	4	Places right hand under and left hand on soap dispenser	−	−	−							
	5	Pushes pump down twice	−	−	−							
	6	Rubs soap between hands for 3 sec	−	−	−							
	7	Rubs back of right for 3 seconds	−	−	−							
	8	Rubs back of left hand for 3 sec	−	−	−							
	9	Rinses hands under water	−	−	−							
M	~~10~~	Turns off hot water	+	+	+	+	+	+	+	+		
M	~~11~~	Turns off cold water	+	+	+	+	+	+	+	+		
	12	Finds hanging cloth towel	−	−	−							
	(13)	Dries palms of both hands	−	−	−					+		
M	~~14~~	Dries backs of both hands	−	−	−	−	+	+	+	+		

Tyshawn has 3 consecutive sessions with no prompts for Step 14 on days 9/21, 9/22, and 9/23. Three pluses indicate Tyshawn has mastered the step and can do Step 14

With Step 14 mastered, parents teach Step 13 on 9/24.

On 9/24, Tyshawn independently completes Steps 13 and 14. Pluses are recorded for each step.

Step 14 is mastered, so the step number is crossed out and an "M" is written in the mastery column to denote the level is mastered.

With Step 14 mastered, Step 13 would be circled to note that this is the next level to focus on.

■ Table 7-7 Task Analysis Data Sheet: Data Tracking Completed for Eleven Sessions

SKILL TARGET   Handwashing

GOAL   When given the instruction, wash your hands, Tyshawn will completely wash his hands independently for three consecutive sessions.

YOUR INSTRUCTION TO CHILD (e.g., "Brush your teeth."):   "Tyshawn, wash your hands."

TEACHING METHOD (Circle)   (BACKWARD)   FORWARD

Mastery	Step	Component Skill (e.g., Turn on water)	9/17	9/18	9/19	9/20	9/21	9/22	9/23	9/24	9/25	9/26	9/26	9/27	9/28	9/28
			BSL	BSL	BSL							1	2		1	2
	1	Turns on cold water	−	−	−											
	2	Turns on hot water	−	−	−											
	3	Places hands under water	−	−	−											
	4	Places right hand under and left hand on soap dispenser	−	−	−											
	5	Pushes pump down twice	−	−	−											
	6	Rubs soap between hands for 3 sec	−	−	−											
	7	Rubs back of right for 3 seconds	−	−	−											
	8	Rubs back of left hand for 3 sec	−	−	−											
	9	Rinses hands under water	−	−	−											
M	1̶0̶	Turns off hot water	+	+	+	+	+	+	+	+	+	+	+	+	+	+
M	1̶1̶	Turns off cold water	+	+	+	+	+	+	+	+	+	+	+	+	+	+
	(12)	Finds hanging cloth towel	−	−	−										−	−
M	(1̶3̶)	Dries palms of both hands	−	−	−	−	−	−	−	+	−	+	+	+	+	+
M	(1̶4̶)	Dries backs of both hands	−	−	−	−	+	+	+	+	+	+	+	+	+	+

Training conducted through 9/28.

With Steps 13 and 14 mastered, parents teach Step 12 on 9/28.

With Step 13 mastered, Step 12 would be circled to note that this is the next level to focus on.

Step 13 is mastered on 9/27 so it is crossed out and an "M" is written in the mastery column.

than once per day in order to give your child more opportunities to practice the skill being taught. For data entry purposes, if you teach a session more than once per day, you can enter the date in multiple columns and then below the date record a one, two, or three to denote what session the data were from for that day. We do realize that there may be days when sessions cannot be conducted. However, inconsistency can make learning more challenging for your son or daughter. Periodically review the sequence of dates and look to see how often you may be missing sessions. If your child is not learning, it could be a result of insufficient practice. This data also should help you evaluate the effectiveness of your teaching. While the example above describes the TADS used with backward chaining, the TADS can also be used to monitor progress when forward chaining is used. The procedures detailed above with regards to marking a "+" or "-" and noting when a step is mastered would be the same. In forward chaining, you will focus on teaching the child to do the first step of the skill independently while helping the child complete all remaining steps after the first step.

The TADS can be used for conducting and monitoring progress for a wide range of skills including personal hygiene, dressing, and eating behaviors. The strategies for teaching these skills are detailed in Chapters 8 and 9. We also have included in Chapter 10, a specific data sheet for tracking toilet accidents and dry pants checks. Details for completing this data sheet are in that chapter.

What Do I Do With the Data?

As we indicated previously, data provide an objective way of evaluating your son's or daughter's progress. But data sheets are only beneficial if you look at them often and try to assess any helpful trends or patterns. If your child has been on the same step (forward or backward chaining) for fifteen sessions or more and is not making progress, then it may be time to consider a change in the program. A change could mean breaking one troublesome step into a series of smaller steps or looking for a more effective reinforcer, and/or examining the type of prompts being used, to name a few options.

You might also find it helpful to be a little more specific in your data collection. Instead of simply recording a minus when a prompt is required for the target step, it may be useful to record what level of prompt is needed. For example, in analyzing the data you may realize that you are slowly but progressively fading the level of prompt. A full physical prompt may have been required two weeks ago, but now only a gesture is required. This is a sign of progress. This level of detailed data also may be useful to uncover any differences between instructors (e.g., you do not need to use a physical prompt but your husband, wife, or child's paraprofessional does). More detailed data collection may illuminate inconsistencies and lead to productive discussions and specific program modifications.

> Data sheets are only beneficial if you look at them often and try to assess any helpful trends or patterns.

There are many ways to collect data and many different instruments. You may find it sometimes useful to develop your own data instruments or to modify the examples that we have provided. Please feel empowered to do that.

■ Troubleshooting Common Problems

We have included some problem-solving suggestions in Appendix B and at the end of several of the chapters, but here are some basics.

My Child Just Can't Get This Step

You may find that your child sometimes gets stuck on one particular step in the program. For example, you have been conducting a dressing program for twenty sessions and you simply cannot fade your prompt entirely for a step that requires your child to button the top button on her shirt. What can you do? The first step is to simply provide more opportunity to practice the step that is not progressing. So, in our example, you could decide to simply run multiple trials (as many as your child will tolerate) on the buttoning step by itself.

Another response is to break the task of buttoning into a series of smaller steps for learning (such as, grab button on shirt with right hand fingers; grab shirt at the button hole with the left hand; push button through hole; grab button with left hand fingers; and so on). Again, you may want to work on this separately from the rest of your dressing program. Basically you would conduct several mini-sessions of the one step your child is not making progress on. Once your child masters the steps within the mini-session, you can go back to teaching the whole skill again.

If a step within a sequence of steps continues to be problematic after days and weeks of trying different possible solutions, then you may want to move on to the next step anyway while continuing to use some of the strategies mentioned above. We have seen examples when simply moving forward seems to take some of the pressure off the child and parent and within the context of the entire sequence, the child's response gradually improves as well. You don't want to hold the child back from progressing through the other steps. There also may be times that you have to settle for a necessary partial prompt for a step, such as a gesture or verbal cue (e.g., pointing to remind your child to complete a particular step). You can continue to work on particular steps even after you move on to teaching other things.

What Do I Do About My Child's Hypersensitivity?

Children with autism often demonstrate odd sensory reactions to objects, textures, visual stimuli, and sounds in their environment. These sensitivities may include a fixation on running water, their refection in a mirror, or moving parts like fans. In these examples, the child will seek these activities and objects as a form of self-stimulation. In other examples, the child may be hyper-sensitive to objects in her mouth, clothing (e.g., long sleeves or a collar tag) on her body, or the texture of towels against her body. In these instances, the child may attempt to escape or avoid the activity.

The simplest thing to do is to set up the environment to prevent your child's seeking or avoiding stimulation. This is particularly true when you first start to teach a new skill. You should attempt to structure the teaching environment without the many annoyances that will interfere with your child's attention. Remove any objects that are unnecessary to the task and make reasonable modifications to materials (e.g., shirts without tags or collars). Consider products that do not increase your child's sensitivities because of their texture, hardness, smell, or touch. If these oversensitivities persist and significantly interfere with learning, you may need to try behavioral strategies to desensitize your child. Procedures described in Chapter 10 for food sensitivities can also be applied here. Similar to a task analysis, you would gradually expose your child to the sensation in small and short increments and then reward her for her ability to stand the brief exposure. Over many trials, you gradually increase the amount of exposure.

In the case of those things that your child seeks (often manifested as self-stimulatory behavior), you cannot remove every potential nuisance. Therefore, you will need another strategy. First, identify the potential problem areas (e.g., flipping the switch to the fan and playing in water). Next, as you begin your lesson to teach a self-help skill, "shadow" your child very closely so that you can quickly intervene when needed. "Shadowing" is a technique in which you remain very close to your child, sometimes with your hands poised near the child's hands or body without touching her. This puts you in a position to quickly intervene. If your child begins to engage in the inappropriate behavior (e.g., turning on the switch to the bathroom fan), immediately "redirect." "Redirection" is a technique that simply means redirecting your child from the inappropriate activity to the desired activity. This typically involves interrupting the undesired behavior and prompting her toward the desired behavior. For example as your child reaches to turn on the fan in the bathroom, you block her from reaching the switch and redirect her hand toward the task to be completed (e.g., toothbrushing). As you can imagine, this requires a lot of alertness on your part. We recommend that you minimize your verbal interaction with your child when redirecting so that your attention does not inadvertently reward the child. This may take a little practice; it is more challenging than it may appear.

Responding To Your Child's Challenging Behaviors During Teaching Sessions

During teaching sessions, it is possible that some children will become unresponsive or uncooperative. It is important to note that if this happens, you should still attempt to complete the session so that your child does not learn that if she acts up, you will stop teaching. If your child becomes resistant while completing the steps of a skill, you should provide the level of prompting necessary to have your child complete the entire sequence of steps. Then, repeat the last step until your child does it independently or with much less resistance. At this point, provide a modified praise statement (e.g., "That's better, nice trying") but the super reward is withheld (it was not earned). In short, you have two objectives: (1) communicate to your child that her behavior will not successfully allow her to avoid the task and (2) end the session on as positive of a note as possible.

As much as possible, you want the session to end on a positive and compliant note. We realize that a resistant child can become even more resistant. There might be an occasion where your child's behavior is so extreme that teaching or hand over hand prompting is not safe for you or your child. In these rare instances, we recommend that the teaching session be temporarily stopped but do not allow her to leave the area. The best approach is to ask her to sit or stand quietly while you take a step back (sitting is usually best). (Note: we recommend that you work on this at other times, so that your child is able to sit and gradually gain control of herself. Throughout the day, ask her to sit for a minute and praise her for responding). If at all possible, do not let your child leave the area. As soon as your child is quiet and calm for at least five to ten seconds then quietly praise her for being quiet, ask her to complete the last step of the program and give her all the assistance she needs, then allow her to leave. This procedure will allow her to achieve the two goals that we discussed earlier (i.e., prevent her from using inappropriate behavior to escape the task and end on a relatively positive note). If you find yourself in this situation a lot, we recommend that you consult with your school staff or other professional with behavioral expertise about conducting a functional behavioral assessment and developing a behavior plan.

I Just Can't Find the Time

We understand that with today's hectic schedules it is a challenge to get everything into a twenty-four hour day. As we discussed earlier, the most natural time for teaching may not be the most convenient time. The most important thing is that you conduct sessions often. Children with autism learn best when they are given repeated opportunities to practice what they are learning. We recommend that you find a time that fits best into your family schedule and when you can devote enough time to do a good job of teaching. It also is important to find a time that is most free of distractions for you and your child. We recommend that you put the session time into your calendar as a standing appointment that will be given high priority. As we mentioned in Chapter 6, you may be able to overlay a systematic instructional plan over what you are doing already. For example, each time your child needs to put on her coat, use that opportunity to conduct the instructional program.

Carving out enough time to teach is critical; children with autism learn best when they are given repeated opportunities to practice.

When I approach a child, he inspires in me two sentiments;
tenderness for what he is, and respect for what he may become.
—Louis Pasteur

8

Teaching Dressing and Personal Hygiene Skills

The Sanford Family

Mrs. Sanford was already on her way to work for the day so it was Mr. Sanford's turn to make sure their three children completed their morning routine (i.e., waking up, brushing teeth and hair, getting dressed, eating, and timely arriving at the bus stop). Being March, you'd expect that the Sanfords would have this routine down with minor problems. However, seven months into the present school year and the only constant was the Sanfords' continuous prodding and yelling for their three kids to complete the various tasks necessary to make the bus. Two of the children, ages six and ten, could complete the tasks; however they had gotten used to responding only after the Sanfords' frequent reminders. Lucas, the eight-year-

old with autism, could not complete any of the tasks despite any of Mr. Sanford's prodding. Time and time again, Mr. Sanford (or Mrs. Sanford, when she was home) would end up just dressing Lucas. Mr. Sanford's prodding would persist until he got the last shoe onto Lucas and the kids were out the door. Several attempts had been made by the

Sanfords to teach Lucas to get dressed independently; however due to time constraints and lack of thoughtful planning, their best laid plans always seemed to result in raised voices and completing the tasks themselves.

The Christopher Family

For the first seven years of Yvonne's life, her parents were resigned to the fact that the only way Yvonne's teeth ever got brushed was if one of them did it for her. Without her parent's assistance, the daily brushing routine consisted of Yvonne putting a lot of toothpaste on her toothbrush, putting it in her mouth, and sucking the toothpaste off. Yvonne's parents had become accustomed to spending part of their morning and evening routines brushing Yvonne's teeth. They never saw it as a problem since they were already in the bathroom to ensure that Yvonne actually washed her hands correctly with soap and water. Sure, the Christophers tried to get Yvonne to brush her teeth and wash her hands independently, but such attempts always ended with lots of prompts and little compliance. It became easier for the parents to just complete the tasks for Yvonne, especially since they wanted these things to be done right. To the Christophers, spending five minutes in the bathroom each morning and evening with Yvonne was not that bothersome and much less of a headache than battling with her to do it correctly. But Yvonne was now seven and they knew it was time for her to become more independent.

▧ Does This Sound Familiar?

These scenarios are not uncommon and many parents will quickly admit: "been there, done that." Specifically, we guess that you have been in a situation when your child's hands were dirty, his teeth needed to be brushed, or he needed to get dressed and you were in a hurry. The easy solution is to just prompt him through the task so that it is done quickly, with little resistance. This is completely understandable. The reality is that getting children with autism to complete dressing and personal hygiene routines can be a very frustrating. Teaching your child to perform these tasks is made even more cumbersome by the fact that most children with autism do not learn to shampoo their hair, brush their teeth, or shave merely by seeing others do these tasks. While doing the routines for your child in the short run is more convenient and timely, in the long run it makes your child more dependent on you. As we mentioned in earlier chapters, this dependence on adults may result in your child's exclusion from school and community events enjoyed by most children their age. Moreover, your child may appear more disabled than he really is. We are here to tell you that it doesn't have to be this way. Your child can learn to care for himself!

Children with ASD can learn to complete a variety of dressing and personal hygiene tasks if taught in a systematic and step-wise way with multiple opportunities to practice and master each step. In this chapter we will focus on helping you to teach your child to complete personal care and hygiene tasks from brushing teeth, dressing, and washing hands to more complex tasks such as taking a shower, shaving, and clipping toenails. While it may seem easier to wash your child's hands than to struggle to get him to do it, if you take the time to teach him, both your child and you will acquire a lifetime of greater independence.

◼ Identifying Skill Deficits

As described in Chapter 3, the first step is to decide what skill(s) to teach. We suggest that you revisit Table 3-1 in Chapter 3 and refer to the Self-Help Inventory in Appendix A. As Table 3-1 indicates, most children by age two years are regularly assisting with basic dressing and most children can remove clothing with little or no help. They can also accomplish simple tasks like assisting with bathing by holding up an arm or pulling up a pair of pants that has an elastic waistband (although they may not be able to do this with great skill or precision). Children without autism seem to show significant progress every month. By the age of four years most children have made a huge leap in their abilities such that they are able to brush their teeth, wash and dry their hands and face, put shoes on the correct foot, and unbutton their clothing. While children at age four still require a lot of reminders and some occasional help, their progress from the ages of two years to four years old is quite remarkable. By the time most children enter first grade or about six years old, they are pretty independent in the completion of dressing skills including many fasteners. They still need frequent reminders to wash carefully and brush their teeth, but they are capable of accomplishing these tasks. By eight years old, most children can coordinate their clothing to match the occasion.

Considering all the self-care and personal hygiene tasks that you help your child complete each day and your desire to help your child become more independent, awareness of these developmental milestones can help you to focus on the right things. As described in Chapter 3, use developmental milestones as a guide, in conjunction with information about your child's developmental readiness, your child's interests and abilities, as well as what is important for your child to know at the time. If your child is a young adult who should start shaving, you may want to consider helping him learn to wash his face first before moving to shaving. If you are a parent who is tired of dressing your five-year-old child, you may want to ensure your child can first pull up his pants, button a shirt, or put on a T-shirt in isolation before you expect him to independently respond to the full implications of the instruction, "Get Dressed."

The bottom line is that there is a whole assortment of personal hygiene and dressing skills that you engage in everyday, from wiping your child's mouth and nose, to wiping his bottom, dressing, and tying laces on his shoes. The importance of learning these skills depends on the setting he is in and its requirements. While parents may not mind helping their child dress after using the bathroom, it is highly unlikely that other adults in school and community settings want to wipe or dress an adolescent child after he uses the bathroom.

Completing the Self-Help Skills Inventory in Appendix A will assist you to pinpoint the self-care and personal hygiene skills that need to be taught. We recommend that as you complete the inventory, you consider how much help you provide now or whether or not you typically complete the task for your child. If you are not sure that your child can complete a particular task, we recommend that you list it as a skill to teach. It is better to cautiously identify all the potential dressing and hygiene skills that your child needs to learn than to assume he can do it but later find you were wrong.

From the list of skills identified with the Self-Help Skills Inventory, we recommend that you choose something simple to get you started. For example, your child may not be able to take a shower, but if he also cannot wash his hands, you should start with handwashing. Likewise, learning to put on and zip his pants is more pressing than learning to put on a belt. Additionally, if you are teaching for the first time, identify only one or two skills to focus on initially. If you try to tackle too many skills at the start, you and your child are likely to get overwhelmed. Experience tells us that when a family tries to teach everything at once, rarely are they successful.

> "Simple" skills will function as building blocks for more complex skills.

Breaking the Skill into Teachable Steps

Now that you have identified the skills your child cannot do independently, we will discuss how to apply the strategies discussed in Chapters 6 and 7 on conducting a task analysis, prompting, shaping, using reinforcement, and collecting data. After identifying the skill you want to teach, one of the first steps is to break the skill into small steps for instruction (i.e., a task analysis). To complete this task analysis, use the Task Analysis Data Sheet (described in Chapter 7). Table 8-1 provides an example of using the TADS to conduct a task analysis for putting on a T-shirt. In this example, the parents identified nine steps. Each step should be clearly written and include observable behaviors that precisely indicate what your child is to do. A step that indicates "wash hands" is pretty vague, but a series of steps that indicates "wet hands," "apply soap to palm," and "rub soap on hands (i.e., front side and back side)" is much clearer.

A good strategy in developing a task analysis is to do the task yourself and make notes of the various actions that are required to complete the skill. Once you do this, test the steps you create on yourself before teaching them to make sure they clearly describe what your child is to do. The completed TADS is largely for you; it is your script for teaching your child. If your child is able to read, it might be used to guide the child as well, but it would have to be faded at some point. If your child is not able to read, you may choose to use visual cues such as line drawings or photographs that depict each of the steps. Again, this support would have to be faded.

> After completing a task analysis, try to act out each of the steps yourself to make sure that the process is logical, understandable, and achievable.

■ **Table 8-1   Task Analysis Data Sheet: Example for Putting on a T-Shirt**

SKILL TARGET   Putting on a T-shirt

GOAL   With the T-shirt laid on his bed and given the instruction to get dressed, Lucas will put on his T-shirt with no prompts for three consecutive teaching sessions.

YOUR INSTRUCTION TO CHILD
(e.g., "Brush your teeth."):   "Lucas, get dressed."

TEACHING METHOD (Circle)   (BACKWARD)   FORWARD

Mastery	Step	Component Skill (e.g., Turn on water)	Date										
	1	Pick up T-shirt with a design on front.												
	2	Place T-shirt flat on bed with the design facing downward. The base (bottom) of the tee shirt should be closest to you.												
	3	Pick up the T-shirt from the base and separate the front and back sides.												
	4	While grabbing the front of the T-shirt at the base with your left hand, slide your right arm through the small hole on the right side. The front of the T-shirt with the design will be in front.												
	5	Bend your right arm to grab the bottom of the T-shirt with your right hand.												
	6	From the bottom of the T-shirt, push your left arm inside the T-shirt and through the hole on the left side of the big hole.												
	7	While still holding the bottom of the T-shirt with your right hand, pull the T-shirt over your head and through the hole in the middle.												
	8	Use your left hand to help the right hand pull the T-shirt down around your head.												
	9	Pull T-shirt down around your waist.												

Have Skill, Need Time and Place to Teach It

Once you have identified a dressing or personal hygiene skill to teach and the steps are delineated in a task analysis, then you must determine when and where you are going to teach. If at all possible, you should choose to teach in the place and at the time in which the skill is needed or expected. For example, dressing in the bedroom in the morning and at night, washing hands at the kitchen or bathroom sink whenever coming in from outside and when it is time to eat, or taking shoes on and off at the front door are all examples of natural locations and times for instruction. If your situation is like the Christophers, you will want to teach your child to brush his teeth in the bathroom sink after breakfast and dinner.

However, let us discuss some important issues that must be considered when deciding location and time to teach a task. For starters, how much time do you have available to teach the skill each day? Brushing teeth in the morning is the ideal time, but will you have time to conduct a lesson if you have to get ready for work yourself and get your child to the bus stop on time? What other tasks must be completed during the time that you are going to teach? If you have other kids, do you have the time to dedicate to teaching buttoning of a shirt, if your eighteen-month-old is awake and wanting to play? What naturally occurring reinforcers are available for the child during teaching? That is, can you teach your child to wash his hands before he is allowed to eat his favorite snack?

These questions are only a sample of the types of questions you must consider in determining when and where you will teach your child. As noted in previous chapters and to be discussed in Chapter 11, the more natural you make the teaching context, the more likely the skill will be generalized and maintained over time. However, there may be situations that prevent you from teaching in the most natural setting and at the most natural time. If there are many time constraints and responsibilities at the most natural time, you should consider teaching the skill at another less stressful time. Take, for example, the Sanfords who are trying to teach Lucas to get dressed in the morning while also attending to the needs of two other children. One option would be for the Sanfords to wake Lucas ten to fifteen minutes earlier each day to give them extra time to conduct the training. They could also consider moving the session to another time when there are fewer time constraints and tasks that have to be done. Note that if the latter option is chosen, they can still use a location for instruction, such as Lucas' bedroom, that is a natural context for dressing.

Conducting a Baseline Assessment of Your Child's Ability

So, you have broken your hygiene skill or dressing skill into steps and have determined the time and place to teach. It is now time to evaluate whether or not your child can complete the identified skill independently. As described in Chapter 7, we recommend that you collect this baseline using the TADS. You will need to identify at least three times when you will ask your child to demonstrate the skill (i.e., "Brush your teeth" or "Wash your hands") and you should do the assessment in the location where you are going to teach it. As noted previously, during the baseline assessment, you should minimize prompts and the use of reinforcers so that it closely matches the conditions that you hope to achieve when the skill is learned. Use the baseline data to help determine whether the skill needs to be taught at all and what steps your child can accomplish already. It is not uncommon during baseline to discover that more or fewer steps may be necessary. If this happens, you should revise the task analysis and conduct a couple more days of baseline before beginning your instruction. Also, remember that your baseline data will serve as a comparison to show whether your child is making progress down the line.

Creating a Lesson Plan: Your Roadmap to Successful Teaching

Once you have determined what you want to teach and have conducted a baseline, the next step is to document how you are going to teach the skill. Specifically, you will need to write an "Instructional Plan" as described in Chapter 6 and in Appendix D. A blank Instructional Plan form is provided in Appendix E and a data sheet template (TADS) is provided in Appendix F. The Instructional Plan will denote whether you will use backward or forward chaining and how you are going to cue, prompt, and motivate (reward) your child to learn the specific dressing or personal hygiene skill. To illustrate how the Instruction Plan works, we once again refer back to the examples of the Christophers and the Sanfords.

The Sanfords have determined that they are going to teach Lucas how to get dressed and, more specifically, they are going to work on teaching Lucas how to put on a T-shirt. The Christophers have decided to teach Yvonne to brush her teeth. Using the Instructional Plan, both the Sanfords and the Christophers identify a functional area and then determine their goal for learning. As discussed in Chapter 6, their goals have four parts (the instructional context, observable behavior, attainable objective, and mastery criteria).

For the Sanfords, their goal is as follows, "*With the T-shirt laid on his bed and given the instruction to get dressed, Lucas will put on his T-shirt with no prompts for three consecutive teaching sessions.*" The Instructional Plan then lays out everything else that is needed for the Sanfords to teach the skill. To complete the Instructional Plan, the family conducts a task analysis of the skill they plan to teach. They also determine and record the place and time for instruction, the materials required, the instructional cue, and any physical accommodations that are made. In addition, they record how they plan to help the skill generalize beyond the teaching session. Lastly, they note whether they were going to teach using backward or forward chaining and how they plan to reward Lucas if he responds correctly. Again, Chapter 6 provides a lot of information about how to address each of these areas.

In Table 8-2 on page 100, notice that the Sanfords are planning to work in Lucas' bedroom, by his dresser twice a day, once in the late afternoon and once at bedtime. They decide not to teach dressing before school because of many time

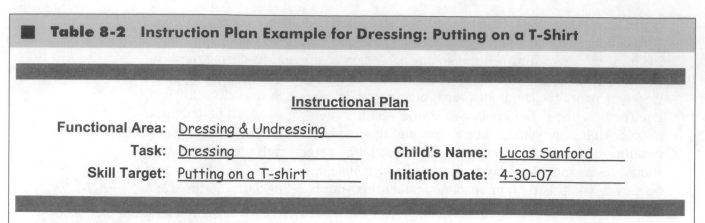

■ Table 8-2 Instruction Plan Example for Dressing: Putting on a T-Shirt

Instructional Plan

Functional Area: Dressing & Undressing

Task: Dressing   **Child's Name:** Lucas Sanford

Skill Target: Putting on a T-shirt   **Initiation Date:** 4-30-07

Goal for Learning

With T-shirt laid on his bed and given the instruction to get dressed, Lucas will put on the T-shirt with no prompts for three consecutive teaching sessions.

Specify Components of the Plan

Check when completed	
✓	**Conduct list of steps required to do the task:** See attached (Table 8-1)
✓	**Place and time for instruction:** At 4:45 p.m. in Lucas' bedroom by his dresser and at bedtime (8:00 p.m.) by his dresser as well
✓	**Materials required:** T-shirt with spaceships on front
✓	**Physical accommodations (if needed):** Lucas has a short attention span so will need to keep sessions short and be ready to reward immediately
✓	**Instructional signal or cue:** "Lucas, it's time to get dressed."
✓	**Data sheet for monitoring progress**
✓	**Steps for generalization:** Will conduct sessions in bedroom where he gets dressed. When successful with late afternoon or nighttime session, will make arrangements to do training in morning. Both parents will conduct sessions.
✓	**Circle which chaining procedure will teach:** (BACKWARD) FORWARD
✓	**Conduct a baseline:** On Data Tracking Form (attached)
✓	**Super reward(s):** Tape player with headphones and choice of music tapes or story tapes to listen to after each session.

constraints. To aid in Lucas' participation in the teaching sessions, the Sanfords chose a T-shirt that is highly preferred by Lucas, specifically one with spaceships on it. The Sanford family is well aware that Lucas wants to wear this shirt every day, even if it is dirty! The Sanfords also know that Lucas has a short attention span, so they plan to keep sessions short and have the super reward identified and clearly available. The Sanfords start each teaching session with "Lucas, get dressed" and they show their son a few photographs of another child completing each step. Mr. and Mrs. Sanford intend to alternate teaching the lesson since they want Lucas to learn to listen to both of them when they ask him to get dressed.

Because Lucas does not show much interest in dressing, the Sanfords decide to teach using backward chaining so Lucas will learn to connect receiving the super reward with completing all of the steps of the task analysis. The Sanfords tell Lucas that he'll be able to listen to his CD player and favorite tapes as the super reward for putting on his T-shirt. They also choose one of his favorite T-shirts in hopes it might help motivate him to pay attention. Notice in Table 8-2, the Sanfords check off each component of the Instructional Plan as they complete it.

Table 8-3 on page 102 illustrates the Christophers' instructional plan to teach Yvonne to brush her teeth in the morning and at night. The parents make adjustments to their morning schedule by waking Yvonne fifteen minutes earlier each morning so they have the time to complete the lesson. They run sessions in the bathroom. Just like the Sanfords, the Christophers key in on Yvonne's preferred materials — a "Barbie" toothbrush. They also use natural toothpaste that does not have any flavor added, to reduce Yvonne's desire to eat it. The Christophers know that Yvonne has difficulty squeezing out the toothpaste, so they built steps into the task analysis to help her be more successful at this. As the program indicates, a step stool is added to ensure that Yvonne is tall enough to reach the sink.

The Christophers start each teaching session with a very simple instruction: "Yvonne, brush your teeth." They decide to teach Yvonne using a forward chaining approach since she seems to understand the relationship between her independent behavior and the reward, even when the super reward is delayed until the very end. Mr. and Mrs. Christopher tell Yvonne that brushing her teeth will earn her a chance to leaf through her favorite magazine (super reward). The Christophers have been controlling Yvonne's access to these magazines at other times of the day in order to maximize her motivation to earn them.

Along with the Christopher's Instructional Plan is the Christopher's completed TADS (see Table 8-4, page 103). We discussed instructions for completing the TADS previously and will not repeat the discussion here. Once the Instructional Plans and the TADS were completed, the Sanfords and the Christophers were ready to start teaching.

■ Putting it All Together

Using the Instructional Plan you have developed, it is time to start teaching. We recommend that prior to each teaching session, you dedicate a few minutes to review the specifics of your plan so that if you experience any difficulty during the teaching session, you will have a specific protocol to guide you.

■ **Table 8-3** **Instruction Plan Example for Hygiene: Toothbrushing**

Instructional Plan

Functional Area: Personal Hygiene

Task: Oral Hygiene   **Child's Name:** Yvonne Christopher

Skill Target: Brushing Teeth   **Initiation Date:** 5-25-07

Goal for Learning

Given an instruction to brush her teeth, Yvonne will brush her teeth with no prompts for three consecutive teaching sessions.

Specify Components of the Plan

Check when completed	
✓	**Create task analysis of steps required to do the task:** See attached (Table 8-4)
✓	**Place and time for instruction:** In the morning at 7:15 a.m. and at bedtime at 8:30 p.m. at the sink in the bathroom. Will wake up fifteen minutes earlier in the morning to allow time to conduct lessons.
✓	**Materials required:** Barbie toothbrush; natural toothpaste that has no flavor
✓	**Physical accommodations (if needed):** Yvonne will need specific steps on how to hold the toothpaste and how to squeeze the toothpaste out. Use stepstool to ensure Yvonne is high enough at the sink to manipulate faucet heads.
✓	**Instructional signal or cue:** "Yvonne, brush your teeth."
✓	**Data sheet for monitoring progress**
✓	**Steps for generalization:** Will conduct sessions in bathroom at the sink in the morning and at night. Also, both parents will conduct sessions.
✓	**Circle which chaining procedure will teach:** BACKWARD (FORWARD)
✓	**Conduct a baseline:** On Data Tracking Form (attached)
✓	**Super reward(s):** Access to House Decorating magazine.

■ Table 8-4 Task Analysis Data Sheet: Example for Toothbrushing

SKILL TARGET Brushing Teeth

GOAL Given an instruction to brush her teeth, Yvonne will brush her teeth with no prompts for three consecutive teaching sessions.

YOUR INSTRUCTION TO CHILD
(e.g., "Brush your teeth."): "Yvonne, brush your teeth."

TEACHING METHOD (Circle)   BACKWARD   (FORWARD)

Mastery	Step	Component Skill (e.g., Turn on water)	Date									
	1	Turn on cold water										
	2	Pick up paper cup and fill with water										
	3	Turn off cold water										
	4	Get toothbrush and toothpaste from holder										
	5	Unscrew lid off of toothpaste										
	6	Hold toothpaste tube at the end with right hand										
	7	Hold toothbrush with left hand										
	8	Squeeze toothpaste onto toothbrush										
	9	Put down toothpaste tube										
	10	Brush teeth in an upward and downward motion (at least ten strokes in outside top, outside bottom, inside top, and inside bottom of mouth)										
	11	Rinse mouth with water from paper cup, then spit out water										
	12	Empty remaining water in cup into sink										
	13	Throw empty cup into garbage										
	14	Turn on cold water										
	15	Rinse toothbrush under running water										
	16	Turn off water										
	17	Screw on lid of toothpaste										
	18	Put toothbrush and toothpaste away										
	19	Pick up towel and wipe mouth										
	20	Put towel back on rack										

We have explained the teaching approach in Chapter 6 but we are going to take just a moment to repeat the explanation here because it is so important. As we discuss the approach, you may want to refer back to Table 6-6, where we detailed backward chaining—what we believe is the most appropriate approach for most children with ASD. Teaching children with autism is never a straight and narrow route and you will likely have to make modifications to your plan as you progress. As we have said before, each session should begin with a clear and concise instruction (e.g., "Brush your hair"). In our opinion, it is then good to prompt the child through all of the steps of the program for two or three sessions — so that the child is immediately successful, he begins to understand your expectations, and he receives the super reward (hopefully beginning to learn the connection between completing the task and receiving the reward). Once you have done a few practice sessions prompting all steps, then begin your first real teaching session. Depending upon your child's cooperation, you may be able to run through the steps more than once within a session. For example, it typically takes only two or three minutes to get through fourteen steps of a handwashing program. If your child is cooperative and interested in earning the super reward, then you might be able to repeat the sequence two or

three times. Another approach is to run a few extra trials on the target step. For example, if you are working on teaching your child to turn on the water, then you could run three or four trials just on that step. To keep it simple, we suggest that you take data only on your first time through the sequence of steps. The other trials are just practice.

If you are using a backward chaining approach, just before the last step, pull your hands back and give your child an opportunity to respond. If he does not respond, then provide a full physical prompt (this is often referred to as the "correction"). Over the course of several sessions, begin to gradually diminish the pressure with each correction so that your child is moving toward greater independence. It is hard to describe to you how this will "look" with your child over time because it takes on a somewhat unique profile for each child. It is safe to say that there is a little trial and error that has to occur. You start with a hand-over-hand prompt then move to less pressure on your child's hand as you observe that he begins to do more. Little by little, over several sessions, you should be able to apply less pressure to his hand or even shadow his hand as he begins to respond (i.e., your hand is near but not touching his hand and ready to help if needed). From that point, you may be able to move to a point prompt (just as it sounds, pointing to where you want your child to place the towel after drying his hands). From one session to the next, you may experiment with giving less help and then have to revert back to a stronger prompt (this is the trial and error we mentioned). It should be noted that you should stand behind your child when prompting. In most situations, you want your child focused on the materials (e.g., toothbrush, mirror, and towel) and not on you. It is also easier to prompt from behind and easier for you to fade your physical proximity as your child gains independence.

For many children it will take a long time to learn the first step you are teaching independently. After you have taught a few steps, you may find that the remaining steps go a little more quickly.

Some Common Problems with Hygiene and Dressing and Possible Solutions

Altering Materials to Enhance Learning

Sometimes when your child is not making progress on a particular step or skill, a good strategy may be to alter the materials that you are using to teach. This is particularly good advice when your child has problems with fine motor skills such as buttoning, zipping, snapping, and tying. There are many commercially available products specifically designed for children with these difficulties. You may want to ask the occupational therapist at your child's school or do a search at the library or online. We also have included some references at the end of this book in a section called "Other Helpful Materials."

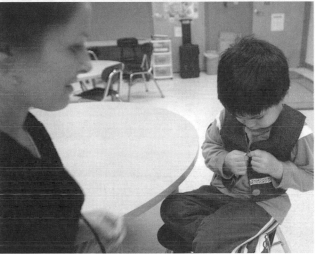

One popular commercial product to aid in teaching your child to dress is a buttoning or zipping vest. The vest is worn by the child and has oversized buttons or easy to grip zippers that provide your child with easier access then a typical shirt or jacket. While adaptive materials are often very helpful, keep in mind that they may lead to problems with generalization to regular clothing. If possible, we suggest trying first to teach your child to dress with regular clothing and moving to adaptive materials only if needed. If you have to adapt the materials, develop an Instructional Plan in the same way as you would if using typical clothing. Once your child has learned with the adaptive materials (e.g., a buttoning vest), you will need to repeat the steps with normal clothing. Fortunately, the transfer rarely takes as long as the initial training.

Another example of altering materials to enhance learning is seen when teaching shoe-tying. Tying shoes often is a big challenge for young children, including children without disabilities. There are a variety of methods to teach shoe-tying and many incorporate stories that help to motivate a preschool child to attend. Whether these stories will work to motivate children with autism has to be individually determined. Nevertheless, the approach these programs use and the modification of materials that are sometimes recommended are often quite helpful for teaching children with autism. One method involves color coding the laces and telling a story about a bunny. Eventually, the child forms loops that look like the ears of a bunny, so we often refer to this as the "bunny ears" method.

We suggest that when teaching shoe-tying, you begin with an over-sized shoe that you place in front of your child on a table. Working on a table makes it easier for your child to reach the shoe and allows you to sit behind him and provide physical prompts as necessary. Another helpful tip is to color one half of a white shoelace one color and the other half another color, then string up your shoe, using this bi-colored lace. Use the "bunny ears" method, involving the following steps, to teach shoe-tying. For the sake of this example, we will say that your bi-colored laces are red and green and the red lace is on the left and the green lace is on the right side of your model.

1. Pick up the red lace with the right hand.
2. Pick up the green lace with the left hand. You will have made an "x" with the laces.
3. While still holding the green lace with the left hand, also hold the middle part of the "x" with the left hand.

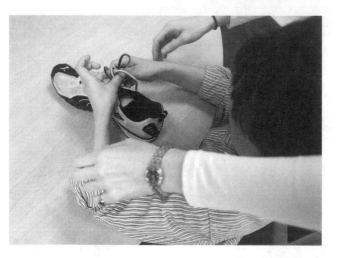

4. Take the red lace in the right hand and put it through the bottom part of the "x" shape.
5. Grab the red lace as you put it through the bottom part of the "x" shape and pull both the green and red lace ends away from each other.
6. Now take the green lace and fold it in half to make a loop that will look like a bunny's ear. Keep the green lace loop upright by holding the green lace loop at the bottom of the loop.
7. While still holding the green lace loop with the left hand, fold the red lace in half to make a loop. Hold the red laced loop with the right hand at the bottom of the loop. (The two loops will look like bunny ears.)
8. Take the green loop and cross it over in front of the red loop.
9. Take hold of both loops with the left hand by grabbing both loops where they cross each other. The loops will form an "x."
10. Using the right hand, take the top of the green loop and bend the loop away from you and through the bottom of the "x" shape.
11. Pull the green loop through, while still holding the loops with the left hand. As you pull the green loop towards you with your right hand, you will pull the red loop away from you with your left hand.

The shoe is now tied. Notice that in this example, you have modified the materials to a level that will make it easier for your child to manipulate the materials. Like the buttoning vest, after training using the oversized shoe on the table, you must transfer this skill to a shoe that your child wears and then to the shoe on his foot.

What About Making Permanent Clothing Accommodations?

What if your child cannot fasten or button, struggles with learning to tie, and cannot figure out the front and back of his shirt despite your modifications in the materials used? Sometimes it is easier just to eliminate the thing that your child cannot do. For example, if your child can not snap or button his clothes then you may choose to use pants with elastic waists or shirts without buttons, or if your child cannot tie his shoes, then you may have them wear loafers or shoes with hook and loops (Velcro). Other accommodations might include using pump dispensers (such as soap, toothpaste, or shampoo), electric toothbrushes or razors, or using a faucet that has only one handle. The question to consider is: What other environments do I expect my child to participate in and will such accommodations be carried over in those settings as well? Such strategies and accommodations may enable you to concentrate on other areas of need, and for this reason they have value. However, while these are good and reasonable short-term solutions, they may not provide long-term independence. If at all possible, you should consider at some point teaching your child to manipulate and manage the different ways and different materials he may have to confront later.

■ Final Tips: Examples of Teaching Dressing and Personal Hygiene Skills

The area of teaching dressing and personal hygiene is very broad and covers many areas. We cannot possibly cover everything. But we have included four more examples of dressing and hygiene skills that may guide you to establish other programs for your child. We have provided a task analysis for these examples but you may need to add additional steps for your child. In each case, we have used the backward chaining approach and provided an example of teaching the last step (i.e., all steps until the last step are prompted).

Putting on socks

Task Analysis
1. Grasp left and right side of the open end of sock with thumb and forefinger.
2. While grasping the sock, use the forefingers to slide the whole sock towards you until the thumbs are touching the end of the sock on the inside.
3. While holding the sock open, pull the sock over the toes of the right foot until the toes are touching the end of the inside of the sock.
4. Continue pulling socks past the heel and up over the heel to the ankle.
5. Once the top of the sock is at the ankle, pull the remaining sock until it is tight on the foot.

Brief description of how to teach
Have your child sit on the floor while you sit behind them with your legs along side his. Using oversized socks, place your hands over his hands then over the sock using thumb and forefinger grasp. Using a backward chain and hand-over-hand prompting, put the sock over your child's toes and pull the sock until it is on his foot and just over his heel. Next, pull your hands slightly back to see if he will pull

the sock up the rest of the way. After three seconds, if no response or an incomplete response occurs, place your hands back over his and pull the sock the rest of the way up. Repeat with second sock.

Putting on pants

Task Analysis

1. Grasp left and right side of pants that have a fastener. Make sure that fastener side of pants is facing away from you.
2. While grasping the pants, fully extend arms downward.
3. Lift right leg up and put into leg opening closest to right foot until the right foot comes out of leg hole.
4. Lift left leg up and put into other leg opening until the left foot comes out of that leg hole.
5. While grasping the pants, pull pants up to waist.
6. While still holding pants, move right and left hands toward the snap.
7. Place right thumb behind the snap and place left fingers over the front of the snap.
8. Push left fingers and right thumb towards each other until the fastener snaps.

Brief description of how to teach

Place your child's pants on the bed with the top end near where he is standing. Stand behind him and place your hands over his hands as you guide him to grasp the right and left side of the top of the pants with the snap facing away from you. Using a backward chain and hand-over-hand prompting, extend your child's hands downward while prompting him to lift and bend his right foot as he puts it into the right pant leg. As he does this, attempt to pull your hands slightly back to see if he completes the step. After three seconds, if no response or an incomplete response occurs, place your hands back over his and pull the rest of the way up. Repeat process with next leg.

Shaving

Task Analysis

1. Take a wet washcloth and wet face with warm water for at least thirty seconds.
2. Close drain in sink and fill the sink with warm water.
3. Put about a quarter size drop of shaving cream onto the palm of your left hand.
4. Spread the shaving cream with your left hand over the bottom right and left side of your face, neck and chin areas, and around lips.
5. Take razor by the handle, with the blade pointing up.
6. Starting at the right side of the face just next to the right ear, shave downward toward your jawbone using light but firm pressure and even strokes.
7. Repeat Step 6, by shaving area directly next to area that was just shaved on the right side.

8. After every two strokes, rinse your razor in the sink to remove cut hair.
9. When the right side of face is shaved, repeat Steps 6 and 7 on the left side of the face.
10. Shave the neck area directly below your chin with firm but light strokes upward.
11. After every two strokes, rinse your razor in the sink.
12. Curl your lower lip over the lower teeth and shave downward the area below your bottom lip to your chin.
13. Curl your upper lip over the upper teeth and shave downward the area above your upper lip to your nose.
14. Rinse face with warm water to remove shaving cream.
15. Check your face for unshaven hairs and use the razor to shave missed hair.
16. Wipe face with washcloth.
17. Dry face with hand towel.

Brief description of how to teach

Have your child stand in front of sink with washcloth. Make sure razor and shaving cream is available. While standing behind him, provide a brief instruction to shave and then prompt him to wet the washcloth and wipe face repeatedly for about thirty seconds. Using a backward chain and hand-over-hand prompting, prompt all sixteen steps and pause before Step 17. After three seconds, if no response or an incomplete response occurs at Step 17, place your hands on his and pick up hand towel and help him dry his face.

Putting on a coat

Task Analysis

1. Place the coat flat on a table or bed with the inside of the coat facing upward.
2. Stand facing the top or collar of the coat or shirt.
3. Put right arm in right sleeve of coat and left arm in left arm of coat.
4. Lift the coat up and over your head.
5. Pull arms down.
6. Zip coat.

Brief description of how to teach

Stand behind child and prompt him to take the coat and lay it flat on table or bed with the inside of coat facing upward. Prompt child if necessary to stand on side of table where the top of coat is located and follow task analysis above. Note this task analysis assumes that your child is able to zip. If not, more steps would be needed to include zipping.

Using a tissue

Task Analysis

1. Take a tissue from tissue box.
2. Lay tissue open and flat in palm of left hand.

3. Bring open left hand with tissue toward face and cup hand over mouth and nose.
4. Press thumb over one nostril.
5. Blow gently through the open nostril.
6. Release thumb and press pointer finger on other nostril and blow gently.
7. Release finger from nostril and cup hand into a fist while keeping tissue in fist.
8. Throw tissue away in the garbage can.

Brief description of how to teach

Make sure a tissue box is available. Instruct your child to blow his nose. While standing behind him, prompt your child to take a tissue from box. Using a backward chain and hand-over-hand prompting, prompt the first seven steps then pause giving your child an opportunity to complete the last step. After three seconds, if no response or an incomplete response occurs to Step 8, place your hands on his and help him to throw the tissue away. Over many opportunities gradually fade your help until your child is completing Step 8 independently. This is a lesson that can be taught many times throughout the day as it should only take from two to three minutes to run.

■ Final Thoughts

This chapter provided you with tools to increase your child's dressing and personal hygiene skills. While every child is different, we firmly believe that if you use an approach that breaks complex skills into small steps and teaches systematically, your child can reach greater independence in the completion of basic self-help skills. The examples here will provide a roadmap for you, but you will have to individualize some of the materials to fit your specific situation. Writing down your plan and sticking to it for a period of time will be important. It is equally important to monitor your child's progress by taking frequent data and using the data to drive your decisions about program modifications.

9

Learning is not attained by chance, it must be sought for with ardor and attended to with diligence.
—**Abigail Adams**

Teaching Eating Skills

The Thompsons

Mr. and Mrs. Thompson's twelve-year-old son, Jeremy, had been a healthy eater, enjoying a wide range of food as a young child. But now nearly a teenager, Jeremy won't eat at the table with the family or use eating utensils without spilling. He will willingly sit for only two or three minutes and rapidly stuff handfuls of food into his mouth. More food ends up on his clothing and the tablecloth than is eaten. Mr. and Mrs. Thompson beg and cajole but can't seem to get Jeremy to cooperate. They've incorporated a number of accommodation strategies including preparing primarily foods that can be eaten with his fingers and cutting food into small pieces. They've

also blocked doors leading to and from the kitchen so Jeremy has to stay put during meals. These actions have made things more tolerable but the absence of age-appropriate eating skills is not acceptable and results in Jeremy's exclusion from the school cafeteria and prevents family trips to restaurants.

The Mintons

Soon after Tammy Minton's birth, she began spitting up profusely after drinking breastmilk or formula. Mr. and Mrs. Minton requested a medical examination and severe gastroesophagael reflux disorder was diagnosed. The Minton's pediatrician prescribed medication to control Tammy's reflux and suggested that her parents start

feeding her rice cereal mixed with breastmilk or formula and then pureed foods as soon as she could coordinate her muscles to swallow them. Tammy initially did well with the transition to pureed food; however, as the Mintons began expanding the menu of solid foods, Tammy refused to eat them. A medical examination found some damage to her esophagus that had resulted from reflux disorder and surgery was successfully performed. Although there was no longer a medical basis, Tammy's eating behaviors improved only slightly after surgery. Her diet consisted of yogurt and a variety of smooth baby foods.

Where to Begin?

Neither the Thompsons nor the Mintons should feel alone. Many children with autism demonstrate significant delays in the acquisition of basic self-feeding skills. Less often, but substantially more frequent than the general population, they demonstrate a narrow range of food preferences and extreme intolerances to many foods because of their texture, color, or smell. This chapter is concerned with teaching basic eating skills such as drinking from a cup, eating with a spoon and fork, and using a knife. However, because so many children with autism also show odd eating preferences and restrictions, we have included a comprehensive section on this as well. Obviously, if your child eats very few foods, then worrying about the use of eating utensils becomes secondary to ensuring a healthy diet.

From Liquid to Solid Foods— The Anatomy of Healthy Eating

Infants of many species, including humans, enter the world with basic reflexes (e.g., suck-swallow and rooting) that enable them to naturally consume an available food source, usually their mother's breastmilk or formula from a bottle. Gradually, they are weaned from their mother's milk or formula and are expected to consume a wider variety of foods. However, the transition from nursing or bottle-feeding to independent eating is not a simple one and it requires that many component skills and complicated chains of behavior be developed.

Children with developmental disabilities may have difficulty making three separate transitions from nursing or bottle-feeding to independently eating solid foods. One transition involves a change in the child's behavior from sucking to chewing. Another transition involves a change from liquids to solid foods. A final change involves social interactions, where close interactions with the feeding adult are replaced with more independent feeding. Delays or problems with the development of self-feeding for the child with disabilities can break down in any or all of these areas.

Problems also arise because of the complexity of the motor skills required for eating (e.g., chewing and swallowing), the need to recognize and discriminate hunger and satiation, and the large number of component skills that are required to reach full independence in this realm. Children with poor attention spans, delays in cognitive and motor development, and auditory processing challenges may not easily develop independent feeding skills.

Before proceeding with this chapter, we want to provide one cautionary note. We encourage you to consult with your child's pediatrician, a speech-language pathologist, or occupational therapist if you notice or suspect that your child may have a physical condition that prevents her from safely consuming food or self-feeding. Seek medical consultation if there is frequent occurrence of gagging, vomiting, rumination (i.e., the voluntary or involuntary regurgitation and re-chewing of partially digested food), nausea, or belching. If these issues exist because of a medical disorder, then the condition needs to be treated before you begin teaching your child to expand her repertoire of foods or increase her self-feeding. As in our example of Tammy, it is not uncommon for eating issues to begin because of a medical condition, but persist long after the medical condition has been corrected. At that point, a systematic plan for intervention is warranted and safe to implement.

> Children with poor attention spans, delays in cognitive and motor development, and auditory processing challenges may not easily develop independent feeding skills.

Early Development of Feeding Skills

Although professional opinion on the best age to introduce solid food varies widely, many parents begin adding solid foods (purees) to their infant's diet at four to six months of age. If food intake is adequate, the typical infant should be expected to triple her birth weight at one year of age and be 50 percent longer than she was at birth (Garwood & Fewell, 1983).

Using broad observations of infant behavior, researchers (Gesell & Ilg, 1937) determined that typically developing infants begin to signal hunger and satiety very early in life. By six months, they may shake their heads if full and by ten months they may throw food when no longer hungry. At eight months, many infants can be heard to vocalize eagerly at the sight of their high-chair or spoon. Carruth, Ziegler, Gordon & Hendricks (2004) surveyed parents of over three thousand children without physical disabilities and summarized the age at which stages of self-feeding emerged. Table 9-1 provides a summary of their findings, indicating the upper end of the age range when most children develop the indicated skills. These findings demonstrate that for the typically developing child, the foundations of self-feeding are pretty well established by the time she is two years old. Furthermore, children appear sufficiently motivated to increase their independence. Carruth & Skinner (2002) reported that children frequently indicate a desire to eat from their parents' plates at as early as ten months old. Contrast this report with the status of Jeremy in our example of the Thompson family. Although Jeremy appears to have the physical ability to self-feed (e.g., sits without support, grasps food with hands, drinks from a cup), he is fixed at the level of an eighteen to twenty-four-month-old child. But continued growth in this area is possible, if a coordinated and systematic approach is used to teach more complex skills.

■ Table 9-1　Stages of Development of Self-Feeding (Carruth et. al., 2004)

General Area of Development	Stages of Development	Developmental Age in Months	Percentage of Children at this age Who Achieved Stage
Physical development	Tongue thrusting ends	6 mos.	majority
	Holds head upright	4—8 mos.	majority
	Sits without support	9—11 mos.	majority
	Most teeth are present	19—24 mos.	majority
Self-feeding skills emerge	Grasps food with hands	9—11 mos.	95%
	Drinks from sippy cup	12—14 mos.	91%
	Consumes solid foods	15—18 mos.	99%
	Removes food from a spoon	19—24 mos.	97%
	Self feeds with a spoon without much spilling	19—24 mos.	88%

■ The Desire for Personal Independence

Teaching your child to eat independently will be one of the most important things that you can do for her. Eating is essential for survival and is a skill that almost all children can master. It can also be one of the easier adaptive skills to teach since food is inherently motivating for most of us. Independent eating not only allows for physical growth and development, it can also facilitate many social opportunities for children. Many birthday parties and holiday celebrations center on the presentation and consumption of food. Additionally, many inclusion opportunities for children with special needs occur in the school cafeteria. A lack of independent eating skills may prevent your child's participation in these activities and limit her opportunities for interaction with peers. Remember our example of Jeremy and his exclusion from the school cafeteria and restaurants?

Not only should your child learn to independently feed herself using utensils, she needs to acquire a wide variety of mealtime-related skills including setting the table, serving herself from a bowl or plate, preparing simple foods, and cleaning up after meals. (Refer to the Self-Help Inventory presented in Appendix A.) Children also benefit from learning how to order food and behave appropriately in a restaurant. When children become young adults, they need to know how to shop for food and monitor their diet. Each of these skills may require individualized direct instruction for learning to occur.

> Teaching your child to eat independently will be one of the most important things that you can do for her.

No matter what level of independence you believe your child can achieve, it is important that the behavior of eating and drinking be related to his or her level of hunger and thirst. It is critical for your child's health and well-being that eating occurs when your child is hungry and drinking occurs only when your child is thirsty. You do not want your child to eat only when you tell them to do so or, conversely, eat every time they see food. The sight of food or your instruction to eat may be required early in your child's development, but should not be the permanent trigger for eating. This transition may be a difficult one, since hunger and thirst are not readily observable behaviors and many children with developmental disabilities also have communication difficulties. Just as it may be difficult for you to ascertain when your child is not feeling well, it may also be very difficult to determine if she is truly hungry. Establishing consistent routines, monitoring your child's diet and eating schedule, and working to shift the signal for eating and drinking to natural internal cues are important to ensure complete success.

First Steps to Independent and Healthy Eating

1. Establish Consistent Times to Eat Meals

Many children with pervasive developmental disorders struggle with transitions and are resistant to change. In fact, inflexible adherence to routines or rituals is a defining characteristic of autism. As a result, many activities of daily living are completed more successfully when they become part of an established routine. Providing your child with a regular, predictable mealtime schedule is the beginning of a good foundation for instruction and will prepare her for common routines in her classroom or at work. An established mealtime schedule will also help regulate your child's hunger and elimination patterns. The nutritional needs for most children will be met with a breakfast, lunch, and dinner meal, along with one or two nutritious snack breaks in the afternoon

> Providing your child with a regular, predictable mealtime schedule is the beginning of a good foundation for instruction and will prepare her for common routines in her classroom or at work.

and evening. For some children, using a time and/or picture schedule may help establish a consistent routine. *Activity Schedules for Children with Autism: Teaching Independent Behavior* by McClannahan & Krantz (Woodbine House, 1999) describes how to develop and use these types of tools.

2. Teach Your Child to Sit Independently

Many children have difficulty at mealtimes because they refuse to sit at the table for more than a few minutes at a time. Rarely do infants have difficulty transitioning from being held by their mother while being fed, to sitting independently in a highchair. However, when they become more mobile, usually before the age of two, many children resist being restrained in their highchair and yet refuse to remain seated in a regular chair. For many parents, ensuring adequate food intake is of primary importance and sitting at the table becomes secondary to eating. Some parents allow their child to walk around while eating and provide nearly continuous snacks throughout the day. Allowing children to "graze," as this is euphemistically called, disrupts the predictable mealtime schedule and throws off hunger patterns. Children who graze often consume large quantities of nutritionally deficient snack food and are less hungry when meals are served. In short, it is very important to teach your child to sit independently while eating and to only offer food during the predictable meal and snack times that you have established.

Referring back to our example of Jeremy, it will be essential that his parents gradually increase the amount of time he sits at the table until he is able to completely eat his meal in one sitting. You may remember that in Chapter 5 we described Mr. and Mrs. Jones and their son, Tom, who had a similar problem. The Thompsons decided to use a similar approach to teaching Jeremy to sit at the table. Although they wanted most of all to focus on teaching Jeremy to use eating utensils, they needed to make sure he could sit at the table before starting anything else. The Jones family began by rewarding Tom for sitting at the table for short periods of time, then gradually increased the length of time that he had to sit before earning a preferred food. It worked quickly and the Jones were eager to move on to teaching the use of utensils.

3. Apply the Strategy of "Mini-Meals" to Promote Learning

Initial attempts to teach independent eating skills should be organized in a manner that will make your child successful and provide multiple opportunities for learning. If your child is one of those children who rarely sits for more than a few seconds, start with a series of "mini meals" throughout the day. Provide highly preferred foods that are divided into small portions. Each portion is provided as a mini-meal and initially your child should be able to consume the entire portion of food within a short time period. The period of time should closely match the average length of time she remains seated for a meal. In a sense, you are matching the length of the meal to your child's attention span. This is a beginning point, not an ending point. Gradually, you begin increasing the portion size, adding less-preferred foods along with highly-preferred foods, and increase the expectation for sitting longer. Working with small portions provides the additional benefit of encouraging your child to communicate to receive additional preferred foods.

Next Steps: Teaching Specific Eating Skills

After considering and using some of the strategies recommended above, it is time to teach specific eating skills. Once again, we encourage you to complete the Self-Help Skill Inventory provided in Appendix A. Start with a skill that is age-appropriate, important for your child to learn at this time, and your child has already shown some ability or interest in learning. Let's reflect once again on Jeremy, the case study we provided in the beginning of this chapter. Once he was reliably sitting for at least ten minutes, it was time for Mr. and Mrs. Thompson to introduce a plan to teach him to use a spoon. They began with a spoon because it is developmentally one of the first utensils children learn to use and he had shown some limited ability with it. Referring to the instructions for writing an Instructional Plan that we provided in Appendix D and discussed in Chapter 6, the Thompsons conducted a baseline assessment of Jeremy's ability that indicated that he was able to complete only some of the steps unaided. Based upon that assessment they decided to select the backward chaining approach and they developed the Instructional Plan provided in Table 9-2.

Progress was slow, but over several months, Jeremy's spoon use increased. Once it was mastered, Jeremy's parents used the same strategies to address eating with a spoon without spilling, using a fork, and wiping with a napkin.

Progress for children with autism is rarely a continuous steady climb. There is commonly a period of growth followed by days and weeks of very little progress. In the end, it may take months to teach some of the most basic skills. Don't get too concerned if your child appears to be making very modest progress after the first couple of weeks. Be patient and continue to conduct the program at each mealtime every day. If progress is not evident after three or four weeks, you may need to tweak the program (e.g., identify better rewards or experiment with a different way of prompting). Typically, there is little to be gained by making radical changes to the program. The most success is going to be made through a slow, methodical approach that continuously evaluates progress and makes changes based on objective consideration of the data.

Children with Significant Feeding Disorders

Abnormal Eating Patterns

Not many things are more frustrating for a parent than a toddler who is an extremely fussy eater. Fortunately, most pediatricians agree that toddlers, even the pickiest, will consume enough variety and quantity of food to survive and grow. The portion size for most toddlers is smaller than many adults estimate and often food is over presented. Additionally, toddlers are famous for "food jags," when they may favor a particular type, taste, or color of food for days or months, and then

■ **Table 9-2   Instruction Plan to Teach Jeremy to Use a Spoon**

Instructional Plan

Functional Area: Eating & Drinking

Task: Use of utensils   **Child's Name:** Jeremy

Skill Target: Eating with a spoon   **Initiation Date:** 4-05-07

Goal for Learning

Given a bowl and a spoon, Jeremy will eat his meal with no more than one prompt for three consecutive opportunities.

Specify Components of the Plan

Check when completed	
✓	**Conduct list of steps required to do the task:** See Task Analysis Data Sheet attached
✓	**Place and time for instruction:** At breakfast, lunch, and dinner time at the kitchen table
✓	**Materials required:** Bowl, spoon, preferred food that has right consistency and texture
✓	**Physical accommodations (if needed):** None; prior to teaching this session, mastered sitting at the table
✓	**Instructional signal or cue:** "Jeremy, time to eat."
✓	**Data sheet for monitoring progress**
✓	**Steps for generalization:** Once Jeremy is reliably using the spoon and bowl provided, begin to introduce other spoons and bowls to ensure generalization across materials. Will begin to introduce other foods of various consistency and texture and probe to see if Jeremy can use his spoon at other tables/eating areas outside of his home and with other people he knows.
✓	**Circle which chaining procedure will teach:** (BACKWARD) FORWARD
✓	**Conduct a baseline:** On Data Tracking Form (attached)
✓	**Super reward(s):** During sessions, will provide access to lighted and beeping toys and after each session will get ten minutes of favorite video

Task Analysis Data Sheet: Using a Spoon

SKILL TARGET   Eating with a spoon

GOAL   Given a bowl and a spoon, Jeremy will eat his meal with no more than one prompt for three consecutive opportunities.

YOUR INSTRUCTION TO CHILD
(e.g., "Brush your teeth."):   "Jeremy, time to eat."

TEACHING METHOD (Circle)   (BACKWARD)   FORWARD

Mastery	Step	Component Skill (e.g., Turn on water)	Date								
	1	Reach toward spoon with dominant hand open									
	2	Place palm of hand on handle of spoon with thumb pointing away from body									
	3	Close fingers around spoon handle									
	4	Pivot hand so thumb points toward food bowl									
	5	Move hand down until spoon is half covered with food									
	6	Pivot hand upward so thumb is perpendicular to body and spoon is horizontal									
	7	Lift dominant arm until spoon is at the height of mouth									
	8	Open mouth									
	9	Turn hand so thumb points toward mouth									
	10	Move arm toward body until entire scoop of spoon is inserted into mouth									
	11	Close lips gently over spoon									
	12	Move arm up slightly and then away from body to slide spoon out of mouth									
	13	Lower arm until spoon is at level of bowl									
	14	Chew food in mouth									
x	x	Repeat steps 5-14 (Record data in adjacent columns each time he repeats this step)									

subsequently refuse it when the jag is over. Typically, over time, most toddlers will develop an expanded repertoire of food preferences.

However, many children with autism continue a food jag for years and often reduce their food preferences over time, instead of expanding them. Surprisingly, many of these children continue to consume enough highly preferred foods to gain adequate weight, although nutritional status may be highly compromised. This restricted food repertoire frequently makes eating in public places difficult and may disrupt the child and family's social relationships. A close working relationship with your child's pediatrician and a nutritionist is essential if your child significantly restricts her food repertoire. These professionals should frequently monitor your child's weight and overall health, and vigilantly watch for symptoms of malnutrition or failure to thrive. Vitamin and mineral supplements may be prescribed; however, these may be difficult to administer. It is also critical to determine whether or not your child may have any medical difficulties or allergies, which can account for her restricted eating patterns. Suggestions for increasing your child's food repertoire will be provided later in this chapter.

> It is critical to determine whether or not your child may have any medical difficulties or allergies, which can account for her restricted eating patterns. A close working relationship with your child's pediatrician and a nutritionist is essential if your child significantly restricts her food repertoire.

Conversely, a large number of children with developmental disabilities are at risk for obesity. Restricted food repertoires may lead to diets high in calories and fats, as most children prefer sweet foods, high in carbohydrates. Some children may have difficulty learning the association between hunger and eating and may choose to eat whenever they see food, when they are bored, or when they are upset. Motor and/or cognitive difficulties may limit participation in physical activities and may lead to a sedentary lifestyle. Finally, some medications commonly used by children with disabilities have weight gain as a side-effect. Consultation with a pediatrician or nutritionist is just as important for children who are at-risk for obesity as it is for those who barely eat. In the following pages we will provide useful advice that you can use to address some specific food intolerances and sensitivities.

Generalized and Specific Sensory Disorders

Many children with developmental disabilities have abnormal sensory responses to common things. Some may be hypersensitive and show exaggerated responses (e.g., *Sam cries uncontrollably when mittens or gloves are placed on his hands*) and others may be hyposensitive and appear to have little reaction to common stimuli (e.g., *Trina did not exhibit any signs of distress after falling off the swing, despite fracturing her leg*). To complicate matters, the same child may show hypersensitivity in one sensory system and with one set of stimuli and hyposensitivity in another sensory system or with different stimuli (e.g., *Although Trina shows no pain response in reaction to a forceful fall, she cringes if another child brushes up against her arm*). All senses may potentially be affected for the child with autism, including the sense of sight, hearing, taste, smell, touch, and proprioception (the ability to sense your body's movement or positioning in space). These sensory processes can exert a direct negative effect on feeding behavior as related to the various characteristics of food listed below.

Sensitivity to Textures

Problems with textures are usually noticed when an infant begins to transition to solid foods. Parents (with the help of baby food manufacturers) begin to slowly move from liquids to purees, to purees with chunks or increased texture, and finally to full solids. Children with autism may refuse purees or soft solids and skip to dry, crunchy foods, which often become a preferred texture. Once a new texture is mastered, old textures may be rejected. Some professionals feel that the transition from liquid to more solid textures may be problematic if not done at the appropriate developmental age (approximately six months). Texture problems may also occur if the parents give up too easily. Typically-developing children frequently reject new textures at first, but will consume them if parents are persistent without forcing food. Sensory issues may also contribute significantly to a child's refusal of certain textures.

Increasing Textures

We recommend changing the texture of a child's diet by very slowly adding a new texture to an already preferred one. If your child prefers pureed textures you need to begin by adding a very small amount of a coarser texture into the preferred food. Once they consume the added texture, you slowly add more until the child is consuming most of the new texture topped off by a bit of puree. The following template suggests the steps to take when trying to get a child who only eats baby food applesauce to begin eating more texture. Typically, this child will eat one cup of baby food applesauce independently using a spoon. Her mother's goal is to have her independently consume an apple cut into bite-sized pieces. This process is outlined below in Table 9-3.

Another way to begin to increase the texture of food, if a child does not even do well with purees, is to add gelatin or other thickening agents that will not change the taste to the food in the early stages of the program. Additionally, we also recommend adding new textures by using foods that are easily dissolved with saliva. When feeding new textures to your child we recommend placing new textures directly onto the teeth on the side of the mouth, as opposed to placing on the tongue, where they are more likely to be expelled by your child.

The same steps are essentially taken when trying to introduce soft or smooth textures to a child that prefers crunchy foods. Sarah loved eating crackers but refused to eat soft, creamy foods. Her mother decided she wanted Sarah to eat peanut butter. She chose peanut butter because Sarah also enjoyed eating peanuts and because it was the color of her preferred crackers. Sarah's mother began by serving Sarah two crackers placed one on top of the other and asking her to eat them without taking them apart (just like a sandwich). Once Sarah was used to eating them this way, her mom added less than one-eighths teaspoon of peanut butter between the two crackers. Sarah never even noticed it was there. More peanut butter was slowly added and Sarah was soon eating peanut butter and cracker sandwiches.

■ Table 9-3 Adding Texture to a Preferred Food

STEP	WHAT YOU DO	CRITERIA FOR MOVING TO THE NEXT STEP
1	Add one tablespoon of adult applesauce (new texture) to one cup of baby food applesauce (pureed). Provide reinforcer if child consumes the food (ideally a preferred toy or activity).	Move to Step 2 when child has consumed food without resistance (e.g., pushing away, gagging) for three consecutive meals. If child is not successful, then reduce the amount of new texture added to one teaspoon.
2	Add 1/4 cup adult applesauce to 3/4 cup baby food applesauce. Reinforce consumption.	Move to Step 3 when child consumes food without resistance (e.g., pushing away, gagging) for three consecutive meals. If child is not successful, then reduce the amount of new texture added to one tablespoon.
3	Mix 1/2 cup adult applesauce with 1/2 cup baby food applesauce. Reinforce consumption.	Move to Step 4 when child eats food without resistance (e.g., pushing away, gagging) for three consecutive meals. If child is not successful, then reduce the amount of new texture added to 1/4 cup.
4	Serve one cup adult applesauce. Reinforce consumption.	Move to Step 5 when child consumes food without resistance (e.g., pushing away, gagging) for three consecutive meals. If child is not successful, then reduce the amount of new texture added to 1/2 cup.
5	Add one tablespoon crushed apple to one cup adult applesauce. Reinforce consumption.	Move to Step 6 when child consumes food without resistance (e.g., pushing away, gagging) for three consecutive meals. If child is not successful, then reduce the amount of new texture added to one teaspoon.
6	Continue in the manner stated above, slowly adding more texture at each step until the child is consuming small pieces of an apple. Reinforce consumption.	Move to next step when child consumes (as stated above). If child is moving along well, you can begin altering food at each meal, backing up steps or reducing the amount of new texture if progress stops occurring.

Once she consumed these regularly, Sarah's mom began slowly breaking away bits of the top cracker until it was no longer present. Soon, Sarah was able to eat peanut butter right off the spoon.

These techniques are examples of shaping procedures that were discussed in Chapter 6. Over time, gradual approximations of the desired behavior are reinforced as the food is systematically altered. Obviously, this is a very time consuming approach, but one that can be very effective. The speed of progress for each child will be different, so as a parent, you must be sensitive to this and modify the approach as needed. As discussed in Table 9-3, if your child stops making progress when you move to a new step, back up and reduce the amount of change that you made to the food. If she moves along rapidly, you can combine steps and make larger changes to the food each time. However, you must be persistent and systematic in your approach. There are some children that will not be successful using these shaping methods and may absolutely refuse to open their mouths or accept new foods. More information about persistent food refusal is presented later in this chapter.

> Shaping procedures for teaching independent eating skills can be very time consuming, but very effective. The speed of progress for each child will be different, so you must be sensitive to this and modify the approach as needed.

Sensitivity to Taste

Taste is an important variable to assess when addressing feeding concerns. Typically-developing children move from a diet with a small number of bland flavors to one of diverse, rich flavors. Children with autism may have strong preferences for a particular flavor or spice. It may help to experiment with your child's food preferences by adding herbs, spices, or other flavoring agents that will not change the texture of the food. You may find that your child, who only ate French fries, may now eat mashed potatoes if salt is sprinkled on them. What was thought to have been a texture issue may only have been an issue related to taste.

Reaction to Temperature

Children with autism may respond negatively when the temperature of the food and utensils are different than their preference. Temperature is a variable that is frequently overlooked when addressing feeding difficulties. If your child seems to prefer a hot, cold, or moderate temperature, it may be helpful to adjust and maintain the temperature of food and utensils to the extent possible. Sometimes refusal to eat midway through a meal may be misinterpreted as a sign of fullness. Instead, your child may be reacting to the fact that the meal has cooled. Placing food in an insulated bowl, putting a hot pack under the plate, or microwaving the plate midway through the meal may help maintain a more consistent food temperature.

Strong Preference or Aversion to a Specific Color

Color and other visual aspects of food are frequently overlooked as possible variables that affect a child's willingness to eat. Some children with autism have strong reactions to the sight of particular colors and may choose foods that do or do not have these colors in them. The colors of the plates, spoons, or other feeding apparatus also may be relevant to food consumption. Some parents have gone as far as using food coloring as a quick and easy way to alter the appearance of less preferred foods. Food coloring is typically available as a paste, liquid, or powder, which makes it useful to change the color of a variety of foods without altering the texture. A small number of children with autism are oddly aware of food packaging and may reject food solely on the basis of its container. One trick is to repackage less preferred foods into preferred food containers. Neither of these tricks offer a long-term solution, but they may provide some help initially. If these aversions become extremely problematic, it may be necessary to introduce a plan to teach greater tolerance of food colors and packaging.

Identifying Food Sensitivities

Determining which areas of sensitivity are influencing your child can be difficult and often times must be determined by trial and error. Parents can systematically determine preferences by making deliberate alterations to food and observing and recording their child's response. However, you are cautioned to not make alterations if your child's diet is restricted to only one food, as you may run the risk of making her refuse it too.

Tammy's favorite food was strawberry yogurt and it was one of the few foods, other than baby food, that she readily accepted. Since Tammy was having a difficult time transitioning off of baby food, Mrs. Minton decided to try to determine if sensitivities were a factor in her food refusal. She did this by making a different change to the yogurt each day and recording Tammy's reaction. On the first day, she cut up very small bits of strawberries and put them into the yogurt, which altered only the texture of the food. Tammy refused to eat it. The next day she put blue food coloring into the yogurt, which turned it a deep purple color but did not alter the texture or taste. After a brief hesitation upon the first bite, Tammy readily consumed the purple yogurt. On day three, Mrs. Minton briefly put the yogurt into the microwave to warm it to room temperature before serving it. Again, Tammy consumed the yogurt. Finally on the following day, Mrs. Minton added a bit of lemon juice to the yogurt and, to her surprise, Tammy consumed it. She repeated this entire sequence two more times to check the reliability of the information. Based on this analysis she determined that Tammy was most bothered by texture and decided to follow the plan in Table 9-3.

◼ Increasing Food Repertoires and Intake

If modifying foods is not effective, there are two relatively benign methods for increasing the variety of food that your child will eat. One is based on the Premack principle, which is sometimes called Grandma's law (Figure 9-1). That is, preferred things and activities (i.e., favorite foods) can be temporarily restricted then provided only if the child demonstrates a less preferred behavior (i.e., eating a nonpreferred food). Hence, if Sally can have a piece of chocolate cake (a highly-preferred food that is always consumed when presented) after she eats her green beans (a nonpreferred food that is consumed at a very low frequency), then the act of eating her green beans will increase. Many parents adopt this technique during mealtimes and it may be effective for children with autism on a bite-by-bite basis. Other parents require that their children consume all of the food from their plates before the highly preferred item can be consumed. Heavy reliance on either method carries the danger of making preferred foods even more appealing, which is generally a problem if the preferred food is nutritionally sparse (e.g., desserts). Additionally, food consumption does not always continue in this fashion when the reinforcer (dessert) is not present. Encouraging children to simply taste each food item, rather than consume it, reinforces the child's willingness to consume new foods and is more effective at maintaining behavior.

Figure 9-1   Example of Increasing Food Preferences Using Grandma's Law

Preferred / Non-Preferred   *Eating non-preferred*

Another approach is based on desensitization procedures and consists of slowly increasing your child's tolerance to novel foods. The program begins by simply placing a piece of new food near your child's plate until she is not bothered by it being there. Over time, you move the food closer to the child while she is eating with no initial expectation that she must consume it. A reinforcer is provided (e.g., a highly preferred food) if you place the food on her plate and she simply allows the food to remain there. Gradually expectations are increased so that the child approximates eating (e.g., picks up the nonpreferred food and brings it to her lips). The child is reinforced after each success. Over the course of days or weeks, the expectation increases until she is required to chew and swallow it. This method can be effectively used to increase the food repertoire of children with autism. However, the method is time consuming and some children never progress to the point where they will place the food into their mouths, without additional physical assistance.

Intensive Treatments

If your child's food intake becomes dangerously limited, she is failing to grow, or her intake does not improve with the procedures listed above, more intensive feeding intervention will be needed. The following interventions should never be attempted without close supervision of a medical professional and an experienced behavior specialist.

Successful intensive feeding interventions based on a combination of behavioral treatment methods and physical guidance have been reported for decades. There are two primary approaches, interventions based on escape-reduction procedures and those based on physical guidance. Escape-reduction procedures attempt to reduce or eliminate the behaviors that prevent eating or the demand to eat, such as the child screaming, pushing away the spoon, and clenching her teeth. To achieve this end, a spoonful of food is presented to the child and held to her lips until she consumes it. All negative behaviors are ignored and the spoon gently follows the child's mouth if she turns her head or tries to move away or push the spoon. It is assumed that the presence of feeding demands is unpleasant to the child and the child will take a bite to remove the demand, even if the demand is removed only temporarily.

The second approach is based on physical guidance techniques and requires that the feeder use jaw prompting to open the child's mouth and insert the food. Swallowing of the food, once in the mouth, is then reinforced with praise, attention, and/or access to preferred toys or activities. In 1996, Ahern, Kerwin, Eicher, Shantz & Swearingin compared the effects of these two feeding interventions, as well as parents' perception of them. The results indicated that both procedures were equally effective at increasing food intake of students who were developmentally disabled. Parents preferred the physical guidance method because it produced quicker results and elicited fewer negative responses from their child. It is beyond the scope of this book to describe these techniques in more detail. Again, we don't recommend you attempt these methods without the support and guidance of medical professionals.

Modifying Materials and Equipment

Adaptations to eating tools and equipment can be made if a child is struggling with feeding. However, parents are cautioned only to introduce these modified devices if needed. Many children with autism may become dependent upon physical adaptations and not generalize to normal conditions. Adaptations can be made to utensils by increasing the width and depth of handles with tape or foam, increasing the length of the utensil and adding cuffs to utensils for children who have poor grips. Bowls and plates can be modified by fitting them with nonslip grips. Cups, bowls, and plates that are shaped to encourage easy scooping and drinking can be purchased. Chairs can be manually modified or specially purchased that provide additional postural support for your child. An occupational therapist is an excellent source of information and ideas for modifying eating utensils and dishes. Additionally, a few resources for these types of adaptive devices have been listed in the *Helpful Materials* section in the back of this book.

Summary

Acquiring appropriate and independent eating skills is important for your child and you for many reasons. The most obvious is that it helps to ensure your child's good physical and mental health. Children with autism often demonstrate intolerances to food that limit their consumption of a well-rounded, healthy diet. Second, the failure to acquire appropriate eating skills may prevent your child from full participation in normal school and community life. Finally, the absence of appropriate eating skills relegates your child and you to a life of interdependence. This chapter provided you with ways to increase your child's ability to feed herself and to expand her repertoire of preferred foods. Through a thoughtful and systematic plan, most children can learn basic skills and many can learn advanced skills that will lead to greater independence.

You can learn many things from children.
How much patience you have, for instance.
—Franklin P. Jones

10

Teaching Toileting Skills

The Coles

Bob and Marcy Cole feel fortunate that their son Jason's autism was diagnosed early (before age three) so they could start an intensive home-based training program while he was still quite young. Now, almost five years old, Jason is doing so well that the consultant to the family recommends that Jason attend a regular kindergarten next fall. As part of her recommendation, the consultant suggests that he first attend a regular prekindergarten (Pre-K) program. Jason appears to have most of the skills needed to be successful in Pre-K, except he hasn't yet toilet trained and the school's attendance policy is that children must be out of diapers in order to participate in the program.

The Coles have noticed that Jason has often been waking up with a dry diaper and wonder if this might be a sign that he is ready to become more independent. But they worry that it may be still too early to begin toilet training since he's shown no other signs of interest or desire to use the toilet. They've also expressed concern that Jason might resist participation in toilet training *efforts and worry that a few unsuccessful interactions might trigger regression in areas where they've just begun to see progress.*

Thinking About Teaching Toileting Skills?

The cost of buying and the patience needed to change what seems like a mountain of wet and soiled diapers are expected and reluctantly accepted by parents of very young children. But when children reach preschool and early school-age years, most parents are expecting a reprieve. However, the mere idea of introducing toilet training can be intimidating to many parents who are keenly aware of the level of commitment required to be successful. This trepidation is heightened for parents of children with autism, who recognize the challenges of overcoming many common symptoms of the disorder, such as insistence on sameness, poor attention, and delays in communication. In addition, children with autism often have significant problems understanding important discriminations and sensing physical changes that may be important for learning, such as feeling and responding to a full bladder or reacting to dampness in clothing. Finally, children with autism may engage in a variety of repetitive behaviors that may interfere with learning, such as playing in water and repeatedly flushing the toilet. Although each of these may be a test of a parent's commitment and resolve, they are not insurmountable barriers.

> Children with autism often have significant problems understanding important discriminations and sensing physical changes that may be important for learning, such as feeling and responding to a full bladder or reacting to dampness in clothing.

There are probably many different ways to wean a child from diapers and there are always plenty of "experts" on the topic—your mother or grandmother might profess to be one of them. The area is wrought with folklore and contradictory information. For example, many professionals recommend that children be allowed to lead the course of learning and that parents should intervene only when the child declares himself ready. Other professionals encourage parents to actively and systematically introduce toilet training. One group of professionals discourages parents from calling the child's attention to a toilet accident for fear that the child might feel shame. In contrast, another group of professionals recommends correcting the child when an accident occurs so that he begins to understand the difference between his behavior and acceptable standards.

So, which approach is right? Well, we are never ones to eliminate any option from our bag of tools. While it is certainly true that you never want a young child with autism to be pushed beyond their ability or feel ashamed, if he does not meet parent expectations, moving from a diaper to independent toileting is rarely achieved without significant intervention. It is not likely to result from simply showing and telling your child what you want him to do. Although we may begin initial toilet training efforts using less directive methods, our recommendations lean toward more active parent direction if progress is slow or absent. In this chapter, we suggest ways for you to evaluate your child's readiness for toilet training and make specific recommendations for helping your child to be more independent. The goal is to provide you with useful ideas and tools that will help you decide the toileting approach that will benefit your child the most and lead to a lifetime of independence.

When Should Toilet Training Begin?

Bladder and bowel control do not happen magically—they are learned (Latham, 1990). Each child has to learn a complex sequence of behaviors that include knowing when, where, and how to relieve his bladder and bowel. At a pretty early age, typically before they turn five years old, children are expected to avoid accidents by using the toilet during the day for urine and bowel movements and to control elimination at night. It has been reported that children typically learn to use the toilet around the age of thirty months to three years old. Most professionals argue that parents should not be too concerned about a child's slow development with toileting unless the child reaches his third birthday and little or no progress is evident. By age five, nearly 85 percent of all children are toilet trained (Latham, 1990) and by age six, nearly all children have complete bladder and bowel control during the day and night.

We do not know of any research showing the typical age of bladder and bowel control for children with autism, but we think it is safe to say that it is much later than the general population. This delay is probably not a result of physical limitations so much as it is part of the general struggle to learn new things. Because all areas of development tend to develop more slowly with children with autism, it makes sense for you to consider starting toilet training with your child a little later than might be expected for the general population. There may be some exceptions to this "rule." If your child is showing signs of readiness, including getting upset by a soiled diaper, beginning to communicate when his diaper is dirty, or sometimes going to the toilet on his own, you should consider toilet training your child. However, it has been our experience that most children with autism, by age six or seven, can acquire significant bladder and bowel control with only occasional accidents. So, in addition to taking into consideration the typical age at which children learn toileting, there are a number of other variables that you should weigh before concluding that your child is ready.

Look for Subtle Signs of Readiness

Look for signs that your child is interested. Consider the following:
- Does he quickly remove his diaper after wetting or soiling it, suggesting that he does not like the wetness against his skin?
- Does your child "hide" or otherwise move to a more private area to urinate or move his bowels?
- Does he attempt to place the soiled or wet diaper into the toilet?
- Does he watch or try to imitate the toileting routines of his siblings or you?
- Does he sit on the toilet without eliminating and look to you to praise him?

- Does he wake up with a dry diaper?
- When he is not wearing a diaper, does he find a diaper and hold it to himself to urinate?
- Does he go for long periods of time without voiding urine or bowel movements?
- Does he tell you or otherwise indicate during or after that he's urinated or moved his bowels?

There are probably many other subtle signs of potential readiness that we have not listed. Many of these behaviors are an excellent signal of readiness and should be recognized as such, and incorporated into some early training efforts. When you observe your child showing interest in the toilet, praise him, label his actions (or the actions of others), and get your child to imitate the word, or exchange the picture of the "potty" if he can. For most children with autism, this level of instruction alone is unlikely to result in your child's learning to use the toilet, but it may help to form some early understanding of the basic component skills.

If your child seems to enjoy the social interactions that occur during diaper changes, that may be good and bad news. Obviously, it is great to observe that your child is socially engaged with you. It also may be a good sign that your attention may serve as a powerful reward (super reward) during systematic toilet training. On the other hand, these interactions may reduce the child's motivation to be more independent. His attitude may be: Why give up a good thing? Although it may be difficult for you, begin to de-emphasize the playful quality of interactions during diapering. It may be helpful if you begin to use a more neutral expression and tone when he has a dirty diaper and show exaggerated happiness when the diaper is found clean.

Determine Your Child's Bladder and Bowel Elimination Patterns

Infants void their bladder and bowel as soon as it begins to fill; this is a reflex (Bettison, 1982). The bladder and bowel capacity are so small that infants void small amounts very frequently. However in the next couple of years, children begin to feel the sensation of a full bladder or bowel and begin holding back for a brief period of time before eliminating. By the end of the second year, their capacity to hold urine and stool has doubled and less voiding occurs. Some of the first signs of control are when the child shows discomfort (crosses legs and fidgets) or moves to a more private area. Sometimes children with disabilities, including autism, fail to demonstrate awareness that their bladder is full, making toilet training more challenging. One of the first things that you need to do is acquire a better understanding of how often your child is voiding urine and bowel.

We recommend that you observe whether your child is beginning to show regular and predictable patterns of elimination. This information will help you measure how often your child is going to the bathroom and may be an estimate of his physical readiness. It will also help to identify the times of day that he is most likely to have a bowel or bladder movement. Record this data, as this information can be used later to determine the frequency and timing of instructions to sit on the toilet. If you can catch him at the right moment, the chances of urine and/or stool finding their way into the toilet is increased dramatically. Sometimes, even the child is surprised to learn what he has just accomplished!

Detecting patterns of urine elimination may be more difficult, especially if your child is still in diapers. Making a note each time your child is wet or dry upon diaper changes may be helpful, but unless you change diapers very frequently, he may eliminate more than once into his diaper before you notice. A more accurate way of documenting your child's elimination patterns (bowel and bladder) is to check him every thirty minutes and simply record whether he is wet or soiled. This is called a "dry-pants check" and we recommend using this method for establishing a baseline of your child's patterns of elimination and as a training technique.

A dry-pants check typically involves reaching down the back of the diaper or under a leg to check for wetness. Dry-pants checks could also be completed by changing from infant-style diapers to toddler-training diapers, which usually have designs or characters that disappear when your child has had an accident. To complete a dry-pants check in a toddler-training diaper, simply check to see whether the images have disappeared. If you find that your child has eliminated each time you check, you should change the dry-pants check interval and check more frequently. Table 10-1 provides a detailed list of steps for conducting a dry-pants check.

Each time you conduct a dry-pants check, summarize the event on the data sheet shown in Table 10-2, page 132. We will show you later how this data sheet can also be used during training to monitor progress. For now, look only at the first two columns: "Time" and "Dry-pants check and child voided." After conducting each dry-pants check, indicate when you did the check in the first column and in the second column indicate whether the diaper or pants contained urine (U), bowel (B), or both (C). If pants were dry, circle "N" for nothing. Continue this procedure over four or five days or until you are confident that you have a fairly typical measure of his urine and bowel patterns.

■ Table 10-1   Steps for Conducting Dry-Pants Check during the Initial Assessment Period

1. Approach your child and in a pleasant voice explain what you are about to do, e.g., "We are going to check and see if you have dry pants."

2. Place the child's hand within your hand and gently check the exterior of his pants first, then the interior, until you have assessed the condition of his clothing.

3. If he is dry, acknowledge that he is dry in a neutral voice and record this data.

4. If he is wet or soiled, acknowledge in a neutral tone that he is wet or soiled and record this data.

5. Quickly and with little comment, change the child's underwear or Pull-Up and pants.

6. Have your child return to what he was doing and repeat sequence every ten minutes.

■ **Table 10-2** **Data Sheet for Tracking Bowel and Bladder Elimination**

Dry Pants and Toilet Training Data Sheet

Child's Name: _____   Date: _____

U = urine   B = bowel   C = combined urine & bowel   N = nothing

Time	Dry-pants check and child voided (accident):	Child was prompted to toilet and voided:	Child self-initiated sitting on toilet and voided:
	U B C N	U B C N	U B C N
	U B C N	U B C N	U B C N
	U B C N	U B C N	U B C N
	U B C N	U B C N	U B C N
	U B C N	U B C N	U B C N
	U B C N	U B C N	U B C N
	U B C N	U B C N	U B C N
	U B C N	U B C N	U B C N
	U B C N	U B C N	U B C N
	U B C N	U B C N	U B C N
	U B C N	U B C N	U B C N
	U B C N	U B C N	U B C N
	U B C N	U B C N	U B C N
	U B C N	U B C N	U B C N
	U B C N	U B C N	U B C N

Is There a Medical Condition that Might Interfere with Learning?

Children with significant delays in many areas (e.g., language, socialization, and learning) may experience temporary and chronic medical conditions that may also interfere with efforts to toilet train. We recommend that you consult with your child's pediatrician before beginning a toilet training program so that you can rule out any undiagnosed medical condition (e.g., kidney infection or immature bladder function). Provide the physician with some of the information that you have gathered (e.g., number of times your child urinates a day). It is also important to consider any physical limitations, such as ambulation (getting up and moving about) and fine motor delays that may prevent your child from achieving full independence. A significant deficit, such as the inability to physically pull ones pants up and down or wipe independently, may not prevent you from going forward with a toilet training program, but special accommodations may be needed and your expectations for level of independence may have to be adjusted.

Does Your Child Have Most of the Component Readiness Skills?

Table 10-3, page 134, provides a list of skills we believe are important for determining readiness for toilet training. Many of the items on this list must be performed only at a very basic level, such as responding to the one-step instructions "stand up" and "sit down." (Again, we refer you to Appendix C in this book as well as other valuable resources in the reference section.) Others on the list are more complex (e.g., discriminating wet and dry) and are important for long-term independence but may not be required for learning to control one's bladder and bowel. As you complete this checklist, think "outside of the box" and consider all the ways that your child may communicate understanding of a specific concept. For example, your child may not yet be able to label "clean vs. dirty" or "wet vs. dry," but if he consistently removes his clothing when soiled, he probably has a basic understanding of these concepts. Use the comments section to document your reasoning when a simple "yes" or "no" is not sufficient. It may be useful to have your child's teacher or other caregivers also complete this chart and make comments. Combining reports may produce a more accurate picture of your child's overall abilities in varying settings and over a longer period of the day.

It is our view that some of these basic skills may be required before you begin, but not all. Examine each of the competencies in Table 10-3 and decide whether your child has a rudimentary understanding of the concept. If your child has four out of the nine readiness skills, he might be ready to begin training. You can always provide support when and where it is needed (e.g., help your child to maneuver on and off the toilet) and you can work on greater independence in the weak areas later. With practice, it is possible that some areas will get better without the benefit of extensive direct instruction.

Table 10-3 A Checklist of Important Component Skills That May Help to Determine Readiness			
Your child has the ability to:	**YES**	**NO**	**COMMENTS**
1. Retain urine for at least an hour without accidents.			
2. Show a predictable and regular schedule of bowel movements.			
3. Sit on the toilet for at least three minutes without the need for frequent prompting and praise. (This can include looking at a book or playing with a simple toy.)			
4. Follow simple one-step directions.			
5. Locate the bathroom independently.			
6. Locate and maneuver on and off the toilet independently.			
7. Pull pants up and down with little or no help.			
8. Discriminate wet and dry.			
9. Communicate need to use the toilet using words, signs, pictures, or voice output device.			

■ Is Everyone Ready?

Another sign of readiness has nothing to do with your child directly. And that is: Are you and your child's other caregivers ready? Planning and conducting a comprehensive toilet training program requires a great level of commitment from all the important people in your child's life. In particular, it will take a lot of your time and emotional and physical energy. Make sure you are in it for the long-haul;

starting and stopping only to start again may be the worse thing you can do. If your child has multiple accidents and you discontinue toilet training, you may have just taught your child that having accidents is an effective way to get what he wants—to be away from the toilet and back in diapers.

In some instances, you may have no choice but to make toilet training a priority, particularly if bladder and bowel control is required for admission or continuation in a preschool, school, or community program. Work closely with your child's teacher to ensure that the school staff is willing to consistently apply important elements of the plan all day. Before beginning toilet training, we recommend that you hold a family-professional meeting (everyone that is involved with your child's day-to-day care) to discuss the program and discern the level of commitment. Share all of the data that you have collected and encourage them to obtain data at school as well. When you are ready to begin, pick a date that makes sense for everyone, considering scheduled vacations and holidays that may hamper your best-laid plans. You might also consider whether any highly anticipated events or stressful family activities might interfere with toilet training (e.g., moving to a new home or the birth of a sibling).

> Before beginning toilet training, we recommend that you hold a family-professional meeting (everyone that is involved with your child's day-to-day care) to discuss the program and discern the level of commitment.

Preparing the Context for Learning

There is a great deal of planning and preparation that has to be done before you begin. As trite as it may seem, one of the most important decisions you'll make involves the toilet itself. The commercial market has an ample selection of children's toilets as well as adaptors for the standard family toilet. As we have mentioned before, accommodations may be required, but whenever you use one, it creates the possibility that your child will be unable to respond appropriately in a more natural context. In this case, generalization from a stand-alone children's toilet to the standard family toilet could be a problem. We recommend that you try to minimize problems with generalization by simply using the family bathroom toilet and, if necessary, purchasing one of the child-sized toilet seats that can replace or lie upon the manufacturer's seat. In addition, a step stool should be available to help your child get on and off the toilet and to provide something to push against when he is forcing a bowel movement. In another attempt to ease generalization and promote independence and success, we recommend that boys sit for both urine and bowel elimination. You can teach your son to stand to urinate after the skills have been acquired.

Next, be sure that your child is able to get himself (ambulate) without distractions and obstacles to and from the bathroom. Remove or place out of reach sundries, medications, and other supplies from the bathroom. In the beginning, you may also want to remove the toilet paper from its dispenser and place it out of reach so your child isn't tempted to fiddle with it. You can provide tissue as needed and wait until later to teach the proper use of toilet paper. Also, gather the sup-

■ Table 10-4 List of Supplies and Actions Needed for Toilet Training	
Items to Get and Things to Do	**Check when accomplished**
1. Container to store, organize, and transport all materials	
2. Clipboard to secure programs and data sheets	
3. Instructional Plan, data sheets, and pencil	
4. Instructional materials and toys that can be used to engage child	
5. Clock or watch	
6. Rubber gloves	
7. Cleaning supplies including antibacterial spray and paper towels	
8. Child-sized toilet seat	
9. Child height step stool	
10. Soap and hand towels	
11. Small toys or snacks to use as rewards	
12. Highly preferred drinks (juice, flavored-water) to increase fluid intake	
13. Cloth underpants (ten to twelve pairs) with elastic waistbands	
14. Pants with elastic waistbands	
15. Remove any obstacles and distractions in path to bathroom	
16. Remove toilet paper from immediate reach of child	

plies and materials that will be needed ahead of time (use the checklist provided in Table 10-4). You might consider limiting your child to certain rooms (e.g., the bathroom, kitchen, and hallway) during the training hours, especially if you are concerned about accidents damaging furniture or flooring.

Finally—and we believe this is very important—get rid of the diapers. For many reasons, if you keep your child in diapers while you are training, it may inhibit the development of independent toileting skills. Diapers mask the sense of wetness for your child and make it challenging for you to know whether an accident has occurred. We strongly encourage you to put your child in underpants. It is important that you do <u>not</u> allow your child to become comfortable having toileting accidents once you begin training. If he becomes comfortable in a soiled diaper, some of his motivation to toilet train will be lost. If a compromise is necessary, isolate

Get rid of the diapers when you are training!

specific times of the day and places in your house for toilet training and use underpants during those times. During other times and in other places, use a diaper. We would prefer to see you set a specific schedule and stick to it than engage in a random schedule of diaper time/underwear time. Some clever parents use waterproof mattress pads, shower curtain liners, plastic table cloths, or tarps on the furniture or carpeting to minimize the damage to household items. Be creative!

Establishing a Consistent Routine

The first action in teaching independent toileting is to establish a consistent toileting routine for your child. By that we mean that your child should expect the same sequence of steps each time he uses the toilet. The events or behaviors that take place in this routine can be conceptualized in the form of a task analysis like the sequence that we have presented in Table 10-5 on the next page. Although this sequence could be taught in a forward or backward chain like we discussed in Chapter 6, we do not recommend it. We simply recommend that you follow this sequence every time, providing whatever level of prompts is needed to get through the sequence. At this point in time, the focus should be on Step 7—How do you teach your child to eliminate in the toilet? As you proceed through the steps each time, informally try to fade prompts and praise your child for his increasingly more independent display of the component skills. We recommend that girls and boys sit on the toilet for urine and bowel training at the beginning. Once successful urine and bowel movement elimination patterns have been established, then it is recommended to move boys to a standing position for urination.

Traditional Toilet Training

Many parent books and materials (e.g., Eisenberg, Murkoff & Hathaway, 1994; Sears & Sears, 1993) recommend an approach that relies heavily upon the child's strong motivation to be more independent. We will refer here to

■ Table 10-5   A Task Analysis for Toilet Training

SKILL TARGET: INDEPENDENT TOILETING

Step	Component Skill
1	Physically recognizes need to eliminate
2	Initiates or communicates to adult the need to use bathroom
3	Locates and ambulates to bathroom
4	Enters bathroom
5	Pushes pants or skirt and underpants down
6	Sits on toilet
7	Eliminates in toilet
8	Wipes self with toilet tissue
9	Pulls up underpants and other clothing
10	Flushes toilet
11	Moves to sink to wash and dry hands
12	Leaves bathroom and returns to task

this approach as "traditional toilet training." According to many experts, toilet training begins as soon as the child initiates some toileting actions on his own (e.g., spontaneously sits on the toilet). Once some initiations have occurred, the parent is then encouraged to use teachable moments, such as transitions (i.e., leaving the house or finishing lunch) or moments when their child shows physical signs of discomfort (e.g., crossing legs and fidgeting), to remind their child to use the toilet. When the child successfully uses the toilet, parents are encouraged to praise their child and reward him with stickers and such. If an accident occurs, the parents are instructed to simply change the child's pants with little or no comment.

As the above description indicates, traditional toilet training is a pretty flexible approach that may look a little different each time it is applied. Although there may be some children with autism who will respond favorably to this approach, it is a rare occasion. First, it assumes that the child will explicitly or implicitly communicate that he is ready to toilet. Unfortunately, many children with autism are unable to communicate basic needs. It also depends upon a highly motivated and social child who is eager to please his parents and continuously strives to learn new things. Again, this does not describe many children with autism. We do not recommend that parents of children with autism try this approach. So what are your alternatives when the traditional approach does not work or you choose not to approach it this way?

■ Systematic Toilet Training

Unlike the traditional approach, systematic toilet training relies heavily upon careful assessment and planning, a high degree of structure, and active parent involvement. Since children with autism often respond best to structure and routine, the systematic method may be the logical choice for your child. Additionally, the systematic approach breaks the complex skill of toileting into many small steps for learning—an approach also found to be important for children with autism. Within a systematic approach, we will discuss two different methods, i.e., *schedule training* and *intensive training*.

Schedule Training

This is the easiest form of systematic training and we often recommend trying it first to see if it works before moving to an intensive program. It consists of three primary parts:

1. Scheduled opportunities for toileting based upon an assessment of your child's elimination patterns;
2. Dry-pants checks; and
3. Gradually extending the length of time between scheduled opportunities for toileting.

Now let's refer back to our opening description of the Cole family and their son, Jason. As you may recall, Mr. and Mrs. Cole are concerned that Jason might be rejected from pre-kindergarten because he is not toilet trained. After studying various methods for toilet training, Mr. and Mrs. Cole decide to begin with schedule training and move to a more intensive approach if it becomes necessary. They begin with the following goal for learning: "*With occasional reminders from his parents and preschool teacher to use the toilet, Jason will have no more than one accident each day for three consecutive days.*" Although the goal does not specify complete independence, everyone agrees that if Jason learns to use the toilet most of the time and has few accidents, it will be a wonderful achievement given his age (four years old) and disability. His parents choose to wait until Jason is a little older to work to remove all cues for him to use the toilet.

The Coles decide to begin the program at home and concentrate their efforts on the period of time from getting out of bed in the morning until 3:00 p.m. in the afternoon. Although they realize it will be a big undertaking, they acknowledge that the program should be conducted from the moment Jason rises in the morning until he goes to bed at night. Mr. and Mrs. Cole take our advice to remove Jason's diapers and use regular underwear until 3:00 p.m. each day, but use diapers on him during the night.

■ Table 10-6   Steps for Conducting Scheduled Opportunities for Jason's Toileting

1. Mr. Cole set a timer for thirty minutes (based on initial assessment data).

2. When the timer rang, Mr. Cole moved toward Jason and got his attention by saying his name. The Coles decided to have Jason point to a photograph of the toilet to indicate his need to go to the bathroom. A photograph or line drawing, or instructing the child to say or imitate "potty," for example, are all acceptable ways to communicate. The goal is for Jason to eventually use the photograph to signal that he needs to use the bathroom.

3. Mr. Cole showed Jason the photograph of the toilet, gestured toward the photograph and used hand-over-hand physical guidance to help him point to the picture to communicate that he needed to use the toilet. (Their initial assessment data indicated that much of the time he *did* have a need to use the toilet.) This and other prompts were faded slowly using an approach similar to that provided in Table 10-10.

4. Once he pointed (prompted or unprompted), Jason was praised ("Nice asking to use the toilet") and instructed to go sit on the toilet, again using a verbal instruction ("Jason, go to the bathroom") and pointing to the bathroom while gently guiding.

5. Once in the bathroom, Mr. Cole gestured toward the toilet for Jason to sit down and used gentle prompting to ensure compliance (verbal instructions were minimized at this point).

6. Mr. Cole required that Jason sit on the toilet for three minutes or until he voided, whichever came first. If he voided in the toilet, Mr. Cole gave him a super reward. If he did not void by the time the three minutes were up, Mr. Cole would say "Nice trying" in a fairly neutral voice and instruct Jason to stand up.

7. Mr. Cole continued to use gestures and gentle prompts through the rest of the sequence (see Table 10-5).

8. Jason was then told that he could leave the bathroom.

9. If Jason voided during the three minutes on the toilet, the timer was reset to thirty minutes. If he failed to void, the timer was set for fifteen minutes.

Next, the Coles conduct a baseline assessment to determine how often bladder and bowel accidents are occurring. Using the data sheet that we provided in Table 10-2, they conduct a dry-pants check every thirty minutes. They follow the steps we provided in Table 10-1 using a neutral, matter-of-fact demeanor. They gather data over several days and examine the information for any clear patterns. Mr. and Mrs. Cole discover that Jason wets his pants on average every hour, but the time between voiding is sometimes as short as thirty minutes and as long as an hour and a half. They also find that he typically has one bowel movement a day, within a couple hours after lunch. Based on this information, they decide to play it safe and set a toilet training interval of every thirty minutes. Table 10-6 provides a description of how the toilet training unfolded.

Initially, Mr. and Mrs. Cole needed to use a lot of prompts to get Jason to complete all of the steps of the program. In the beginning, Jason also did not want to stay on the toilet for the full three minutes, so his parents had to praise and use food rewards for staying on the toilet. After about the third day, it finally happened—Jason urinated in the toilet. You could hear the screams and hoots a block away! In addition to his parents' praise, hugs, and kisses, Jason was also immediately rewarded with his favorite candy—the super reward.

Along with the thirty minute toilet schedule, the Coles applied another important component—the instructional dry-pants checks. These were more than simply opportunities to gather information; these were now opportunities to reward desirable behavior and give corrective feedback. Table 10-7, below, provides a revised version of the dry-pants check sequence that we initially showed you in Table 10-1. Following the instructions provided in Table 10-7, Mr. and Mrs. Cole conducted a dry-pants check every ten minutes. If Jason was discovered to be wet during one of the dry-pants checks, the timer was reset to another full thirty minutes once his clothes were changed.

■ Table 10-7 Steps for Conducting Dry-Pants Checks during Training

1. Approach and in a pleasant voice explain what you are about to do, e.g., "We are going to check to see if you have dry pants."

2. Place the child's hand within your hand and gently check the exterior of his pants first, then the interior, until you have assessed the condition of his clothing.

3. If he is dry, praise enthusiastically (e.g., "Wow! You have dry pants!") and offer a super reward.

4. If he is wet, help him to feel the area again, and then provide corrective feedback in a firm voice (e.g., "You have wet pants"). Indicate that he has not earned the super reward, and quickly change his pants with little or no social interaction. Require that he apply as much effort as he can in changing his clothes, even if he has never had to help before.

5. Have your child return to what he was doing and repeat this sequence every ten minutes.

The Coles consistently maintained a record of dry-pants checks and successful toileting events using the data sheet in Table 10-2. Each day they used a new sheet. When they instructed him to use the toilet, they recorded the time of the incident (sitting on the toilet) and recorded whether elimination occurred and what kind (urine or bowel). They also continued to record dry-pants checks on the same sheet. Within and across days, they compared the number of toileting accidents to the number of successes. In spite of their best efforts, Jason rarely eliminated in the toilet and often was wet when the dry-pants checks were conducted. Although the

Coles felt they had made some progress—for example, physical prompts were rarely required to get Jason to and from the toilet—the number of accidents remained high. After about four weeks of trying, the Coles decided to try a more intensive approach. Depending on your child's typical rate of learning, it may be appropriate to wait more than four weeks before intensifying your approach.

Intensive Training

Intensive toilet training typically has six basic components:

1. a dedicated time and place for training;
2. frequent scheduled opportunities for toileting;
3. increased fluid intake;
4. dry-pants checks;
5. systematic fading of prompts; and
6. reinforcement of successes.

Table 10-8 provides a list of things that need to be done in preparation for intensive toilet training. As you can see, the first thing to do is identify an area in or near the bathroom for training. Typically, a large block of continuous time is set aside for training and toilet training becomes the primary goal for learning. We recommend that at least four hours be set aside each day for toilet training and that all other activities be secondary. Although there are some opportunities to interact with your child while waiting, the focus should be on toileting. We recommend placing chairs for you and your child in the bathroom or just outside the bathroom door, with the toilet clearly visible to the child and no obstructions between the child's chair and the toilet. Although this may sound extraordinary, it is a nearly errorless approach with scientifically demonstrated effectiveness (Foxx & Azrin, 1973).

We recommend that your child be in regular underpants—not diapers, Pull-ups, or thickly padded cotton training pants. Initially, we suggest that your child

---

■ Table 10-8   Things to Do in Preparation for Intensive Toilet Training

1. (Refer again to Table 10-4 for supplies to gather.)

2. Identify area for child to sit near bathroom.

3. Identify possible reinforcers (food and toys).

4. Identify variety of fluids that child will drink.

5. Make sure child is in regular cotton underwear.

6. Make available some simple activities that the child has already mastered so that he can remain occupied between toileting trials.

7. Make sure the child is wearing easy to pull up and down pants or skirt (i.e., with an elastic waistband) without fasteners.

8. If your child gets upset when asked to sit on the toilet, consider running a few trials in which he is instructed to walk to the toilet, sit for two or three seconds, and rewarded for following instructions.

■ Table 10-9 Intensive Toilet Training Sequence

1. Direct child to sit down in the chair you've set out in view of the toilet.

2. Sit yourself in the chair opposite your child.

3. Give child as much fluid as he will drink while seated in the chair.

4. Wait one minute.

5. Direct child to walk to toilet using a verbal instruction, gesture, and gentle physical guidance (see Phase 1 in Table 10-10 for further explanation).

6. Direct child to pull down pants and then sit on the toilet using a gesture and gentle physical guidance (try to avoid verbal prompts from this point forward).

7. When child voids, give super reward and praise while seated, then direct him to stand.

8. If child does not void within three minutes of sitting on the toilet, direct him to stand using a gesture and gentle physical guidance. Neutrally state, "You didn't have to pee."

9. Direct child back to chair using a gesture and gentle physical guidance.

10. After five minutes of sitting, conduct dry-pants check.

11. Check pants every five minutes.

12. After thirty minutes, begin the sequence of steps again, starting with Step 3.

(Adapted and printed with permission from Foxx & Azrin, 1973, *Toilet training persons with developmental disabilities*. Harrisburg, PA: Help Services Press)

wear only underpants, a short shirt that will stay out of the way when he sits, and socks for warmth. After some success, pants or a skirt can be added but they should be easy to pull up and down (i.e., with an elastic waistband) and without fasteners.

Similar to scheduled training, in intensive training you need to give your child many opportunities to use the toilet. The bladder training sequence has a thirty minute cycle (see Table 10-9). First, your child is encouraged to drink as much fluid as he will drink. Over the course of each day, this will significantly increase the probability of elimination in the toilet. If your child refuses to increase fluid intake, give him salty snacks and reassess preferred drinks. It is recommended that the increased fluids be discontinued at least two hours before bedtime, so as to avoid nighttime accidents. Once again, it is acceptable to place a diaper or Pull-Up on your child during the night-time hours. You will then need to address night-time toileting as a separate task.

Periodically praise your child for sitting on the toilet, but avoid engaging in a lot of social interaction. Remember that independence is the goal, so it is wise to minimize social stimulation that your child may become dependent upon for success with toileting. Your child should not be reading, playing with toys, or interacting socially with you while he is sitting on the toilet. Ultimately, he should not be dependent upon your prompts and cues to use the toilet. Initiation should be a result of his awareness of a full bladder or bowel. If he voids in the toilet, give him enthusiastic praise and a super reward, direct him to stand and return to the chair. If your child fails to void in the toilet after three minutes, direct him to return to the chair, while saying, "You didn't have to pee."

During the remaining portion of the thirty minute interval (probably about eighteen to twenty minutes remain), while you are seated in the chairs, you can engage him in some simple tasks that are mildly stimulating and easy for him to accomplish (e.g., he plays quietly with simple toys or you read to him). Again, he should focus on the physical awareness of his bladder and bowel, not you and the materials. Every five minutes, conduct a dry-pants check as we described in Table 10-7. After the thirty minutes is up, begin the entire sequence again. We recommend that this intensive training sequence be used for at least four hours daily.

Fading Prompts

This combination of fluid intake, dry-pants checks, and rewards continues until your child is having few accidents and is consistently voiding in the toilet. You should be able to see success within a few days. Once he has accomplished a couple of successive days with one or no accidents per day, we recommend expanding the toilet schedule from thirty minutes to forty-five minutes while gradually replacing items of clothing to be worn during the remainder of training (to aid generalization). When he has once again had success on a forty-five minute schedule for three consecutive days, expand it to one hour. At this point, you also need to begin fading prompts, as outlined in Table 10-10. As he continues to progress, move the chair farther away from the bathroom and eventually eliminate the chair all together and return to a normal schedule of activities.

◼ Reinforce Successes

Reinforcement for successes with the toilet and for keeping clothes dry and unsoiled is essential for toilet training to be successful. The reinforcers, or super re-

wards, that you choose should be highly preferred by your child and restricted solely for use with toilet training. Because bowel control sometimes takes a little longer to learn, it may also be helpful to identify one highly-prized reinforcer for urination and another even more highly-prized reinforcer for successful bowel movements. You may have to conduct periodic reinforcer assessments (refer back to Chapter 5) to ensure that you are using the most effective rewards.

In our clinical practice, we have found it helpful to keep the reinforcer in the bathroom, in view, but out of reach. For some children, this is an effective motivator. If your child becomes pre-

■ Table 10-10 Recommended Sequence for Fading Prompts

PHASE	LEVEL OF PROMPT	EXAMPLE
1	Verbal instruction + gesture + touch or gentle physical guidance	Parent says, "[Child's name], go to the bathroom" and points to the bathroom while touching child's shoulder or gently guiding to the toilet.
2	Verbal instruction + gesture	Parent says, "[Child's name], go to the bathroom" and points to the bathroom.
3	Reduced verbal + gesture	Parent says, "[Child's name], bathroom" and points to the bathroom.
4	Further reduced verbal + gesture	Parent says, "Bathroom" and points to the bathroom.
5	No verbal + gesture	Parent points to bathroom and motions with head.
6	Reduced gesture	Parent points to bathroom with arm partially extended and motions with head.
7	Further reduced gesture	Parent motions with head toward bathroom.

(Adapted and printed with permission from Foxx & Azrin, 1973, *Toilet training persons with developmental disabilities.* Harrisburg, PA: Help Services Press)

occupied with getting the reinforcer, then the reinforcer may need to be hidden out of view until the point at which it is delivered. We have found that some children are especially motivated to work for rewards that are wrapped in colorful paper or hidden in a lunch bag.

Many children with autism appear to enjoy watching the water swirl downward as the toilet flushes. This can be a good thing *and* a bad thing. For some children, earning the privilege of flushing the toilet can be a huge motivator. However, since the flushing lever is often right next to the child, some children will repeatedly reach and flush. There are also children who like to throw things in the toilet before they flush. In short, if you chose to use flushing as a reinforcer, you have to restrict the child's ability to flush the toilet to only those occasions after he has successfully voided in the toilet. If flushing serves as a reinforcer for your child, it would be helpful to assume that any time your child is near the toilet, he will try to flush the toilet. We recommend physically blocking the attempt to flush and gently guiding your child's hands into a more appropriate waiting activity (e.g., hands on lap). In the most challenging situation, the water to the toilet can be temporarily turned off (most toilets have an easy to turn valve under the toilet tank) while you are working on toileting and appropriate flushing can be introduced at a later time.

Accidents Happen

Nobody's perfect and everyone has accidents as they learn to use the toilet. In fact, accidents are almost as important as successes because they help children learn the difference between acceptable and unacceptable behaviors. This is where your vigilance becomes so important. As the implementer of toilet teaching, it is your responsibility to watch carefully for accidents and attempt to turn them into successes. If your child is dressed only in a t-shirt and cotton underpants, you should be able to view the beginnings of an accident right away. If your child begins to have an accident, try to mildly startle your child by saying his name or the word "Hey!" loudly. This should make your child's muscles contract thereby stopping the flow of urination or the release of the bowel movement. You should then immediately direct your child to the toilet so that he can finish eliminating in the appropriate place. If he completes the elimination in the toilet, you should consider that incident of elimination a success on the data sheet, rather than an accident. However, if the startle technique does not work and he voids in his pants, it is considered an accident and should be scored as such. If your child has some accidents (five or fewer), but over time, the data show that they are decreasing, continue your current toileting approach. Children should not have more than five accidents per day. If that is the case, your procedures should be examined and changes to the toileting protocol should be made and further individualized to your child.

> If your child has some accidents (five or fewer), but over time the data show that they are decreasing, continue your current toileting approach.

If your child is having frequent accidents and you are finding it challenging to catch him in the act of urinating in his pants, you might consider the use of a pants alarm (Azrin & Foxx, 1971). Pants alarms are safe and easy to use (Mercer, 2003). They can be sewn into your child's clothing: the alarm is attached to the pants or shirt and the sensor is attached where urination is most likely to be detected on the underpants. The alarm sounds when urination is detected and serves to alert the person that the urine is releasing, thereby teaching him to recognize the feeling of having a full bladder and potentially serving to startle the person enough to hold the urination until he reaches the toilet. Most pants alarms are intended for use during nighttime to detect bedwetting, but can be used during daytime toileting sessions (Lancioni & Markus, 1999).

Nighttime Toilet Training

Nighttime control is a different skill than daytime control and may be learned much later by children with and without developmental disabilities. Nighttime control requires a strong bladder, the ability to sense when your bladder is full, and the ability to sometimes wake yourself and independently eliminate in the toilet. Not an easy sequence of sub-skills. Toileting is difficult enough to teach when your child is awake; night training is a real challenge for many children and parents.

The first thing we recommend to parents is that you consider whether you are ready to begin. You'll likely experience many interrupted nights until you are successful, so you must be highly motivated to start. Until you are ready, we recommend that you continue to have your child wear a diaper at night, even if he goes without diapers during the daylight hours.

When you are ready to begin nighttime toilet training, we recommend not using a diaper at night, just like the recommendation we made for daytime toilet training. Using a plastic mattress, waterproof mattress pad, or plastic sheets will help protect your child's bedding and shouldn't interfere with training. Your initial steps toward teaching your child nighttime control are pretty easy. First, reduce fluid intake during the late afternoon and evening hours and discontinue fluids altogether at least two hours before your child's normal bedtime. Make sure your child empties his bladder before going to bed. Before going to bed, ask your child to select a special super reward (e.g., a special breakfast or privilege to be completed in the morning) that he earns the mornings that he wakes up with a dry bed and pants. Also, review the steps to complete if your child wakes and needs to use the toilet. If these simple techniques are not enough, consider more intensive methods.

First, you need to know your child's pattern of bedwetting. We recommend that you conduct dry-bed/pants checks every thirty minutes after your child goes to sleep until you go to bed, extending your bedtime as late as is practical for you. Then resume dry-bed/pants checks every thirty minutes in the morning before he wakes up. In between, we realize that checking his pants every thirty minutes is pretty unrealistic, but ask yourself what you are capable of doing. For a few days, are you able to wake yourself and conduct a dry-pants check every sixty minutes? How about every seventy-five minutes? The more, the better. If you take notes, you should have a pretty good picture of his bed-wetting pattern within three to five days. It is not necessary to wake your child up for dry-bed/pants checks, but you need to change his pants when he is found wet so that when you conduct the next dry-pants check you can tell whether he has voided again. Analyze the data collected by looking for a consistent pattern of elimination (e.g., he typically voids once at night between 1:00 a.m. and 2:00 a.m.).

Once you have determined your child's common pattern of elimination, set your alarm clock so that you wake fifteen to thirty minutes before your child is likely to void. Slowly wake your child, giving him an opportunity to feel the sensation of a full bladder. When he wakes, instruct him with few or no words to use the toilet. Keep the lights low and minimize social interaction. Whether you deliver a reward at night depends on your child's progress with daytime toilet training. If you have decided to address day and nighttime toileting at the same time, then use the super reward during the day and night. If you have decided to wait to attempt nighttime training until all prompts and rewards have been faded during the day, then it would be appropriate to reward successful nighttime toilet use in the morning.

If your child wakes up in the morning with a dry bed, enthusiastically praise him and give him the super reward that you identified before going to bed. After several successive nights of success, move the middle of the night wake-up time a little later, giving him an opportunity to wake himself first. Initially, you may have to use a subtle technique of very gentle touching so that he gradually wakes and eventually opens his eyes and moves without much prompting from you. It has been our experience that many children who experience nighttime bedwetting also sleep extremely soundly and may not recognize the feeling of a full bladder. By extending the time fifteen to thirty minutes ahead each night, you give them an opportunity to wake up before you intervene and you are probably strengthening their bladder as well.

■ Some Common Problems with Toileting Training and Possible Solutions

My Child Won't Sit on the Toilet

It is not uncommon for children with autism to resist sitting on the toilet. As soon as you get them on the toilet, they are trying to crawl back off. If you keep trying, they eventually won't walk to the bathroom at all. First, make sure that the child feels secure on the toilet seat. Make sure it is not too big or too small, make sure his feet are firmly planted on the ground or a stool. Modify the seat if necessary by adding or removing other toileting seats.

The next step is to simply teach the child to approach and sit on the toilet. Don't worry about bladder and bowel training at this stage. Begin by making it as fun as possible. It might begin with a race to the bathroom door. Whomever gets there first and touches the door (and remember your child always wins) gets a super reward. After he is successfully accomplishing this, move farther into the bathroom and have him touch the toilet. Conduct many trials throughout the day. Next, have him walk or run to the bathroom and sit on the toilet with his clothing on. After he is successful at this step, then require that he pull his pants and underpants down and sit for only few seconds. Continue in this manner until he is a willing participant.

There are several books and videos for children that address toilet training. These might be helpful resources for modeling the toileting sequence. Siblings and parents should frequently model the toileting process for your child.

My Son's Urine Stream Goes Straight Up

First, attempt to teach your son to push and hold his penis down. Sometimes this is not as easy as it sounds, primarily because he'll want to use both hands for balancing securely on the toilet seat. (Remember, you start training boys sitting on the seat for urinating and later move to a standing position.) While somewhat messy, we've also had some success with placing a towel over the child's lap so that it deflects the urine down. Although a reasonable solution, you must be more vigilant to know when he is urinating so that you can immediately praise him and deliver the super reward if he is successful. Some children's toilet seats also can be purchased with a deflector for urine, but it would be more advantageous to teach your child to control his own urine stream. We have also had success in teaching children to "tuck" themselves down during urination. The least desirable alternative—but sometimes effective—is to have your son sit backward on the toilet. The shape of the toilet usually forces him to lean forward so the urine stream goes into the toilet.

My Child is Successfully Eliminating Urine but not Bowel

Successful bowel control may take longer than urine control. The best solution is to carefully analyze your child's pattern of bowel movements and try to catch them at the most likely time. This may require that he sit on the toilet for longer than three minutes. Also, observe your child frequently and if you catch him beginning to have an accident, startle him by saying his name loudly (or "Hey!") and quickly get him to the toilet and hope he'll finish there. In the beginning, even if only a small amount makes it into the toilet, praise enthusiastically and withhold corrective feedback for a soiled diaper. If a child is avoiding making bowel movements for long periods of time, talk with your pediatrician about medical interventions that might assist with bowel training. For example, it has been recommended that an enema be administered and the child placed on the toilet very frequently until they void (e.g., every fifteen minutes); however this is an extreme intervention and should be used only with close medical monitoring. We recommend that you consult your child's pediatrician before using this approach. Another, more natural approach, may be to include more fiber in your child's diet. You might also practice the pushing or grunting actions during motor imitation trials. Once your child has had one or two bowel movements in the toilet and receives praise and a super reward, the frequency of successes will increase.

My Child is Retaining Urine Until the Toilet Training Session is Over

There are some children who will go several hours without voiding and as soon as the toilet training session is over for the day and the diaper is back on, then they go! There are no easy solutions to this but you might consider lengthening sessions a couple more hours and increasing fluid consumption. We recommend that you consult with your child's physician before you extend the session or increase fluids.

Planning for Generalization

When your child demonstrates appropriate toileting in a variety of settings (e.g., home and school), with varied equipment (e.g., toilets vs. urinals) and with many different people (e.g., parents, grandparents, and teachers), you can conclude that the skill has been learned and "generalized." We talked about generalization a little in some of the previous chapters and we will discuss it in more detail in Chapter 11. For practical reasons (e.g., privacy), you cannot teach toileting in a variety of settings and with a number of people. Therefore, we teach in one setting and hope that it generalizes. When it does not, we then actively train in each desired context (i.e., setting, equipment, and people). Typically, once it has been learned in one context it takes much less time to ensure that it generalizes.

As we will discuss in Chapter 11, one of the first things you must do to program generalization is to make a list of all the places, people, and equipment that must be evaluated to determine if generalization has occurred. Once the skill is taught, you can then begin to test the occurrence or nonoccurrence of generalization to each of the new conditions. If newly acquired skills transfer only a little, then you must conduct additional training in additional settings, with a wider range of people, and using equipment found in other environments (e.g., automated flush toilets). Also, remember that any supports that you have added in the form of instructions, physical prompts, and rewards are okay when your child is just beginning, but must be faded in order for your child to be truly independent. Finally, make sure that your child's community of family, friends, and professionals support and reinforce his growing independence. If they continue to physically do things for him, there is little or no motivation for him to generalize and maintain newly acquired skills.

■ Summary

Toilet training a child with a significant disability will be one of the most challenging things you will attempt to accomplish. The good news is that thousands of children have successfully acquired bladder and bowel control and most have become independent at it. As we have indicated, traditional toilet training methods begin with an assumption that children are naturally interested and highly motivated to learn prior to any formal intervention. Although this certainly describes some children, it does not accurately describe many children with autism. It has been our experience that a successful approach must be very structured and systematically implemented. The two systematic approaches that we have described—schedule training and intensive training—are often very effective; however, they are labor and time intensive. It is highly likely that you may need a little help from someone who has implemented one or both of these strategies before. Begin by checking with your child's teacher to see what experiences he or she may be able to offer. There are also a number of toilet training resources that we have identified at the end of the book.

One generation plants the trees;
another gets the shade.
—Chinese Proverb

$\mathcal{P}$lanning for Generalization

The Marco Family

The Marcos are determined to teach their fifteen-year-old daughter, Anita, to dress herself independently. Although Anita provides some assistance with dressing, such as raising her arms to put on a blouse, she never initiates and rarely completes any steps on her own. To this end, the Marcos began by developing a detailed plan to teach Anita to put on a pullover shirt that did not require buttoning. After successfully teaching this skill, they assumed that Anita would be able to put on a blouse (as long as she was not required to button it) or a sweater with little or no help. But, surprisingly, they discovered that there was little or no transfer of learning from the pullover shirt to the blouse or sweater.

The Marcos learned that Anita experienced similar confusion when it came to putting on other articles of clothing. Anita learned to put on pants more quickly than she learned to put on underwear, but while she was able to pull up pants that had an elastic waistband, she struggled to pull up pants that had a fastener (even though she *was not expected to fasten it). It was the same story with socks and shoes. Although similar actions, each required direct teaching and little or no learning appeared to transfer from one skill to the other. Fortunately, Anita readily participated in dressing and, when instructed to get dressed, would happily respond for persons other than her parents.*

Must You Teach Everything?

As we have discussed previously, children without developmental disabilities seem to learn to dress themselves fairly easily. And once a child has learned some general principles about where arms and legs go, understands front from back and left from right, she learns how to apply these rules and in a short time can put on a wide variety of clothing. Along the way, the parents' job is to encourage and supervise to ensure that their son or daughter dresses appropriately for the day. This seems to be equally true for the development of personal hygiene, eating, and toileting skills.

For many families that have a child with disabilities, it is not so simple. As our example of Anita illustrates, children with autism may learn a new skill under one set of conditions and not generalize it to another situation. In fact, almost every skill may have to be individually taught and systematically linked to other learned skills. The good news is that for many children with ASD, after learning a new skill, the amount of teaching required to learn the next, similar skill, is often less. So in our example of Anita, Mr. and Mrs. Marco can expect that although the skills learned to put on a pullover shirt did not automatically transfer to putting on a sweater, they can take some comfort knowing that it may take less time to teach this additional related skill.

We have discussed generalization in several of the chapters in this book, but we feel it is important enough to talk about in a little more detail here. Although we have placed it at the end of the book, we do not want to mislead you into thinking it is the last thing you do. In fact, generalization should be one of the first things you consider before starting to teach, an ongoing consideration as your child learns, and the last thing you must ensure is accomplished before you conclude a job-well-done.

A newly learned skill is said to "generalize" when it is taught under one set of conditions (materials, people, and setting) and the child is able to apply the same skill in a different situation (different materials, people, and settings). For example, after learning to groom their hair with a brush, most children without autism quickly display the ability to use a comb (different material) to accomplish the

> A newly learned skill is said to "generalize" when it is taught under one set of conditions (materials, people, and setting) and the child is able to apply the same skill with different people, in a new place, and using other materials.

same thing and they are able to display this skill at school (different setting and people). In our example of Anita, her parents are dealing with a complex set of skills that we collectively call "dressing." Within each component skill (e.g., putting on a shirt), Anita may or may not demonstrate generalization to a variety of pullover shirts, persons other than her parents, and to a variety of places other than her bedroom. In short, generalization may not happen without some thoughtful planning and direct intervention by her parents.

Planning for Generalization

We recommend that before you begin to teach, take a few minutes to think about the matter of how to maximize generalization. Using the example of Anita, Mr. and Mrs. Marco wrote the following objective for learning: "With clothing arranged on her bed, Anita will dress (not including fasteners) with two or fewer prompts for three consecutive opportunities." When most of us think of dressing, we think about socks, underwear, pants, shoes, and a shirt. However, each article of clothing also has many forms (e.g., a shirt can be a blouse or pullover style and it can have long or short sleeves). Likewise, Anita may have to dress at home, school, and the local recreation center. And, she may have to respond to requests to dress from her parents, grandparents, teachers, and coaches. If Mr. and Mrs. Marco decide to use a particular set of clothing to teach the skill in Anita's bedroom, the objective may be achieved with little or no generalization to other clothing, places, or people. On the other hand, limiting the complexity of clothing and the variety of settings may help to promote initial learning. The key is to find the balance point that leads to the fastest learning but does not inadvertently restrict generalization. We will discuss this further in the paragraphs to follow.

In the example of Anita, the first step in addressing the matter of generalization is for Mr. and Mrs. Marco to simply list each form of clothing Anita needs to learn to put on and list the places that she will need to dress herself (e.g., home, school, Grandmother's house, and community swimming pool). In addition, they need to write down all of the caregivers

> The key is to find the balance point that leads to the fastest learning but does not inadvertently restrict generalization.

who come in contact with her in a typical day and week. Once all of these things are known, the full scope of the problem of planning for generalization becomes clearer and the Marcos have a decision to make. Do they plan from the beginning to include every form of clothing, location, and caregiver in hopes of maximizing generalization? Or, do they knowingly leave some scenarios out because teaching them all is simply not practical and may confuse Anita? (In Chapter 10 we gave the example of toilet training and argued that it would be impractical, even inappropriate, to teach in all potential situations where the skill will be needed.) Not surprisingly, the Marcos decide that it is not practical to teach Anita how to deal with every possible situation from the very beginning. Instead, they try to incorporate some basic strategies that have been shown to indirectly encourage expansion of a behavior beyond what is directly taught. If some generalization is not evident at that point, they will directly intervene where necessary. For example, if Anita fails to generalize how to dress and undress at the community swimming pool, her parents will directly teach her in that context. If she is not able to dress at her grandmother's house, they will incorporate Grandma into some of their training efforts. The following paragraphs will provide other useful alternatives and examples for programming generalization.

Some Specific Strategies for Encouraging Generalization

There are ways to teach self-help skills that may encourage greater generalization without having to teach everything the child needs to know directly (Stokes & Baer, 1977; Baer, 1999). Stokes and Baer (1977) identified several strategies that we have borrowed, modified some, and will present here. These should be considered before you begin any initial teaching. Most of these strategies are things that you apply from the beginning to encourage generalization. However, some professionals may advise that you restrict the range of materials, places, and people until your child is beginning to show some success at the skill that you are trying to teach. This approach may minimize your child's confusion.

Teach in the Most Natural Context with the Most Common Materials

All things being equal, the natural environment is the best place for instruction. This is something you can do from the beginning. For example, teaching a child to brush her teeth in the bathroom is the most natural environment. Doing so promotes generalization to other settings (in this case, bathrooms) because those environments are likely to contain similar equipment and materials (e.g., a mirror, vanity, and sink). If generalization fails across settings, one strategy is to bring some of the stimuli (people and materials) from the successful setting into the setting where generalization has not been realized. For example, if liquid soap is used at home and bar soap is used at school, learning to wash hands at home may not completely generalize to school. When generalization fails, you have the option of setting up the bathroom at school with similar materials (in this case, liquid soap) or introducing bar soap at home. Similarly, if handwashing is successful at home with you as the instructor but not at school with the classroom aide, then generalization may be achieved if you conduct a few sessions at school with the aide present then allow the aide to conduct sessions while you observe. Ensuring generalization may not take a lot of effort, but it often needs a little push.

Teach Lots of Examples

It is not unreasonable, and may be necessary, to restrict materials, settings, and instructors to a small number of things, places, and people— at least initially. This is often done to keep things simple and to avoid confusing the child. Although this may make sense on one level, as we mentioned before it may also inadvertently communicate to the child that this is the only place, person, and materials needed or important. The result can be a failure to generalize to a variety of non-instructional situations. You can avoid this potential snag by using many forms of materials, objects, and places. We recommend that you begin in a more restrictive situation, but as soon as the child is beginning to show progress (especially with her attention and motivation), begin to vary some of the materials, settings, and instructors a little. For example, this does not mean you will jump from teaching a short-sleeved pullover shirt to a long-sleeved button-down shirt, but you may begin to introduce a variety of pullover garments.

If the Marcos are to apply this approach with Anita, they will begin to vary the shoes, pants, socks, and shirts used each day. Although most of the instruction might occur in Anita's bedroom, they will also use the bathroom and other bedrooms to dress. Mrs. Marco can work with Anita on some days and Mr. Marco will pick up the task on other days. They can even get Anita's older sister involved. A little later, they might identify a couple of other settings outside the home where they feel comfortable conducting lessons. They still may hope for some generalization to public settings (e.g., the community swimming pool) without the benefit of direct instruction. This is not an unreasonable expectation. There is ample research demonstrating that most children generalize after three or four examples have been taught. For example, after learning the skill at home, Grandma's house, and school, Anita may dress herself in the clubhouse at the pool.

Vary the Things That Don't Matter

Stokes and Baer refer to a strategy called "teach loosely." We have taken the liberty of modifying their strategy a little by recommending that you frequently vary all of the small things that are irrelevant to helping your child generalize the skill that you are teaching. In fact, if you don't vary them, your child may incorrectly believe that they are important for defining their behavior. It is sort of the strategy of "teach many examples" gone wild. Whenever you teach you should use different materials, vary teachers, teach in more than one place, vary your tone of voice and choice of instructions, dress at different times of the day, vary reinforcers, teach in noisy and quiet conditions and do all of this as unpredictably as possible. In short, none of these things are really needed in order to accomplish most self-help skills— they are irrelevant (e.g., the time of day is irrelevant to completing the task of dressing). This is not to suggest that you teach using materials, places, or people that are not the most natural context for the target skill.

This may seem to contradict what we have been saying about starting slowly with one or maybe a few examples. Yes, it is a contradiction. But we decided to discuss it in part to demonstrate all of the things that are not really relevant to your child's ability to complete self-help tasks (e.g., time of day). The point to be made is that you should begin to vary these irrelevant things as soon as you can. It may take a little trial and error to know what works and doesn't work for your child.

Don't Introduce Things You Don't Need

Throughout this book we have recommended that you avoid introducing things that your child really doesn't need to successfully learn a new skill. The most common error is for parents to either talk too much or physically help too much. This error is understandable given your desire to help your child be successful as quickly as possible. But remember that the ultimate goal is to achieve the greatest level of independence possible for your child. If her parents start each day with: *"Anita, let's get dressed. Come over to the bed and put your clothes on. I know you can do it. Okay, get started. If you need help, let me know,"* their verbal prompts and encouragements become the cues to get dressed and Anita may need them forever. Therefore, we encourage you to minimize your words and actions as much as possible. There will be time after the task is done to talk.

Some professionals may encourage you to verbally label each of the items (e.g., toothpaste, toothbrush, water and so on) as you teach. We understand that from a language perspective, the materials used in completing self-help skills present wonderful teachable moments; however, you must set your priorities. There will be other opportunities to teach the names of things.

Fade Rewards

Rewards are necessary and important tools for teaching self-help skills, but they must be faded. We talked about how to fade reinforcers in Chapter 5 but we think it is worth repeating again here. Imagine if you had to praise your child forever for completing each and every step of toothbrushing. For some children, receiving rewards in one setting but not in another setting may be enough to prevent generalization. The easiest method is to slowly reduce reinforcers in the teaching setting until they are absent or less prominent. Another strategy to attempt when generalization fails is to reduce the amount and quality of reinforcers in the teaching setting and to provide the super reward in the generalization settings (at least temporarily). Your ultimate goal is to reduce the need for rewards that are delivered by someone else so that the child is motivated simply by completing the job and by natural contingencies such as fresh breath and clean clothes.

Make Sure Everyone Supports Your Efforts

Far too often we teach a skill and the people and conditions in the generalization settings do not support the new behavior. Stokes and Baer (1977) refer to this as the "natural community of reinforcers." For example, if we teach a child to wash her hands at home but she is very slow at completing the task, a busy classroom aide may choose to wash and dry the child's hands so that it takes less time. This raises two concerns. The first is that the skill is not learned well enough to satisfy the demands of the school environment. Since it is not demonstrated often, it is halting and effortful. The second is that the classroom aide is perhaps not fully aware of the expectation for the child's independence. One approach is to help the child learn to respond more quickly and accurately and then to probe to see if generalization has occurred. A second is to work with the classroom team to ensure that it is willing and able to support the child's effort by allowing sufficient time and avoiding unnecessary prompts. Both may be necessary.

■ Summary

An inability to generalize is often stated as a common characteristic of children with autism. Skills may be learned in one very specific context and fail to generalize across materials, people, and settings. Sometimes in our efforts to simplify learning, we begin in highly controlled conditions that help the child learn the skill but may prevent generalization from occurring. The challenging task is to balance the need for simplification with the requirement to help the child apply newly learned skills in a variety of situations. As we have indicated, the first step is to clearly identify what is to be learned and where, when, and how it must be used. With that information in hand, you can see the full scope of the problem and decide how much direct teaching you will do to program generalization. You can also apply some strategies while you are teaching that may facilitate greater generalization without the need to do direct teaching in all contexts. In most cases, the combination of direct and indirect strategies results in significant and generalized learning.

The most difficult thing is the decision to act, the rest is merely tenacity.
The fears are paper tigers. You can do anything you decide to do.
You can act to change and control your life;
and the procedure, the process is its own reward.
—Amelia Earhart

Conclusion

We end this guide by repeating something we said in the introduction: We are surprised by how much one needs to know to teach self-help skills. We hope that we have given you enough of the necessary skills and motivation to be successful. It is so important to your child and to you.

As parents and professionals who work with children with ASD, we often focus on the early development of core skills in communication, socialization, and play. These not only form the very foundation of how children learn, but also reflect the core deficits for children with ASD. Surely, severe deficits in these areas prevent full participation in family and community. But we strongly encourage you to remember that the failure to develop basic self-help skills will also contribute greatly to your son's or daughter's ability to make friends, find and sustain a job, and participate in normal family and community activities.

The good news is that there is great hope for teaching greater personal independence. The area of self-help development is often an area of strength for individuals with ASD and significant improvement and independence is possible. Although their road to achieving success may be a different one, when skills are broken into small steps and taught systematically, most children with ASD make significant progress. The result is not only independence and confidence for your child but also greater independence for you as their primary caretaker.

We know that carrying out the methods we have discussed in this book may require hundreds of hours from you. We recommend that you start early and take it slowly. Pick one or two things to work on and try to do them consistently every day.

Often, it will be possible to take the things that you do all the time (like dressing and bathing your child) and try to do them a little more systematically and with greater focus on what you expect to accomplish in the long run. As we have said, children who accomplish these skills are more likely to fit in at school and in their community and later at work and in their personal friendships. Making the decision to act is a big step and one that you will never regret.

References

Ahearn, W.H., Kerwin, M.E., Eicher, P.S., Shantz, J. & Swearingin, W. (1996). An alternating treatments comparison of two intensive interventions for food refusal. *Journal of Applied Behavior Analysis, 29,* 321–332.

Anderson, S.R., Taras, M. & O'Malley Cannon, B. (1996). Teaching new skills to young children with autism. In C. Maurice, G. Green, and S. Luce, (Eds.), *Behavioral intervention for young children with autism: A manual for parents and professionals.* Austin, TX: Pro-Ed, Inc.

Azrin, N.H. & Foxx, R.M. (1971). A rapid method of toilet training the institutionalized retarded. *Journal of Applied Behavior Analysis, 4,* 89–99.

Baer, D.M. (1999). *How to plan for generalization.* Austin, TX: Pro-Ed, Inc.

Baker, B.L. & Brightman, A.J. (2004). *Steps to independence: Teaching everyday skills to children with special needs.* Baltimore, MD: Paul H. Brookes Publishing.

Bandura, A. (1969). *Principles of behavior modification.* New York: Holt, Rinehart and Winston.

Bettision, S. (1982). *Toilet training to independence for the handicapped: A manual for trainers.* Springfield, IL: Charles C. Thomas Publisher.

Bredekamp, S. & Copple, C. (Eds.) (1997). *Developmentally appropriate practice in early childhood programs (revised edition).* Washington, D.C.: National Association for the Education of Young Children (NAEYC).

Carruth, B.R. & Skinner, J.D. (2002). Feeding behaviors and other motor development in healthy children (2–24 months). *Journal of the American College of Nutrition, 21,* 88–96.

Carruth, B.R., Ziegler, P.J., Gordon, A. & Hendricks, K. (2004). Developmental milestones and self–feeding behaviors in infants and toddlers. *Journal of the American Dietetic Association, 104,* S51–S56.

Cicero, F.R. & Pfadt, A. (2002). Investigation of a reinforcement–based toilet training procedure for children with autism. *Research in Developmental Disabilities, 23,* 319–331.

Cohen, M.J. & Sloan, D.L. (2007). *Visual supports for people with autism: A guide for parents and professionals.* Bethesda, MD: Woodbine House.

Delmolino, L. & Harris, S.L. (2004). *Incentives for change: Motivating people with autism spectrum disorders to learn and gain independence.* Bethesda, MD: Woodbine House.

Dyer, K. (1987). The competition of autistic stereotyped behavior with usual and specifically assessed reinforcers. *Research in Developmental Disabilities, 8,* 606–626.

Dyer, K., Santarcangelo, S. & Luce, S.C. (1987). Developmental influences in teaching language forms to individuals with developmental disabilities. *Journal of Speech and Hearing Disorders, 52,* 335–347.

Eisenberg, A., Murkoff, H.E. & Hathaway, S.E. (1994). *What to expect the toddler years.* New York: Workman Publishing.

Fisher, W.W., Piazza, C.C., Bowman, L.G. & Amari, A. (1996). Integrating caregiver report with a systematic choice assessment to enhance reinforcer identification. *Journal on Mental American Retardation, 101,* 15–25.

Foxx, R.M. & Azrin, N.H. (1973). *Toilet training persons with developmental disabilities.* Harrisburg, PA: Help Services Press.

Garwood, S.G. & Fewell, R.R. (Eds.) (1983). *Educating handicapped infants: Issues in development and intervention.* Rockville, MD: Aspen Publishers.

Gesell, A. & Illg, F.L. (1937). *Feeding behavior of infants.* Philadelphia: JB Lippincott Co.

Harris, S.L. & Weiss, M.J. (1998). *Right from the start: Behavioral intervention for young children with autism: A guide for parents and professionals.* Bethesda, MD: Woodbine House.

Individuals with Disabilities Education Act (IDEA) (2004). U.S. Department of Education, Office of Special Education and Rehabilitative Services, Public Law 108–446, 108th Congress.

Lancioni, G.E. & Markus, S. (1999). Urine–triggered alarm signals and prompts to promote daytime urinary continence in a boy with severe intellectual disability. *Behavioral and Cognitive Psychotherapy, 27,* 261–265.

Latham, G. (1990). *The power of positive parenting.* North Logan, UT: P&T Ink.

Leaf, R. & McEachin, J. (Eds.) (1999). *A work in progress: Behavior management strategies and curriculum for intensive behavioral treatment of autism.* New York, NY: DRL Brooks. LLC.

Lifter, K., Sulzer-Azaroff, B., Anderson, S.R. & Edwards Cowdery, G. (1993). Teaching play activities to preschool children with disabilities: The importance of developmental considerations. *Journal of Early Intervention, 17,* 139–159.

Lovaas, O.I. (2003). *Teaching individuals with developmental delays: Basic intervention techniques.* Austin, TX: Pro-Ed, Inc.

Maurice, C., Green, G. & Foxx, R.M. (Eds.) (2001). *Making a difference: Behavioral intervention for autism.* Austin, TX: Pro-Ed, Inc.

Maurice, C., Green, G. & Luce, S.C. (Eds.) (1996). *Behavior intervention for young children with autism: A manual for parents and professionals.* Austin, TX: Pro-Ed, Inc.

McClannahan, L.E. & Krantz, P.J. (1999). *Activity schedules for children with autism: Teaching independent behavior.* Bethesda, MD: Woodbine House.

Mercer, R. (2003). *Seven steps to nighttime dryness: A practical guide for parents of children with bedwetting.* Ashton, MD: Brookeville Media.

Schnell, M.E. & Farlow, L.J. (1998). Self-care skills. In M.E. Schnell (Eds.), *Instruction of students with severe disabilities.* New York: Macmillan Publishing Company.

Sears, W. & Sears, M. (1993). *The baby book: Everything you need to know about your baby from birth to age two.* New York: Little, Brown and Company.

Sebastian, S. (1998). *How to teach through modeling and imitation.* Austin, TX: Pro-Ed, Inc.

Shore, R. (1997). *Rethinking the brain: New insights into early development.* New York, NY: Families and Work Institute.

Stokes, T.F. & Baer, D.M., (1977). An implicit technology of generalization. *Journal of Applied Behavior Analysis, 10,* 349–367.

Wheeler, A.J., Miller, R.A., Springer, B.M., Pittard, N.C., Phillips, J.F. & Myers, A.M. (1997). *Murdoch Center Program Library, 3rd Edition.* Butner, NC: Murdoch Center Foundation, Inc.

Self-Help Curricula and Other Resources

Self-Help Curricula

A few commercially available materials exist for teaching self-help skills. Most of these materials are not designed for children specifically with autism, but much of the information still applies. Furthermore, most of these manuals and materials cover all areas of development (e.g., domestic, motor, cognitive, and social) and provide only a brief discussion of self-help skills. Nevertheless, you may find these materials helpful.

Baker, B.L. & Brightman, A.J. (2004). *Steps to independence: Teaching everyday skills to children with special needs.* Baltimore, MD: Paul H. Brookes Publishing.

Foxx, R.M. & Azrin, N.H. (1973). *Toilet training persons with developmental disabilities: A rapid program for day and nighttime independent toileting.* Harrisburg, PA: Help Services Press, 2349 Forest Hills Drive, Harrisburg, PA.

Johnson-Martin, N.M., Jens, K.G., Attermeier, S.M. & Hacker, B.J. (1999). *The Carolina curriculum for infants and toddlers with special needs, 2nd edition.* Baltimore, MD: Paul H. Brookes Publishing Co.

Schopler, E., Lansing, M. & Waters, L. (Eds.) (1983). *Individualized assessment and treatment of autistic and developmentally disabled children: Teaching activities for autistic children, Volume III.* Austin, TX: Pro-Ed, Inc.

Wheeler, A.J., Miller, R.A., Springer, B.M., Pittard, N.C., Phillips, J.F. & Myers, A.M. (1997). *Murdoch Center Program Library, 3rd Edition, Volume 1.* Murdoch Center Foundation, Inc, P.O. Box 92, Butner, NC 27509.

Other Resources

Clothing and Bed Alarms

The Bedwetting Store
P.O. Box 337
Olney, MD 20830-0337
Phone: 800-214-9605 or 301-774-1495
Internet: www.bedwettingstore.com

Educational Materials

Different Roads to Learning, Inc.
37 East 18th Street, 10th Floor
New York, NY 10003
Phone: 800-853-1057 or 212-604-9637
Internet: www.difflearn.com

Super Duper® Publications
P.O. Box 24997
Greenville, SC 29616 USA
Phone: 800-277-8737 or 864-288-3536
Internet: www.superduperinc.com

Picture Communication Symbols

Mayer-Johnson, LLC
P.O. Box 1597
Solana Beach, CA 92075
Phone: 800-588-4548.
Internet: www.mayer-johnson.com

Appendices

■ Appendix A Self-Help Inventory

Instructions: Although completing the entire form may serve as a good baseline of your child's ability, you may decide not to fill out every section of this survey. Instead, search down the list of Functional Areas (Column 1) and identify the areas that interest you most. Once you have selected one or more Functional Areas, proceed as follows:

1. Move down the list of Skill Targets (Column 3) and indicate by marking the small box if your child already demonstrates that skill.

2. Next, in the column labeled Level of Independence, indicate how much help your child needs to complete the task. Circle the corresponding number as defined in the box below. If your child completes the task with little or no help, don't bother to complete the other columns in that row.

3. On the other hand, if your child cannot complete the task at all or requires significant help, complete the next two columns. In the case of a young child, some help in completing self-help tasks is expected so a high rating (meaning a lot of prompts are needed) does not necessarily mean the skill needs to be taught now.

4. As you can see, the column labeled Age Appropriate asks you to consider whether another child the same age would be able to perform this task with little or no help. If you need to do so, refer to Chapter 3 for further guidance in this matter.

5. The column labeled Functional asks you to indicate whether this skill is essential to your child at this moment in time. Does not possessing the skill prevent him from participating in school, community, or work opportunities (e.g., not being toilet trained excludes him from swimming in the school pool).

6. Once you have completed the relevant parts of the survey, narrow the list down to five or six Skill Targets. Then consider these within the larger picture of other goals you are currently addressing or want to address (e.g., academic, social, and play) and try to prioritize them.

SELF-HELP SKILLS INVENTORY

FUNCTIONAL AREA	TASK	SKILL TARGET	LEVEL OF INDEPENDENCE			AGE APPROPRIATE	FUNCTIONAL
Eating & Drinking	*Basic Skills*	☐ Eats finger foods	0 1 2		3	Yes / No	Yes / No
		☐ Eats solids	0 1 2		3	Yes / No	Yes / No
		☐ Holds and drinks from cup	0 1 2		3	Yes / No	Yes / No
		☐ Eats meal with spoon and cup as main utensils	0 1 2		3	Yes / No	Yes / No
	Use of Utensils	☐ Scoops with spoon	0 1 2		3	Yes / No	Yes / No
		☐ Eats with a fork	0 1 2		3	Yes / No	Yes / No
		☐ Eats without spilling	0 1 2		3	Yes / No	Yes / No
		☐ Spreads with knife	0 1 2		3	Yes / No	Yes / No
	Advanced Use of Utensils	☐ Cuts with knife	0 1 2		3	Yes / No	Yes / No
		☐ Cuts with edge of fork	0 1 2		3	Yes / No	Yes / No
		☐ Puts jelly or butter on bread	0 1 2		3	Yes / No	Yes / No
	Other	☐ Pours liquid from one container into another	0 1 2		3	Yes / No	Yes / No
		☐ Uses napkin	0 1 2		3	Yes / No	Yes / No
		☐ Sets table	0 1 2		3	Yes / No	Yes / No
		☐ Serves self from serving dishes	0 1 2		3	Yes / No	Yes / No
		☐ Orders from menu	0 1 2		3	Yes / No	Yes / No

Level of Independence
0 = performs skill with no help
1 = performs skill with one or two prompts
2 = performs skill with at least three but fewer than five prompts
3 = performs skill with five or more prompts

Age Appropriate
Is this a skill that children the same age as your child would normally know how to do?

Functional
Does your child need this skill at this time to fully integrate and participate in home, school, or work?

SELF-HELP SKILLS INVENTORY

FUNCTIONAL AREA	TASK	SKILL TARGET	LEVEL OF INDEPENDENCE				AGE APPROPRIATE	FUNCTIONAL
Eating & Drinking (continued)	*Snack Preparation*	☐ Fixes snacks (e.g., milk & cookies)	0	1	2	3	Yes / No	Yes / No
		☐ Makes toast	0	1	2	3	Yes / No	Yes / No
		☐ Fixes sandwich	0	1	2	3	Yes / No	Yes / No
Undressing & Dressing Skills	*Undressing Basic – Removes:*	☐ Shoes (Velcro or slip off)	0	1	2	3	Yes / No	Yes / No
		☐ Socks	0	1	2	3	Yes / No	Yes / No
		☐ Underpants	0	1	2	3	Yes / No	Yes / No
		☐ Undershirt	0	1	2	3	Yes / No	Yes / No
		☐ Pants (elastic waistband)	0	1	2	3	Yes / No	Yes / No
		☐ Shirt (pullover style)	0	1	2	3	Yes / No	Yes / No
	Undressing Advanced – Removes:	☐ Shoes (lace-up style)	0	1	2	3	Yes / No	Yes / No
		☐ Pants (belt, buckle, snap, button, zipper)	0	1	2	3	Yes / No	Yes / No
		☐ Shirt (button-up style)	0	1	2	3	Yes / No	Yes / No
		☐ Dress (steps out)	0	1	2	3	Yes / No	Yes / No
	Dressing Basic – Puts on:	☐ Underpants	0	1	2	3	Yes / No	Yes / No
		☐ Undershirt	0	1	2	3	Yes / No	Yes / No
		☐ Socks	0	1	2	3	Yes / No	Yes / No

Level of Independence
0 = performs skill with no help
1 = performs skill with one or two prompts
2 = performs skill with at least three but fewer than five prompts
3 = performs skill with five or more prompts

Age Appropriate
Is this a skill that children the same age as your child would normally know how to do?

Functional
Does your child need this skill at this time to fully integrate and participate in home, school, or work?

SELF-HELP SKILLS INVENTORY

FUNCTIONAL AREA	TASK	SKILL TARGET	LEVEL OF INDEPENDENCE	AGE APPROPRIATE	FUNCTIONAL
Undressing & Dressing Skills (continued)		☐ Pants (elastic waistband)	0 1 2 3	Yes / No	Yes / No
		☐ Shirt (pullover style)	0 1 2 3	Yes / No	Yes / No
		☐ Shoes (Velcro or slip on)	0 1 2 3	Yes / No	Yes / No
	Dressing Advanced – Puts on:	☐ Shoes (without tying)	0 1 2 3	Yes / No	Yes / No
		☐ Sandals / Boots	0 1 2 3	Yes / No	Yes / No
		☐ Pants (without fastening)	0 1 2 3	Yes / No	Yes / No
		☐ Button-up shirt	0 1 2 3	Yes / No	Yes / No
		☐ Bra (without fastening)	0 1 2 3	Yes / No	Yes / No
		☐ Dress (pulls overhead)	0 1 2 3	Yes / No	Yes / No
		☐ Sweater	0 1 2 3	Yes / No	Yes / No
		☐ All articles of clothing	0 1 2 3	Yes / No	Yes / No
	Other	☐ Dresses promptly (by the clock or a timer)	0 1 2 3	Yes / No	Yes / No
		☐ Tucks in shirt	0 1 2 3	Yes / No	Yes / No
		☐ Chooses and color-coordinates clothing	0 1 2 3	Yes / No	Yes / No
	Fasteners	☐ Buttons articles	0 1 2 3	Yes / No	Yes / No
		☐ Snaps articles	0 1 2 3	Yes / No	Yes / No
		☐ Zippers articles	0 1 2 3	Yes / No	Yes / No

Level of Independence
0 = performs skill with no help
1 = performs skill with one or two prompts
2 = performs skill with at least three but fewer than five prompts
3 = performs skill with five or more prompts

Age Appropriate
Is this a skill that children the same age as your child would normally know how to do?

Functional
Does your child need this skill at this time to fully integrate and participate in home, school, or work?

SELF-HELP SKILLS INVENTORY

FUNCTIONAL AREA	TASK	SKILL TARGET	LEVEL OF INDEPENDENCE				AGE APPROPRIATE	FUNCTIONAL
Undressing & Dressing Skills (continued)		☐ Ties shoes	0	1	2	3	Yes / No	Yes / No
		☐ Buckles belt	0	1	2	3	Yes / No	Yes / No
		☐ Affixes hook and eye (bra)	0	1	2	3	Yes / No	Yes / No
	Outerwear – Removes and puts on:	☐ Coat	0	1	2	3	Yes / No	Yes / No
		☐ Sweater	0	1	2	3	Yes / No	Yes / No
		☐ Hat (baseball / knit)	0	1	2	3	Yes / No	Yes / No
		☐ Mittens	0	1	2	3	Yes / No	Yes / No
		☐ Gloves	0	1	2	3	Yes / No	Yes / No
	Other	☐ Detects clean vs. dirty clothes	0	1	2	3	Yes / No	Yes / No
		☐ Changes clothes when dirty or soiled	0	1	2	3	Yes / No	Yes / No
		☐ Chooses different clothes each day	0	1	2	3	Yes / No	Yes / No
		☐ Monitors own appearance throughout day	0	1	2	3	Yes / No	Yes / No
	Accessories	☐ Wears belt when needed	0	1	2	3	Yes / No	Yes / No
		☐ Wears watch	0	1	2	3	Yes / No	Yes / No
		☐ Carries wallet / purse (with identification)	0	1	2	3	Yes / No	Yes / No
		☐ Wears glasses / sunglasses	0	1	2	3	Yes / No	Yes / No
		☐ Wears jewelry or ID bracelet	0	1	2	3	Yes / No	Yes / No

Level of Independence
0 = performs skill with no help
1 = performs skill with one or two prompts
2 = performs skill with at least three but fewer than five prompts
3 = performs skill with five or more prompts

Age Appropriate
Is this a skill that children the same age as your child would normally know how to do?

Functional
Does your child need this skill at this time to fully integrate and participate in home, school, or work?

SELF-HELP SKILLS INVENTORY

FUNCTIONAL AREA	TASK	SKILL TARGET	LEVEL OF INDEPENDENCE	AGE APPROPRIATE	FUNCTIONAL
Toileting	Daytime *(stays dry)*	☐ Follows schedule (bladder) initiated by an adult	0 1 2 3	Yes / No	Yes / No
		☐ Follows schedule initiated by an adult (bladder and bowel)	0 1 2 3	Yes / No	Yes / No
		☐ Indicates need to eliminate	0 1 2 3	Yes / No	Yes / No
		☐ Independent (bladder and bowel)	0 1 2 3	Yes / No	Yes / No
	Other	☐ Uses toilet paper effectively	0 1 2 3	Yes / No	Yes / No
		☐ Urinates while standing (male)	0 1 2 3	Yes / No	Yes / No
		☐ Pulls clothing down (rather than removing) when toileting	0 1 2 3	Yes / No	Yes / No
	Nighttime (stays dry)	☐ Follows schedule initiated by an adult	0 1 2 3	Yes / No	Yes / No
		☐ Gets up to use the bathroom independently	0 1 2 3	Yes / No	Yes / No
Personal Hygiene	*Menstrual Care*	☐ Recognizes beginning of period	0 1 2 3	Yes / No	Yes / No
		☐ Maintains cleanliness of clothing	0 1 2 3	Yes / No	Yes / No
		☐ Places pad on underpants	0 1 2 3	Yes / No	Yes / No
		☐ Uses tampon	0 1 2 3	Yes / No	Yes / No
		☐ Disposes of pads / tampons appropriately	0 1 2 3	Yes / No	Yes / No
		☐ Maintains cleanliness of personal area	0 1 2 3	Yes / No	Yes / No
		☐ Carries supplies in purse during outings	0 1 2 3	Yes / No	Yes / No

Level of Independence
0 = performs skill with no help
1 = performs skill with one or two prompts
2 = performs skill with at least three but fewer than five prompts
3 = performs skill with five or more prompts

Age Appropriate
Is this a skill that children the same age as your child would normally know how to do?

Functional
Does your child need this skill at this time to fully integrate and participate in home, school, or work?

SELF-HELP SKILLS INVENTORY

FUNCTIONAL AREA	TASK	SKILL TARGET	LEVEL OF INDEPENDENCE				AGE APPROPRIATE		FUNCTIONAL	
Personal Hygiene (continued)	Bathing	☐ Washes hands	0	1	2	3	Yes / No		Yes / No	
		☐ Dries hands	0	1	2	3	Yes / No		Yes / No	
		☐ Washes and dries face (without washcloth)	0	1	2	3	Yes / No		Yes / No	
		☐ Washes and dries face (with washcloth)	0	1	2	3	Yes / No		Yes / No	
		☐ Washes body (shower or bathtub)	0	1	2	3	Yes / No		Yes / No	
		☐ Washes hair	0	1	2	3	Yes / No		Yes / No	
		☐ Showers	0	1	2	3	Yes / No		Yes / No	
		☐ Uses body lotion or moisturizer	0	1	2	3	Yes / No		Yes / No	
	Hair Care	☐ Combs or brushes hair	0	1	2	3	Yes / No		Yes / No	
		☐ Blow dries hair	0	1	2	3	Yes / No		Yes / No	
		☐ Styles hair and keeps out of face	0	1	2	3	Yes / No		Yes / No	
		☐ Uses hair accessories (female)	0	1	2	3	Yes / No		Yes / No	
	Ear Care	☐ Uses Q-tips	0	1	2	3	Yes / No		Yes / No	
	Other	☐ Cleans glasses	0	1	2	3	Yes / No		Yes / No	
		☐ Cares for contact lenses	0	1	2	3	Yes / No		Yes / No	

Level of Independence
0 = performs skill with no help
1 = performs skill with one or two prompts
2 = performs skill with at least three but fewer than five prompts
3 = performs skill with five or more prompts

Age Appropriate
Is this a skill that children the same age as your child would normally know how to do?

Functional
Does your child need this skill at this time to fully integrate and participate in home, school, or work?

SELF-HELP SKILLS INVENTORY

FUNCTIONAL AREA	TASK	SKILL TARGET	LEVEL OF INDEPENDENCE			AGE APPROPRIATE	FUNCTIONAL
Personal Hygiene (continued)	*Toothbrushing*	☐ Applies appropriate amount of toothpaste to toothbrush	0 1 2 3			Yes / No	Yes / No
		☐ Brushes all teeth (front, back, inside, outside, sides)	0 1 2 3			Yes / No	Yes / No
		☐ Rinses out mouth	0 1 2 3			Yes / No	Yes / No
		☐ Flosses teeth	0 1 2 3			Yes / No	Yes / No
		☐ Uses mouthwash	0 1 2 3			Yes / No	Yes / No
	Other	☐ Applies deodorant	0 1 2 3			Yes / No	Yes / No
		☐ Wipes and blows nose	0 1 2 3			Yes / No	Yes / No
		☐ Applies hand lotion / lip balm	0 1 2 3			Yes / No	Yes / No
		☐ Clips and files fingernails	0 1 2 3			Yes / No	Yes / No
		☐ Clips and files toenails	0 1 2 3			Yes / No	Yes / No
		☐ Cares for cuts, wounds	0 1 2 3			Yes / No	Yes / No
		☐ Shaves face (male)	0 1 2 3			Yes / No	Yes / No
		☐ Shaves legs and underarms (female)	0 1 2 3			Yes / No	Yes / No

Level of Independence
0 = performs skill with no help
1 = performs skill with one or two prompts
2 = performs skill with at least three but fewer than five prompts
3 = performs skill with five or more prompts

Age Appropriate
Is this a skill that children the same age as your child would normally know how to do?

Functional
Does your child need this skill at this time to fully integrate and participate in home, school, or work?

■ Appendix B Troubleshooting: Common Problems and Possible Solutions

Note: Chapters 6–11 include other potential solutions.

Problem	Possible Modification	Examples
Your child does not appear to be interested in completing the task.	1. Modify reinforcement by altering the type, amount, and/or frequency of rewards. 2. Make the task more appealing by pairing it with more desirable consequences (e.g., earning a favorite activity) or using more interesting materials.	Sam rarely initiated dressing in the morning despite performing the skill quite well during teaching trials. His mother implemented a token system whereby he earned tokens for dressing without being asked. She also purchased some new T-shirts with pictures of Sam's favorite cartoon characters on them.
Your child keeps making multiple errors.	1. Utilize an errorless prompting sequence (e.g., hand-over-hand prompting that is gradually faded). 2. Break the task into smaller steps.	Jane becomes very agitated when her mother pulls a spoon out of the drawer. She has been unsuccessful with self-feeding for several months now. Her mother decides to provide a most-to-least prompting strategy and increase the steps in her task analysis from five to ten.
Your child's performance is highly inconsistent.	1. Ensure that teaching methods are applied consistently. 2. Increase the consistency of reinforcement and complete a reinforcer assessment to determine the best rewards.	Ricky would go for a few days without toileting accidents and then have multiple accidents on the same day. His mother determined that his daycare provider was not using the same error correction procedures she was when Ricky had an accident. She also determined that she had faded rewards too quickly so she returned to reinforcing him after each success and then began a more gradual fading of rewards.
Your child is becoming dependent on prompts.	1. Reduce verbal prompts. 2. Give reinforcers for increasingly greater independence (fewer prompts) in the completion of the task. 3. Fade prompts in a systematic manner.	Giovanni rarely remembered to brush his teeth unless reminded to do so by his mother. She stopped reminding him and instead placed a picture of his toothbrush on the bathroom mirror. After Giovanni consistently responded to the picture, his mom began cutting away 1/8" of the picture each day, until it was no longer present.
Your child needs continuous prompting on one particular step of a task.	1. Modify that step by breaking it into smaller steps. 2. Provide physical modifications to make the step easier for your child.	Martina got stuck when she had to turn on the faucet to wash her hands. Her teacher's aide determined that she was not tall enough to get the leverage that she needed to turn the handle. Placing a small step stool beneath the sink allowed her to complete this step without physical assistance.
Your child is not generalizing skills.	1. Teach skills in multiple settings with various adults present.	Mr. Cruz made sure that he took Ricky to the restroom each time they went to the mall or a restaurant to practice his toileting skills.

■ Appendix C Five Readiness Skills Your Child Should Learn

The following are five skills we believe your child should acquire before you begin teaching self-help skills. Although all are important, the first three (attending, responding to your name, and following directions) are probably the most important. We have briefly provided some strategies for teaching each skill. As we indicated in Chapter 3, other useful resources for teaching these important skills include Harris & Weiss (1998), Lovaas (2003), and two books edited by Catherine Maurice & colleagues (1996, 2001).

■ Attending to an Activity

Rationale: For your child to learn self-help skills, he needs to be able to attend to your instructions and remain focused on the task with only a few gentle reminders.

Behavioral Goal: When given a new task or activity to complete with a supervising or participating parent, your child will remain engaged in the task/activity for at least ten minutes with two or fewer reminders from you to pay attention or to finish the activity, for three consecutive opportunities.

Instructional Plan: Begin by teaching your child to sit and respond in a highly structured situation when there is nearly continuous one-to-one attention. Start in a quiet room with two chairs and a table that will eventually be used as a work surface. Instruct your child to come to the table and sit down, providing as much physical assistance as needed to get your child to sit in the chair. Praise enthusiastically and provide the child with access to a super reward. Give a few seconds to consume or play with the reward, then remove it and allow him to leave the area. Repeat this approach many times and gradually require and reward your child for staying longer periods of time seated in the chair. Begin to provide simple tasks for your child to complete while in the chair and reward him with praise and a small treat (typically a small piece of desired food that can be eaten in four or five seconds) for working on the task. After the task is done, reward him with the super reward and allow him to leave the chair. Do not increase the time in the chair too rapidly, which could lead to a series of failed trials. Praise frequently for "good sitting" and "good working" while your child is sitting and attending.

■ Responding to His Name and the Instruction "Look"

Rationale: Your child's ability to attend to you and the instructional materials is important for learning. Although not a guarantee, making eye contact with you and/or looking at the materials certainly increases the likelihood that your child is attending and listening. Eye contact is also the foundation for other important skills such as looking at another individual when socializing.

Appendix C continued on next page

Behavioral Goal: When an adult says the child's name followed by the instruction, "Look," the child will look at the adult within three seconds eight out of ten times for three consecutive sessions.

Instructional Plan: Find a quiet room and place two chairs facing each other with you in one and your child in the other. Say your child's name, then instruct him to look (i.e., "Ricky [pause two seconds], look.") If your child looks at you (even fleetingly at this point), praise him enthusiastically. If he fails to respond, gently place a hand on each side of his face and prompt him to look. Some children may resist by pulling away or intentionally avoiding eye contact by looking away. If this happens, don't struggle with him. Simply try another way.

One alternative method is to hold a desired item or food near your face and call his name again. When he looks towards the item (which will now be in the general direction of your eyes), praise him and give him the item to eat or to explore for fifteen to thirty seconds. If you reward him for looking at something he really wants, he will learn to look at you as well. You are trying to establish yourself as a reward. You want him to learn that looking at and interacting with you results in good things (warm smiles, fun activities, and desired toys and materials). Over many trials, your child's desire to make eye contact will increase.

Once he is reliably looking at the object, partially conceal the object in your hand and continue to conduct instructional trials. Over the course of many trials, conceal the object entirely in your hand, but continue to place your hand near your eyes. Finally, place your right empty hand near your eyes (as if the object is concealed within it). When your child looks at you, praise and provide the object now concealed in your left hand. Continue many trials in this manner until he is reliably responding. Finally, use your right hand to gesture or point to your eyes, while giving the instruction to look. Eventually, over many trials you may be able to fade this gesture as well, but don't worry about this early on.

Once he is beginning to look at you regularly, gesture toward objects (with a point or head nod) that you have placed near you on a table and praise him for looking at the object that you have identified. Practice this drill multiple times per day at the table (along with the other skills listed here). As a general rule, once your child is responding correctly on his own for the majority of the trials, and can do so for two to three days in a row, you can begin practicing the skill away from the table. Then you may take advantage of the hundreds of natural opportunities that occur throughout the day and ask and reward him for making eye contact.

■ Learning to Follow Directions

Rationale: It is helpful if your child is able to reliably respond to simple spoken directions such as those provided in the table below (C-1). These instructions, along with other skills that we advocate should be taught, establish a base of learning-to-learn skills and increase your child's general responsiveness to you. The good news is that understanding complex, multi-step directions ("Pick up the toothbrush and toothpaste.") will be helpful, but not required, to learn many self-help skills. By using the principles of task analysis, chaining, and reinforcement, children learn to sequence small steps to form more complex behavior (e.g., putting together all the steps of toothbrushing without parents directing each step).

■ **Table C-1** **Simple One-Step Instructions Your Child Should Learn**	
Come here	Stand up/down
Give me _____	Look at me
Hands down on table or in lap	Jump
Clap hands	Point to _____
Give me a hug	Go/Stop
Put in trash	Give me "five"
Get your _____	Open/close door
Touch your head	Pick up _____ (with gesture)
Turn on/off light	Open _____

Behavioral Goal: After hearing his name followed by a commonly used instruction (e.g., "Jon, come here"), the child will follow the instruction within five seconds eight of ten times each day for three consecutive days.

Instructional Plan: In many cases, the ability to follow directions involves both understanding what your words mean and learning what your expectations are. It is not uncommon for most children to test the limits of their parents' authority, and the same can be said about children with autism. One of the first things you will need to teach your child is that your words mean something. It is as simple as *"look – listen – do."* Each time you make a request, you have the opportunity to teach your child what your words mean and establish expectations for responding. The more you practice the skills of *look – listen – do*, the more your child will understand your expectations. It is challenging to discern whether some children with autism understand the instruction but choose not to follow it, or do not understand the instruction at all. In our opinion, this distinction may be irrelevant as long as you are consistent in following a sequence that provides a clear indication of expectations, and supports your child to respond.

The following sequence ensures that if your child does not understand the instruction you have just given him, he will be shown the desired response. If he does understand, but chooses not to respond, he will learn that a nonresponse is unacceptable.

1. Gain your child's attention.

Appendix C continued on next page

2. Provide a clear, simple instruction in a neutral tone of voice.
3. If you child responds, praise him ("Good job following directions."). In the beginning, you may want to deliver a super reward, but over time praise should be enough.
4. If your child does not respond, repeat the instruction and physically prompt him.

From the instructions provided in Table C-1, select one instruction that you would like to teach first. Begin as we described above, sitting in two chairs facing each other. Say your child's name, deliver a simple instruction (e.g., "stand up") and immediately physically prompt him to comply (e.g., stand). Use only the amount of energy necessary to assist him, allowing him to make as much effort as he will at this point. With each consecutive trial, gradually decrease the amount of help you provide until your child is following the instruction on his own. Once he is correctly following directions without assistance for the majority of the trials, and can do so for two to three days in a row, you can begin delivering simple instructions throughout the day whenever opportunity occurs naturally.

Next, pick a second instruction and randomly alternate between the two requests (e.g., "stand up" and "sit down"). Praise your child when he responds to either instruction, but provide the super reward only when your child responds to the newly introduced request. Continue adding one direction at a time until all are learned. Begin to incorporate them into everything you do throughout the day. You will be surprised to see how quickly your child begins to learn new instructions.

◼ Imitating the Actions of Others

Rationale: Most children spend a large portion of their day watching their parents, siblings, and friends, and they often do what they see. This "watching" and then "doing" is called imitation and it forms the basis for learning. As we indicated in Chapter 2, many children with autism do not naturally or easily develop imitation skills. Some children seem to lack component behaviors such as monitoring the behavior of others and translating the behavior of others into their own actions. Without these skills, imitation fails to develop or remains very limited, and these children lack an important tool for efficient and effective learning. This doesn't mean they can't learn, but if modeling (showing) cannot be effectively used, then the instructional challenges are greater.

Behavioral Goal: When given the instruction, "Do this," followed by a simple motor action (e.g., clapping hands), the child will imitate the modeled action within three seconds eight out of ten times each day for three consecutive days.

Instructional Plan: A first step in teaching imitation is to teach children with autism to imitate simple motor movements, for example clapping hands. This is a good place to start because you can easily physically help your child to complete the action if he fails to do it on his own. Table C-2 provides a list of commonly taught motor movements.

■ Table C-2 Simple Motor Actions Your Child Should Know

Clap hands together	Wave
Touch nose with index finger	Stomp feet
Touch table	Jump
Touch head with palm of hand	Shake head back and forth or up and down
Touch eyes with index fingers	Raise arms
Stand up	Touch ears with index fingers
Touch mouth with index finger	Touch arm with palm of hand
Pat legs using both hands	Touch feet with both hands

Again, an instructional lesson begins with the parent and child facing each other. You simply say your child's name and provide an appropriate request (e.g., "Amelia, do this") while modeling the specific action. If your child initially makes any close approximation of your actions, praise and deliver an identified reinforcer. If not, physically assist (prompt) your child to complete the task. Begin with one action and slowly over several days or weeks add more as the child progresses. Typically, you want your child to demonstrate the new action eight out of ten times within a session and to repeat the session three times over at least two days. Ideally, you want your child to learn the rule "Do as I do" rather than learning a list of isolated responses. As you add motor movements, each one should take less time to teach until he eventually is able to imitate an action the first time it is modeled. At that point, you know your child has learned the rule "Do as I do." Over time, you can begin to expand the number of actions and add them together to form two- and three-step actions (e.g., touch your nose, head, and knee and ask him to imitate the three actions in order). You also can begin to embed trials within music (for example, imitating the related actions in the song, "Head, Shoulders, Knees & Toes") or imitating the steps of a vocational program (e.g., matching a model's demonstration of how to sort objects by shape, size, or color). The opportunities are limitless once your child learns how to imitate.

■ Learning to Make Simple Choices

Rationale: At this point you are probably wondering why "making simple choices" is a readiness skill for learning self-help skills. We acknowledge, from among the things that we have discussed so far, it is a distinctly different kind of

Appendix C continued on next page

skill. However, we think it is important because it can be used to help identify what rewards your child most values. We often begin a lesson by asking the child the following question, "What do you want to earn?" The child then selects by pointing to one object from a choice of two to four items. Throughout the session, we remind him what he is earning. This often is important when you are looking for the most natural and effective ways to motivate a child to complete self-help tasks. For example, if you can ask your child to select what he wants for breakfast, it might function as strong encouragement to dress each morning.

Behavioral Goal: When given a choice of preferred and nonpreferred objects, the child will point to the preferred item eight out of ten times each day for three consecutive days.

Instructional Plan: Using the reinforcer assessment methods we described in Chapter 5, identify a group of five to ten items (preferred) that your child typically chooses when given a variety of things to select. Choose another five to ten items (nonpreferred) that are unlikely to ever be desired by your child. (Probe your child's interest by making these items available and see if he chooses them.) These could include disliked foods, nonfunctional objects (for your child) like paper and paper clips, and so on. Begin each trial by holding up two objects (one preferred and one nonpreferred) and ask your child to "Show me what you want." Whichever item he selects, give it to him for a minute either to consume or use. If he selects the nonpreferred item, he will likely give it back to you immediately or set it down. At that point you may want to correct his response by repeating the request and helping him to point to the preferred item. Praise him for choosing the correct item and remind him that he needs to select the preferred item the first time. Pause for three to five seconds, and then repeat the request again. This time, if he points to the preferred item, give it to him (note: no other rewards are necessary). Mix the choice of preferred and nonpreferred items.

■ Appendix D How to Write an Instructional Plan

Instructional Plan

Functional Area: (Refer to Self-Help Skills Inventory in Appendix A)

Task: (Refer to Self-Help Skills Inventory)　　**Child's Name:** _____

Skill Target: (Refer to Self-Help Skills Inventory)　　**Initiation Date:** _____

Goal for Learning

Specify a context, observable behavior, attainable goal, and mastery criteria (see Chapter 6). For example: *Given an instruction to set the table, Brian will place a spoon, fork, knife, cup, and plate on the table in correct position with one or fewer prompt for three consecutive meals.*

Specify Components of the Plan

Check when completed	
	Conduct list of steps required to do the task (attach Task Analysis Sheet): *Break target skill into smaller steps for learning. (See Chapter 6 regarding developing a task analysis.)*
	Place and time for instruction: *Identify the most natural place and time to maximize your child's strengths, utilize existing routines, and reduce the need to program generalization later. If this time is not doable, choose a period of the day that will not likely be interrupted.*
	Materials required: *Indicate what materials will be needed to complete this task.*
	Physical accommodations (if needed): *Indicate what setting and material modifications may be necessary to accommodate attention and motor deficits.*
	Instructional signal or cue: *Identify the most natural cue and don't add cues that are unnecessary and will have to be eliminated later. Keep it brief.*
	Data Sheet for monitoring progress (attach): *Develop a data sheet for tracking progress on individual steps. (See Chapter 7.)*
	Steps for generalization: *Identify places, materials, and people that are important for generalization and teach using many examples of each. Fade prompts and rewards, and get everyone involved.*
	Circle which chaining procedure you will use: **BACKWARD**　　**FORWARD** *Select a plan template from Chapter 7 (backward and forward chaining).*
	Conduct a baseline (describe): *Collect data over the course of two or three days to determine how many of the steps your child can complete before you begin formal teaching.*
	Super reward(s): *Identify a food, activity, or toy that your child will be motivated to earn as a reward for completing targeted steps of the program.*

◼ Appendix E Blank Instructional Plan Form

Instructional Plan

Functional Area: _____

Task: _____   Child's Name: _____

Skill Target: _____   Initiation Date: _____

Goal for Learning

_____

_____

_____

Specify Components of the Plan

Check when completed	
	Conduct list of steps required to do the task (attach Task Analysis Sheet):
	Place and time for instruction:
	Materials required:
	Physical accommodations (if needed):
	Instructional signal or cue:
	Data Sheet for monitoring progress (attach)
	Steps for generalization:
	Circle which chaining procedure you will use: BACKWARD FORWARD
	Conduct a baseline (describe):
	Super reward(s):

■ Appendix F Blank Task Analysis Data Sheet

SKILL TARGET _____

    GOAL _____

YOUR INSTRUCTION TO CHILD
(e.g., "Brush your teeth."): _____

TEACHING METHOD (Circle)   BACKWARD   FORWARD

Mastery	Step	Component Skill (e.g., Turn on water)	Date																
	1																		
	2																		
	3																		
	4																		
	5																		
	6																		
	7																		
	8																		
	9																		
	10																		
	11																		
	12																		
	13																		
	14																		
	15																		
	16																		
	17																		
	18																		

$\mathcal{I}$ndex

Page numbers in italic indicate tables or figures.

■ About the Authors

Stephen R. Anderson is the Executive Director of Summit Educational Resources in Tonawanda, New York, which serves children and young adults with developmental disabilities. He is a licensed psychologist and Board Certified Behavior Analyst.

Amy L. Jablonski is a licensed psychologist and Summit's Chief Operating Officer which includes oversight of educational and diagnostic services.

Marcus L. Thomeer is a licensed psychologist and Director of Research and Evaluation at Summit. His responsibilities include Connections, a summer treatment program for children with Asperger's disorder.

Vicki Madaus Knapp is Summit's Chief Clinical Director and a Board Certified Behavior Analyst.